C Standard Library

Jack Purdum
Timothy C. Leslie

Que™ Corporation
Indianapolis, Indiana

C Standard Library.

Library of Congress Catalog No.: 86-62528

ISBN 0-88022-279-4

91 90 89 88 87   8 7 6 5 4 3 2 1

Interpretation of the printing code: the rightmost double-digit number is the year of the book's printing; the rightmost single-digit number, the number of the book's printing. For example, a printing code of 87-1 shows that the first printing of the book occurred in 1987.

Dedication

To Kay and Paul and my friends at Tilden Lake.

Jack Purdum

To Pat, who gets me into trouble, and Emma, who gets me out of trouble.

Timothy C. Leslie

Product Director
Chris DeVoney

Editorial Director
David F. Noble, Ph.D.

Managing Editor
Gregory Croy

Editor
William H. Ball

Technical Editor
Anthony Skjellum

Production
Kelly Currie
Jennifer Matthews
Dennis Sheehan

About the Authors

Jack Purdum

Jack Purdum wrote Que's *C Programming Guide* and *C Self-Study Guide* and coauthored *C Programmer's Library*. He received his M.A. and Ph.D. degrees in economics from Ohio State University. Purdum has taught seminars on the C programming language and microcomputers in business. He has made presentations on teaching C and the philosophy and methodology of benchmarks. Purdum is president of Ecosoft, Inc., a software house that specializes in C compilers and statistical software.

Timothy C. Leslie

Timothy C. Leslie is the Director of Software Development at Ecosoft, Inc. and the principal author of the Ecosoft C Compiler. He is coauthor of *C Programmer's Library*. His background includes the development of medical image analysis, operating systems, and system utilities software.

Table of Contents

1 Introduction to C Standard Library

2 Summary of the ANSI Language Enhancements

3 Standard C Library Header Files

4 Converter Functions

5 String and Character Operations

6 Math Functions

7 Input/Output Functions

8 Miscellaneous Utility Functions

9 Time and Internationalization Functions

Foreword

The C language has undergone substantial changes in the past few years. Perhaps the most influential force in these changes is the work of the X3J11 committee of the American National Standards Institute (ANSI). A second force is work done over the years by the UNIX™ community. In particular, AT&T® has been a leader in defining what UNIX and C are supposed to look like in the UNIX System V (SYSV) environment. Indeed, AT&T's *System V Interface Definition* document (AT&T, Indianapolis, IN) clearly defines what resources are found in a UNIX SYSV implementation.

The result is a proposed standard by the ANSI X3J11 committee for the C language. At this time, that document is out for public review. The proposed standard defines all elements of the C language, including enhancements (for example, structure passing and assignment, new data types, etc.) and the contents of the standard library. Because many of the proposed changes to C make sense, there is little doubt that the major elements of the proposed standard will be adopted.

The purpose of this book is to explain the resources available to the C programmer in the proposed ANSI standard library. This book is not designed to teach you the C language; we assume you're familiar with pre-ANSI C. But, out of necessity, this book discusses a number of the C language enhancements proposed by ANSI that affect the use of the standard C library.

The proposed C standard library contains almost 200 functions. As complete as the list is, no library can cover all needs. For that reason, we have included several functions available in the SYSV library, but not part of the ANSI library. Therefore, the driving force behind the list of functions covered in this book is the ANSI standard C library, with a few additional functions included from the SYSV library definition.

We identify C library functions unique to ANSI, those unique to SYSV, and those common to both. In some cases, even though a function is common to ANSI and SYSV, there may be slight differences between the two specifications. We have tried to point out these differences when they occur.

Each function description includes a prototype (a new enhancement discussed in Chapter 2) of the function, a list of required header files, a discussion of how the function works, and a simple program that uses the function. We have tried to keep the example programs as simple as possible so that you can type them in and exercise the function easily.

The book begins with a general discussion of the proposed standard, some of the enhancements to the language, and a discussion of common trouble spots programmers run into when getting started with C. Chapter 2 expands the language enhancements for readers not familiar with them. Chapter 3 discusses the header files the proposed ANSI standard expects. Some of these are new and aren't specified in the SYSV specification.

The remainder of the book discusses the function definitions. These are presented in chapters arranged by function use. The areas covered are converter functions (Chapter 4), string processing functions (Chapter 5), math functions (Chapter 6), input/output functions (Chapter 7), utility functions (Chapter 8), and time functions (Chapter 9). Within each chapter, functions are arranged in alphabetical order for quick reference. In addition, we have spent considerable time cross-referencing the functions; the index at the back of the book is useful for locating a function by name or task.

Acknowledgments

We would be remiss if we did not mention several people who have contributed to this book.

We would like to thank Chris DeVoney, who served as technical advisor, for his insight and careful eye to detail.

Thanks to Anthony Skjellum, who did yeoman service reviewing the text and testing the program code.

Also, thanks to Dave Cooper, Don Dunine, Chuck Lieske, Craig Miller, and Jim Rheude for keeping us on the straight and narrow.

Lastly, thanks to all of the people at Que, who consistently weave burlap into silk.

Trademark Acknowledgments

Que Corporation has made every attempt to supply trademark information about company names, products, and services mentioned in this book. Trademarks indicated below were derived from various sources. Que Corporation cannot attest to the accuracy of this information.

AT&T is a registered trademark of AT&T.

Hewlett-Packard is a registered trademark of Hewlett-Packard Company.

IBM is a registered trademark of International Business Machines Corporation.

UNIX is a trademark of AT&T.

1
Introduction to C Standard Library

The C programming language has come of age. C has gained wide acceptance in all sectors of the programming community: in industry by professional programmers because of C's power and portability among hardware environments, in educational institutions for teaching modern programming techniques, and in the home by programmers who find pleasure in programming in C.

American National Standards Institute (ANSI) and X3J11

One reason why C has become so popular is that C has not been fragmented by "dialects" which plague other languages, such as BASIC. Although many programmers take C's commonality among compiler vendors for granted, others do not. A nucleus of C vendors and programmers petitioned ANSI to form a committee to write a formal definition for the C language. The result was the creation of ANSI's X3J11 committee.

The goal of X3J11 was to create a standard for the C language that would formally define the language, clear up several gray areas, and add enhancements most C programmers felt would benefit the programming community. The X3J11 committee wanted to meet these goals and also ensure that the standard "would not break existing C code" being used in the field.

The key to understanding the work of X3J11 is the word *portability*. X3J11's work is to establish a minimum base for the C language and library which works across all computing systems. If a function or feature cannot be implemented on all computers, X3J11 either does not incorporate the function or feature in its proposal or makes the item implementation-defined (meaning the vendor is at liberty to handle the item in any way but must document how the item is handled).

A conforming ANSI compiler will compile an ANSI-conforming program. If you are concerned about porting a program to a variety of machines or compilers, X3J11's work will have a profound impact on you. If you are less concerned about portability (you work with only one machine or one compiler), X3J11's work has less significance. X3J11's proposal will add useful features and functions to the language, but the extensive use of extensions for items as screen addressing and console input remains outside the jurisdiction of X3J11.

The public comments from the first formal proposal by X3J11 are being reviewed by the committee. Most C programmers who have read the document for the proposed standard feel that the next iteration of the proposal by committee, in late 1987, will be adopted as an ANSI standard in early 1988.

The standard C function library is not part of the formal definition of C. Although much of the effort expended by X3J11 was (rightfully) directed to the language definition and other aspects of the language, the committee has also proposed a minimal standard C library.

UNIX System V and X3J11

The X3J11 committee is not alone in promoting a standard C library. Three forces are pushing for a standard C library. The first is the standard C library defined in the report by the X3J11 committee. The second is the standard library under UNIX System V (defined in the *System V Interface Definition*). The third is the 1003 standards committee of the Institute of Electrical and Electronic Engineers, IEEE. The 1003 working standard is nicknamed POSIX, and the 1003 effort is to standardize the UNIX operating system for non-AT&T computers. These forces are important, but their standards are different. Hence, the problem: What is "the" standard library when there are three important, although different, forces influencing the standard?

Although X3J11's primary duty was not to standardize the standard C function library, our opinion is that the standard C library in the proposed ANSI standard will form a base standard C library and will be supported by vendors of C compilers in the future. We also believe that many of the library functions in UNIX System V will be offered in addition to those in the X3J11 report. The 1003 working standard states that the X3J11 draft is the base document for the 1003 C library and only offers an extension to X3J11's work. Therefore, it seems likely that "the" standard C library will be a blend of the ANSI X3J11 committee report, the UNIX System V standard library, and the 1003 final standard, which will be close to the current UNIX standard library.

This book, therefore, covers the standard C library functions in the proposed ANSI standard presented by the X3J11 committee report. We have also included functions that have gained popularity as part of the UNIX System V standard library, but are not part of the ANSI standard library. The work of 1003 is covered under our discussion of UNIX System V.

Until the future gives us the standard library, we offer this text as a guide to the complete proposed ANSI standard C library, plus many System V standard library functions that have proved useful in the past. There are enough functions between the two libraries to ease our programming tasks significantly until the "ultimate" standard library arrives.

Why the Standard Library Is Important

The first reason for having a standard library is that the functions are known and behave in a predictable manner. It is somewhat amazing that, despite an absence of a formal definition of the standard C library, almost all compiler vendors implement the majority of standard C functions by using the same function name, argument sequence, return values, and behavior. But variations exist and can lead to surprises when you try to port code between environments.

A second reason for having a standard library is so that programmers can move their code easily between one hardware environment and another. If programmers could write code for one system and never worry about changing equipment, the need for portability wouldn't be much of an issue. Computing needs seem to grow over time, however, and rewriting code is expensive and disruptive to users. Because the standard C library functions behave in a well-defined manner, changing environments becomes easier.

A third reason for using the standard library is that the functions have already been debugged (at least that's what we're told when we purchase a compiler). Although bugs creep in once in a while, programmers who use the standard library will be more productive because they don't have to reinvent the wheel.

A fourth reason for using the standard C library is that it reduces the cost of maintaining code. You can reduce your programming time and make your code easily read and understood by others.

In a nutshell, using the C standard function library increases programmer productivity over what it would be if the library did not exist.

The Purpose of This Book

We doubt that any C programmer would question the value of the standard C library. A standard library is crucial to efficient program development. We also think most programmers agree that the conventions and uniformities in the standard function library owe their consistency to the UNIX operating system. The work by X3J11 is concrete testament to the early (and continuing) importance of UNIX. Indeed, if there were major disagreement between the X3J11 report and the conventions found in UNIX, this book would not have been possible. The tie with UNIX, however, has made the programmer's task more difficult.

First, UNIX has changed substantially over the years. It has become more sophisticated and powerful. The standard library had to change to keep pace with the operating system. The second problem relates to the first: As the power of UNIX increased, so did the level of sophistication of the programmers developing software under UNIX. As a result, understanding UNIX documentation requires a fair amount of computer knowledge and the ability to read technical descriptions accurately.

Formal definitions, however, are not easy to read. There is a big difference between reading a function's technical description and using a function correctly.

The purpose of this book is to define the proposed ANSI standard C function library and present examples that show how to use the library's functions. We have tried to keep each function's explanation easy to understand while describing how the function behaves. Each function is accompanied by a short C program.

This approach has two direct benefits: (1) you have a reference that describes the behavior of the function in an understandable manner, and (2) you have a program to test whether your manufacturer's version behaves in the described manner. Finding a difference in a function's behavior in a simple program under a controlled environment is much easier than detecting the same difference in a piece of application software.

The Reader of This Book

In a book like this, we must make certain assumptions about you, the reader.

First, we assume that you are familiar with C. We don't expect you to be an expert, but you should be able to read C code and have some C programming experience. We have used some of the ANSI enhancements to the C language, such as prototyping. We encourage you to adopt prototyping if it is supported by your compiler.

Second, we assume that you have a C compiler. We do not expect you to have a specific hardware system or compiler. We have tried to avoid hardware-software specific elements in the book wherever possible.

We should also mention that we assume the proposal by the ANSI X3J11 committee on the C programming language will be approved with minor modifications. Because many compilers already support a number of the enhancements in the X3J11 document, we have used the new features where we think they're appropriate. However, until the X3J11 document is an ANSI standard, some minor elements of the proposal *can and will* change. This book is not a definitive reference to the X3J11 work. An update to this book will be periodically issued. See the back of this book for more information.

Finally, we have made assumptions about the type of programming you do. Our goal is to discuss functions a typical programmer uses daily. If your programming needs are unique, we may have missed some of your favorite functions. On the other hand, we have seen hundreds of thousands of lines of C code and think that the C library functions presented in this book cover the broadest spectrum of programmers' needs.

Some Common Questions Asked about the Standard Library

In the course of teaching C seminars, plus working with students and customers, we have been asked many questions about the standard C library. Depending on the amount of the questioner's C experience, some of these questions seemed obvious, while others were more subtle. Yet, each person asking the question was sincere. Perhaps you have similar questions. Therefore, in this section, we present and answer some of the questions we've been asked most often.

How Many Functions Are in the Standard Library?

Until the ANSI X3J11 proposal becomes a formal standard, there is no standard number or coverage of the functions in the function library. Further, after the X3J11 proposal becomes a standard, the standard proposes only a "minimal" standard library. Vendors may offer additional functions as part of their standard library.

Therefore, the number of functions in the standard library that ends up being distributed with your compiler is not known. We are aware of compilers with fewer than a dozen functions in their standard library, while other compilers have several hundred. The more library functions you have, the better, because you will have to write less code.

Is a Function Implemented as a Macro Different from a Function Call?

Chapter 3 discusses header files and completely answers this question. Briefly, macros generate "in-line" code in your program. This avoids some of the overhead associated with a function call and often results in slightly faster code. This also means, however, that whatever code is needed to implement the macro is duplicated throughout the program each time the macro is used. Hence, you gain speed at the expense of increased program size.

Another difference is that, because a macro generates in-line code each time it is used, there is no unique address associated with a macro. Therefore, you cannot initialize a pointer to point to a macro, as you can a pointer to function. Macros aren't functions.

Finally, argument(s) used in a macro are data inspecific. A macro that squares a number, such as

```
#define    sq(x)      ( (x) * (x))
```

can use any data type for argument `x`. `x` might be an `int`, `long`, `float`, or `double`. Therefore, because there is no fixed data type for a macro, you cannot use a prototype with a macro.

Does It Matter What We Call Our Own Functions?

Yes. First, if you write a function that uses the same name as one that exists in the standard library, you will have two different functions with the same name. Which version of the function ends up in the program is the responsibility of the linker. In most situations, the version that appears in the program's source code (that is, not the one in your function library) is used in the program.

Avoid naming functions with a leading underscore character. Compiler writers have adopted the convention of prepending an underscore character to variables and function names used by the compiler. If you avoid naming functions (and variables) with a leading underscore, you will reduce the likelihood of colliding with a special function or variable name reserved by the language.

Why Doesn't My Square Root Routine Work Properly?

Quite often, you haven't given the square root function what it expects. (In this answer and elsewhere, we assume that data is passed back to the caller on the stack. Not all compilers may work this way, but an illustration may help answer the question.) The following displays a common mistake:

Program 1.1

```
#include <stdio.h>

int main()
{
      double x;

      x = sqrt(5);
      printf("square root of 5 is %f", x);
}
```

Now view things as the compiler would. When the compiler reads the line

```
x = sqrt(5);
```

it believes that it has an integer constant of 5 as the argument for the `sqrt()` function. Because the compiler thinks that it has an integer data type, only enough bytes to hold an integer data type are set aside for the constant 5. Typically, this means that the constant 5 will be formed as two or four bytes and placed on the stack in preparation to the call to `sqrt()`.

Once we are in the `sqrt()` function, the function takes whatever information it needs from the stack, does its job, and sends the return value back on to the stack. So where did we go wrong?

Because something isn't working properly, we look up the `sqrt()` function in our documentation and find that `sqrt()` expects a double as its argument. Therefore, `sqrt()` also expects to find a double data type (usually eight bytes) on the stack. The `sqrt()` code dutifully pops eight bytes off the stack and tries to find the square root of that value.

Now we can see the problem. We stuffed a two- or four-byte integer on the stack when we wrote the call to `sqrt()`, and `sqrt()` tries to pull off an eight-byte double from the same stack. Using an integer when a double is expected usually doesn't work well. The value returned from the routine will depend on how floating-point values have been implemented, but it's almost certain to be wrong.

We need to inform the compiler that we're working with a double data type, not an integer. To do this, make the following minor, but important, change to the program:

```
x = sqrt(5.0);
```

This change tells the compiler that the value being passed to `sqrt()` is a double data type. The compiler can now recognize `5.0` as a floating-point constant and will allocate the proper amount of stack space for the constant.

Always make sure that you pass the proper data type to a standard library (or any other) function.

I Made the Previous Correction, and It Still Doesn't Work. Why?

This is a common mistake made by C programmers. At one time or another, every function in the standard library that does not return an integer value has suffered the same fate as the one presented here. The fix is easy; remembering the fix seems to be another issue.

Because square root returns a double and you did not tell the compiler, the compiler thinks that it is getting the default data type of integer back from the square root routine. Frequently, 75 percent of the answer from square root is still on the stack. Let's see why.

The rule and solution are simple: Prior to calling a function, always declare any function that returns a noninteger data type. For example,

Program 1.2

```
#include <stdio.h>

main()
{
     double sqrt();
     double x;

     x = 5.0;
     printf("square root of 5 is %f", sqrt(x) );
}
```

works fine because we have declared that `sqrt()` returns a double. Because we made the declaration before calling `sqrt()`, the compiler knows to pop enough bytes off the stack to form a double data type as the value returned from the function call. If you leave the declaration out of the program, the compiler will only pop "int bytes" from the stack.

There is a better and easier solution, however. All we have to do is add one #include directive.

Program 1.3

```
#include <stdio.h>
#include <math.h>

main()
{
        double x;

        x = 5.0;
        printf("square root of 5 is %f", sqrt(x) );
}
```

If your compiler supports prototyping, the math.h header file will contain the prototype for sqrt() (plus other math functions). The declaration of sqrt() becomes unnecessary because the prototype takes care of the declaration for you.

If your compiler has header files, use them. Using header files will increase your productivity by letting the compiler catch more programming errors for you, especially if your compiler supports prototyping.

Is There a Header File That Gives the Prototypes for the Standard Library Functions?

There is no single header file that covers all functions. The ANSI proposal has a header file for every function in the library, and some of the header file names are different between ANSI and System V. Those functions, it appears, which do not require header file information (for example, symbolic constants), are being placed in the header file named stdlib.h.

These and related issues are discussed in detail in Chapter 3.

Is There an Important Difference between a Data Declaration and a Data Definition?

Yes.

In Program 1.2, the line

```
double sqrt();
```

is a declaration. It tells the compiler that the function `sqrt()` returns a double data type. Declarations do not cause any storage to be allocated; they simply provide information needed by the compiler to do its job properly.

In Program 1.2, we see

```
double x;
```

which is a data definition. In this case, we tell the compiler to create a variable called `x` for subsequent use in the program. Data definitions cause enough storage to be allocated to hold the requested data type (a double in the example).

Declarations are not limited to function names. For example

```
extern int fred;
```

is a data declaration that says: "Okay compiler, you should know about a variable named `fred` even though you won't necessarily find it defined anywhere in this file. Whenever you reference it, however, treat `fred` as an integer data type."

Until now, you probably have function declarations scattered throughout your code. Life's about to change. Because of prototyping and ANSI's extensive use of header files, you need to declare only your own "custom" functions (that is, the functions you write). A few `#includes` are going to replace a bunch of function declarations in the future.

The new proposed ANSI standard mandates that the header files declare functions in the standard library. Whenever you define a function, you are writing the function yourself—it is not in the standard library.

Are There Any Tips for Remembering the Order of Arguments for Standard Library Function Calls?

As you gain experience with C, many of the function arguments will become second nature to you. However, in the interim, some of the standard library functions have a pattern to the order of their arguments.

For example, many of the "str" functions have their arguments formed in the order in which we write assignments in C. That is, the assignment operator takes the right-hand expression and assigns it into the left-hand expression:

```
left-hand         right-hand
destination   =   source;
```

which assigns source into destination. The string copy function has the same ordering of arguments:

```
strcpy(destination, source);
```

If you think of the comma as an equal sign between the arguments, you can easily remember the order of the arguments to strcpy().

String functions with the letter *n* in the middle (for example, strncpy(), strncat(), strncmp(), etc.) tend to have the integer value last in the argument list. For example:

```
strncat(destination, source,  elements);
```

Functions that deal with high-level file input/output are another example. These functions use FILE pointers (fp's for short) and often begin with the letter f. Common functions in this category are fclose(), feof(), ferror(), fflush(), fopen(), fread(), and fwrite(). Several have multiple arguments, and the (fp) FILE pointer argument is usually last in the function call's argument list. Of course, there are exceptions [such as fscanf() and ftell()].

As you look through this text, you'll see that groups of functions tend to have a pattern to their arguments. If you are just beginning to program in C, knowing which functions are available and how they are used is more important than memorizing function arguments and their order. If you know what you want to do and what functions in the standard library are capable of doing that task, you will have solved most of the problem.

It's easy to look up the arguments and their ordering. Knowing which arguments are needed and their order assumes that you already know the function name. Therefore, the first task for the beginner is to find out what's available in the standard function library.

Using This Book

The library functions in this book are grouped according to usage. You may know what you want a function to do, but not the name of the function that can do it. Grouping the functions by task should make your search easier.

It makes sense, in many cases, to discuss a number of functions simultaneously. For example, the "is's" (such as `isalpha()`, `isdigit()`, etc.) are discussed together, as are most of the "str" functions (for example, `strcpy()`, `strcat()`, etc.). This is done to avoid repetition.

Each function or group of functions is discussed in a uniform manner. The format is presented in Table 1.1.

Table 1.1
Format for Function Discussions

1. Function Name
2. Standard Met
3. Purpose
4. Prototypes
5. Required Header
   ANSI
   SYSV
6. Usage
7. CAUTION
8. Illustration
9. Program Comment
10. Miscellaneous Comments

Let's discuss each section.

1. Function Name

The function name section may contain one or more functions that are being discussed. If more than one function name is given in a section, a common thread ties the functions together.

2. Standard Met

"Standard met" refers to whether the function(s) are described in the proposed ANSI or System V standard library, or both. "ANSI" means that the function is defined in the ANSI standard library. "SYSV" means that the function is found in the System V standard library. If the function(s) are in both libraries, you will see ANSI and

SYSV in this section. Any differences in function behavior between the two libraries will be noted in the Caution section.

3. Purpose

This section, kept as short as possible so that you can peruse each function quickly, lets you know what the function does.

4. Prototype

This section presents the function's prototype. Since prototyping is included in the ANSI specification and appears certain, prototyping is used throughout this text. (We think it is important that you read Chapter 2, which discusses several of the ANSI enhancements to C. Even if you're familiar with the concept of prototyping, we encourage you to read Chapter 2.)

The proposed ANSI standard states that, wherever possible, if a library routine is implemented as a macro, it will also have a function that accomplishes the same task. Therefore, even though `getchar()` is implemented as a macro, there will also be a `getchar()` function. (Chapter 3 shows how to prevent macro substitution.) Although prototyping a macro is incorrect, we present the prototype in each case for clarity.

5. Header Files

Each ANSI library function is associated with a header file. This is true for many, but not all System V functions. The ANSI header file will always be given if the function exists in the ANSI library. (If a header file is not present in the ANSI column, that function is not in the ANSI library.) Many header files contain symbolic constants used by the function (such as `EOF` in `stdio.h`).

Because prototyping will be a standard feature of C compilers from now on, a file that contains the prototypes for the functions should be provided with your compiler. If a function has a required header file (for example, `printf()` and `stdio.h`), the prototype will be in the required header file. A function without a required header file will have its prototypes in the `stdlib.h` header file. In the function discussions in subsequent chapters, **if a required header file is not needed, we assume that you will `#include` the `stdlib.h` header file**.

As a general rule, if a header file is given, it should be `#included` into the program.

6. Usage

This section contains the formal definition of the library function and tells what the function does and what it returns. If the return values have special meaning (for example, one value for a normal return condition, and another for an error condition), these are mentioned. Deviations between ANSI and System V behavior are pointed out.

7. Caution

Sometimes a caution section discusses errors you might make with the function. One possible error might be caused by misusing the function because of a difference between the ANSI and System V interpretations. Another might be caused by making an assumption about the function not warranted by its formal description. There won't be many such cautions, but they're presented if we know the function has caused trouble for programmers in the past.

8. Illustration

This section shows how a function might be used. We have tried to make these programs: (1) as short as possible so that they can be typed in easily; (2) simple so that they are easy to understand, yet still show what the function does; and (3) modular where necessary. By making the program modular, you can, for example, see how `strtok()` works without having to type in all of the str function code.

Another point should be stressed about the program examples. As stated earlier, ANSI and System V have had an important influence on C's development. Several problems arose in writing the programs, because some functions are common to ANSI and System V, but use different header files. Also, there are functions in ANSI not found in System V, and vice versa. We had to compromise for some of the program examples.

There are three rules of the compromise. First, when a function is in both the ANSI and System V standard libraries, the program example uses the ANSI header file. If you need the System V header and if one applies to the function, you can substitute the appropriate header as stated in the Required Header (see Table 1.1, #5) section of the function discussion. If a header file is not required for the System V version of the function, the Required Header will be blank for the System V header file.

Second, if the function is not in the ANSI standard library, we'll tell you in the Program Comment section (see Table 1.1, #9) of the example. Another way to check is to look at the ANSI Required

Header field. Because ANSI has a header file for every function, a blank header file means that the function pertains only to System V.

Finally, there are a few cases where ANSI specifies a function not presently part of the System V library. In those rare cases, we will tell you that the function is not available as part of System V in the Program Comment section.

9. Program Comment

Following each function example is a comment about how the code works or a discussion of the output generated by the program. Because the programs are short and simple, a detailed discussion is not usually necessary.

We have also tried to anticipate problems. If experience tells me that a certain function may surprise you, we have tried to use a sample program that shows why the unexpected behavior occurs. In other cases, the functions are so simple that the program examples may not need explanation. Once you read the formal function description, you may not have to read the program description. On the other hand, if you read the technical and program descriptions and are still unsure how a function behaves, you may want to type in the example and test the code to see whether the function performs as expected.

10. Miscellaneous Comments

Finally, we have reserved a section for miscellaneous comments. In some cases, we may point out that the function is gradually being replaced by a new function with a different name. If there is a clever use for the function, or anything else pertaining to the function that we think may help you as a programmer, it will be presented in this section.

Some Closing Thoughts

Chapter 2 discusses several enhancements that the proposed ANSI standard will add to C. You should read this chapter carefully, because the function discussions draw on information presented there.

If your compiler does not support the ANSI standard, chances are it will in the near future. To whatever extent you can, try to implement the new C language enhancements supported by your compiler into your coding style as soon as possible. ANSI has added some useful enhancements to C, and you're robbing yourself if you don't take advantage of them.

As a final thought, we suggest that you read the book from start to finish, especially if you're just getting started in C. Even if you are interested in only one aspect of the standard library, you might learn something along the way. Also, you'll develop a better grasp of the variety of programming problems already solved for you.

2

Summary of the ANSI Language Enhancements

This chapter discusses several of the C language enhancements that have been added by the ANSI X3J11 standards committee. Although the standard has not yet been approved, the features discussed in this chapter will almost certainly be part of the final standard.

Prototyping

A number of changes will be made to the C language as a result of the X3J11 committee of the American National Standards Institute (ANSI). One of these changes is prototyping. Prototyping allows for type checking of the data types used as arguments to function calls. Although prototyping is relatively new, it will emerge as part of the ANSI standard for the C language, so we have used prototyping throughout this text.

An example is the best way to show how prototyping works. In the past, if you used the `fseek()` function, it was defined as:

```
int fseek(fp, offset, position)
int position;
long int offset;
FILE fp;
{
        .
        .
}
```

Beginning programmers tend to make two mistakes with this function. The errors are illustrated in code fragment 2.1.

Code Fragment 2.1

```
int where;
.
where = fseek(fp, Ø, position);
.
```

The first mistake is to forget to pass `offset` as a `long int` data type to the function. In code fragment 2.1, the second argument should be a `long int` data type, but the argument will be passed as an integer because the `long int` modifier is missing. This error is corrected in code fragment 2.2.

Code Fragment 2.2

```
int where;
int fseek();              /* Declare to return long */
.
where = lseek(fd, ØL, position);
.
```

Notice that the second argument to `fseek()` has the L modifier after the Ø.

A second error that might be made is to forget one of the arguments and simply pass two arguments to `fseek()`. Although this error is less frequent, it does occur occasionally.

Prototyping helps eliminate these types of problems. C compilers that support the proposed ANSI standard and prototyping will have a header file which contains the prototypes for each function in the standard library. Although the names of the prototyping header files are not etched in stone, the functions in the standard library are grouped into headers according to the purpose of the functions. For example, most of the string-related functions are in `string.h`, the mathematical functions in `math.h`, and so on. A catchall header named `stdlib.h` is for functions that don't fit into a single category.

If a function has a required header, the header should be `#included` into the program. As a general rule, functions without a currently required header file will have their prototypes in the `stdlib.h` header file.

Regardless of where the prototype is located, a typical prototype declaration might look like:

```
int fseek(FILE, long int, int);
```

The `int` that appears at the start of the declaration is the type specifier for the function. The type specifier tells the data type returned by the function and is identical in purpose to the current rules for function declarations and definitions. The next declaration is the function name or identifier (id)—`fseek()` in the example.

The change that prototypes represent appears between the parentheses for the function and tells the compiler the number of arguments to the function and the data type for each of the arguments.

Use prototyping to allow the compiler to: (1) check the data types of the arguments used in the function; (2) allow usual conversions of the arguments to the function; and (3) check the number of arguments you use versus the number expected by the function. The type specifier permits checking of the return data type. Prototyping allows the compiler to look for mismatched data types and other programming errors.

Prototyping with Identifiers

We should also point out that prototyping permits identifiers to be used in the prototype. See, for example, the following:

```
int fseek(FILE fd, long int offset, int position);
```

These identifiers are for documentation purposes and help the reader to understand what the arguments are supposed to do. The identifiers used in the prototype declaration are not defined; the argument identifiers are meaningless. (Identifiers in prototype function definitions are meaningful. This is explained later in this chapter.)

Data Types and Conversions with Prototypes

ANSI has proposed several extensions to the current data types and rules for converting data types. The full range of data types are:

signed char, unsigned char, char (the "signedness" of the char is left to the programmer)

int bit-fields, unsigned int bit-fields

short int, unsigned short int

int, unsigned int

long int, unsigned long int

float, double, long double

array, structures, unions, enums (actually integers), pointers (including void *), and void

Another feature of prototyping is that "usual" conversions are performed on the arguments. Providing precision is not lost, one arithmetic data type can be converted to another. Given the previous example for fseek(), under prototyping, passing a 0 as the offset would cause the 0 to be converted to a long int data type.

Note that pointers do not mix. Previously, programmers freely interchanged pointers. Under ANSI C, any pointer can be converted to a void * and back to the original pointer; however other pointers cannot be freely converted (you cannot pass an int * to a function expecting a char *).

Other Prototypes

What if a function doesn't need an argument? For example, the clock() function doesn't need an argument. A prototype for clock():

```
clock_t clock(void);
```

says that an argument should never be passed to clock(). Prior to prototyping, this error could not be checked. (Also notice that clock() returns a clock_t data type. An explanation of clock_t is in Chapter 3.)

What if a function has a variable number of arguments? The printf() function is an example. This prototype contains a new C symbol called an ellipsis. The ellipsis is three periods. The prototype for printf() becomes

```
int printf(char *control_string, ...);
```

The prototype says that `printf()` will always have a pointer to `char` data type (that is, the control string), followed by zero or more additional arguments.

Creating Your Own Prototypes

If you are developing your own functions, you should start using prototyping in your code. For example, a function without prototyping:

```
double matrix(x, y, error)
int error;
double x, y;
{
       .
       .
}
```

and written in prototype form becomes

```
double matrix(double x, double y, int error)
{
       .
       .
}
```

In this case, because you are defining the function and not declaring it, the variables `x`, `y`, and `error` exist. These identifiers may be used in the function just as if they were defined in the nonprototyped version.

To create the prototype declaration of the function, the first line of the function is copied and a semicolon added. For the example function, the prototype declaration is:

```
double matrix(double x, double y, int error);
```

You should become familiar with prototyping. It is here to stay.

enum Data Type

An `enum` data type is a data item that has a defined set of legal values. The following is an example:

Code Fragment 2.3

```
enum color {red, white, blue};

enum color flag, cloth;

flag = red;
cloth = blue;

if (flag != red)
     printf("The colors for flag and cloth don't match");
```

The first line of code fragment 2.3 establishes an `enum` tag called `color`, followed by a list of enumerated items that are part of the set belonging to `color`. The second line defines two variables of type `color`. This means that `flag` and `cloth` can legally assume only the values associated with `red`, `white`, and `blue`.

Unless otherwise assigned, each item that belongs to the set `color` starts with 0 and is increased by one for each item in the set. In the example, therefore, `red` equates to 0, `white` to 1, and `blue` to 2. If we changed the enumeration to:

```
enum color {red, white = 100, blue};
```

`red` would still equal 0, `white` would now be 100, and `blue` would be 101. Notice that the new value for `blue` is determined by the initialized value of `white` (that is, `blue` is 1 greater than `white`). If you want `blue` to retain the value of 2, you would have to use:

```
enum color {red, white = 100, blue = 2};
```

An item in the enumerated set can be assigned a nondefault value by simple assignment. The only assignment restriction is that the assigned value should not exceed the signed value of an integer on the host machine. That is, if an `int` is 16 bits, assigning 40,000 to `blue` would be an error because 40,000 is larger than that `int` can hold (+32,767).

The next two lines assign the value of `red` into the `enum` variable named `flag`, and `cloth` is assigned to the value `blue`. This is the proper use of an `enum` data type. On the other hand, it is improper to use:

```
flag = 0;
cloth = 1;
```

because 0 and 1 are not in the set of the enum data type—only red, white, and blue belong to the set.

Also note how the if test uses an enumerated item that belongs to the set. This test is not correct:

```
if (flag != 0)
```

because flag should properly test for the items in the enumerated list, not the values the items assume. At the present time, the ANSI standard does not specify the improper use of the enum data type as an error.

The enum data type is presented here because there are a few functions that expect enum data types to be passed as function arguments.

const and volatile

The proposed ANSI standard also states that const and volatile are new keywords in C. Both keywords are type specifiers to be used in data definitions and declarations. For example,

```
const int port = 0x10;
```

defines the variable port and states that port's value should not be changed anywhere in the program. In other words, port is like read-only memory: you can read port, but can't allow anything to alter the value held in port (for example, increment, decrement, etc.).

If we declare port as:

```
const int *port = 0x10;
```

we now say that whatever is stored at 10 hex cannot be changed.

If we declare port as:

```
int * const port = 0x10;
```

we now say the port can be used to change location 10 hex, but port cannot point anywhere else (the pointer is constant).

You will also see const used in function prototypes. For example, the atoi() prototype:

```
int atoi(const char *nstr);
```

is used to convert the string representation of a number in nstr to an integer value. The use of const in the prototype says that the atoi() function should not change what nstr points to. That is, we want to leave the string representation of the number unaffected after atoi() has finished its task.

The volatile keyword in a data definition tells the compiler to maintain the sequencing associated with this variable in any expression as the sequencing is stated in the code. In other words, the compiler will generate the code in the exact sequence that we state in the expression. This approach may be necessary to prevent the compiler from performing optimizations that might alter the sequence in which operands are evaluated. The volatile keyword, therefore, prevents unknown side effects that might be caused by compiler optimizations.

For example, if you define i as a volatile integer in the following code fragment,

Code Fragment 2.4

```
volatile int i = 0;

i = i + 1;
```

an optimizing compiler would probably change the code to the equivalent of ++i. But because i is volatile, the compiler must read i, add 1 to it, and then store the result back into i.

The Terminology of ANSI

There are two terms frequently used by the X3J11 document you should know. *Implementation-defined* behavior depends on how the compiler writers implement the function or feature. Behavior that is implementation-defined is not consistent across all compilers. However, each compiler must document how it handles implementation-defined behavior.

Undefined behavior is a program that uses nonportable or erroneous constructs, or uses indeterminately valued objects. The compiler implementor is at liberty to compile the undefined construct (with or without any message) or issue a fatal error.

Basically, undefined behavior is from potentially compilable constructs that have no predictable or specifiable results. Implementation-defined behavior is behavior that may change from compiler to compiler and compiler writers must document how that behavior is handled.

These two terms appear frequently throughout the book. View implementation-defined items as items that X3J11 cannot specify in a uniform, portable fashion but that can be implemented on all machines in some fashion. Undefined behavior is nonportable and potentially, but not always, erroneous behavior that X3J11 cannot specify.

Transition Problems

There is going to be a time lag between formalizing the ANSI standard and seeing compilers meet the formal standard. In fact, a number of compilers already meet a good part of the proposed ANSI standard even though ANSI's standard has not been finalized. Many compilers already support structure passing and assignment, the `enum` and `void` data types, and prototyping because these enhancements make sense and will likely be part of the formal standard.

On the other hand, significantly fewer manufacturers have as yet implemented `const` and `volatile`. There is no elegant way to handle the absence of `const` and `volatile` on a compiler that doesn't support them. A "dirty" way to prepare for those features is to use the following:

```
#define const
#define volatile
```

at the top of the program. This interim technique permits the compiler to parse `const` and `volatile`, but the features associated with these keywords are lost. That is, the compiler can still change a `const` variable and optimize on a `volatile` variable. Removing the `#define`s and recompiling the code with an ANSI compiler would activate these enhancements.

In the interim, we suggest that you try to use as many of the proposed ANSI enhancements as possible; you will be comfortable using the new enhancements when they become available.

3
Standard C Library Header Files

The proposed ANSI standard library uses header files extensively. The purpose of this section is to discuss header files in general, and then to present information about the ANSI header files. The proposed ANSI standard makes extensive use of the information contained in its header files, so you should understand the information in this chapter.

What Is a Header File?

A header file is a collection of function prototypes, symbolic constants, plus parametized macro definitions that are necessary for using a group of related functions properly. Each header file is designed to cover a general area of programming so that unnecessary header files need not be included in the program. For example, if your program uses a lot of string processing, you will want to `#include` the `string.h` header file. Since the program doesn't use floating-point operations, the `math.h` header file may be unnecessary.

The Difference between a Library Function and a Macro

Library functions in the standard library normally exist in relocatable format as a separate file and are not part of the program source code or any header file. If a program calls a function implemented as a library function, the compiler notes where the function is referenced (used) in the program. After the program is compiled, the linker moves the relocatable function code from a library file to the appropriate location in the executable program. The code for a library function, therefore, appears only once in a program even though the function may be called many times.

A macro normally is a `#define` directive in a header file and results in a textual substitution, called a macro expansion. The classic example of a macro is one that squares a number. Consider, for example, the following:

```
#define square(x) ( (x) * (x) )
```

We might use the `square()` macro in a program as

```
i = square(j);
```

After the preprocessor finishes its pass, the `square()` macro is expanded to

```
i = ( (j) * (j) );
```

A number of implications result from the macro expansion. First, each time we use the `square()` macro, we substitute the associated macro expansion. In other words, macros generate in-line code.

Second, because each call to the macro generates in-line code, you cannot have a pointer to a macro. While you can create a pointer to a function, because a function exists as a chunk of code in the program, you cannot create a pointer to a macro since a macro doesn't "exist" at any one place in the program.

Third, because macros result in in-line code, a macro will execute slightly faster than a function—there is no function-call overhead to process. The price of this speed is the potential to generate more code, because each use of a macro generates code at that point in the program.

Fourth, macros are data inspecific. That is, in the previous example, variable `j` could be a `char`, an `int`, or a `double`, and the macro will work correctly. If `square()` is a function, the argument's data type is declared as part of the function definition. Therefore, one `square()` macro can do the work of several `square()` functions because we don't need one function for each data type we want to square.

Fifth, because macros are data inspecific, data type checking is impossible with a macro. This means that you cannot have a prototype for a macro or use a data type specifier as part of the macro definition. For example, you should not use

```
#define isdigit(int) ((int) >= 'Ø' && (int) <= '9')
```

even if the compiler will process the macro correctly. You forgo some of the type-checking protection with macros that is not true for functions with prototyping.

Sixth, any operation on a parametized macro may produce side effects. For example, if you called the `square()` macro as

```
i = square(j++);
```

there is no guarantee how j is treated after expanding the macro. The macro `square()` expands to

```
i = ( (j++) * (j++) );
```

which may not be what we want to do. Because of possible side effects, you should determine whether a function is a function or a macro. Read the contents of each header file supplied with your compiler.

Forcing Functions over Macros

As suggested in the previous section, there are advantages, such as speed, and disadvantages, such as code size, associated with using macros rather than function calls. Because such trade-offs exist, the proposed ANSI standard states that any macro appearing in a header file should have an equivalent function in the standard library whenever possible. This equivalency lets you decide whether to use the macro or function for a task. There are exceptions, however. Some macros, such as `assert()`, cannot be implemented directly as a function.

If you do nothing to the contrary, the preprocessor pass will replace all function calls with the appropriate macro if the macro exists. What can you do to force a function call over macro replacement?

There are several ways to force the selection of a function over a macro; some are better than others.

The no-brainer way of forcing the function call is to delete the #include for the header file that contains the macro. Deleting the #include is not a wise choice for several reasons. First, the header file may be necessary for other parts of the program to work properly. Leaving out stdio.h because you don't want the putchar() macro, for example, also prevents you from doing any buffered file input/output. Second, you lose the safety provided by type checking for those functions prototyped in the header you have deleted. In short, not including the header file is an unsafe choice to solve the problem.

A common alternative is to #undef the macro that you want replaced with the function call. For example, if you don't want putchar() implemented as a macro, then

```
#include <stdio.h>
#undef putchar
```

has the effect of removing the macro substitution of putchar() in the code.

A final and perhaps best alternative is to use a form of syntax that forces the function to be called even though a header file has a macro in force. There has been no #undef for the macro, for example. The syntax is

```
#include <stdio.h>
.
.
i = (putchar)(c);          /* Note the parentheses */
.
```

This works correctly because the preprocessor can only expand a parametized macro substitution when the macro identifier is followed by either white space or an opening parenthesis. The parentheses around putchar, therefore, turn off macro substitution but have no effect on function invocation and leave intact the call to the putchar() function.

Although the other alternatives work, the last alternative has the advantage of (1) maintaining the availability of the macro and (2) providing direct documentation that a macro was not used.

Using #include

You may usually `#include` header files in any order in your program, but they should be included in the source program prior to referencing any variable, function, or macro appearing in the header.

Keep in mind that including a header file may bring unwanted information into the program. You may, for example, want to replace a macro with your own macro or function. If so, then `#undef`, followed by the macro name after the header file is included in the source file, has the effect of removing the macro definition contained in the header file.

ANSI Standard Header Files

Header files under the proposed ANSI standard contain information not found in their prestandard counterparts. The most notable addition will be function prototyping.

What follows in this section is a list of the header files expected to be in the final ANSI standard. Header files that are part of the ANSI standard are followed by the ANSI abbreviation. All others are not part of the ANSI standard, but are often included with a C compiler. (Most other header file names are derived from UNIX System V, or SYSV from now on.) Because some functions may not be possible on all operating systems (for example, the time functions under CP/M), some compilers may not support all the header files presented in the list.

Although we expect the ANSI standard header files to prevail, several non-ANSI header files are presented to help you locate where the information under the pre-ANSI standard is now found. Be aware that some information in the ANSI header files may be changed slightly before the X3J11 standard is finalized.

List the contents of each header file supplied with your compiler. These listings can be used for reference during program development and while you read this chapter.

assert.h ANSI/SYSV

This header file contains the `assert()` macro definition, which may be used to test an expression in a program. This macro's argument is an expression to be tested. For example, suppose a program, called `atest.c`, contains the following code fragment:

```
int a, b;

a = 3;
b = 2;

assert( (a + b) == 6);
```

When the compiled program is run, you would see the following displayed on the `stderr` output device:

```
assertion failed: (a + b) == 6, atest.c, line xxxx
```

in which `xxxx` is the line where this `assert()` macro was called. (The capitalization of the assertion line may vary between compilers and operating systems.)

The advantage of the `assert()` macro is that it allows debug code to be toggled into and out of the program, using the `-d` command line argument to the compiler. We assume that your compiler has an equivalent `-d` or `-D` command line switch, which inserts `#define` commands into the source code. If, for example, the command line uses

```
-dNDEBUG
```

at compile time, the line

```
assert( (a + b) == 6);
```

is not compiled into the program. You can "remove" the `assert()` test code from the program source code without having to edit out instances of the `assert()` macro.

Most compilers that support the `assert()` macro will support the use of `NDEBUG` from the command line, but there may be compilers that don't.

ctype.h ANSI/SYSV

This header file contains the macro definitions for the "is" macros [for example, `isalpha()`, `isdigit()`], and the "to" macros [such as, `toupper()`, `tolower()`], plus their related function prototypes. The list of functions includes

`isalnum()`	`isalpha()`	`iscntrl()`
`isdigit()`	`isgraph()`	`islower()`
`isprint()`	`ispunct()`	`isspace()`
`isupper()`	`isxdigit()`	`tolower()`
`toupper()`		

(Note that X3J11 is considering proposals to handle multibyte character sequences, which are used to handle foreign languages like Kanji, the Japanese character set. The resolution of these proposals will force some change on `ctype.h`, but the scope of the change is unknown. An additional ctype header will probably be created to supplement the current one.)

errno.h ANSI/SYSV

This file contains a declaration of `int errno`, an integer that is set to reflect various error conditions by functions in the standard library. ANSI declares `errno` to be a `volatile int`.

The `errno` variable is set to zero at start-up and may be changed by a library function to an error number. The error number selected depends on the function that generates the error.

The file also contains numerous `#define`s for error conditions that may be detected by the library functions. For SYSV, the constants associated with each type may be used with `sys_errlist[]` to print an error message. If `EBADF` is `#define`d in `errno.h` as:

```
#define EBADF  4
```

if `errno` equals 4 in a program, the statement

```
printf("%s", sys_errlist[errno]);
```

would display the error message associated with a bad file number.

For ANSI, the only constants guaranteed to be defined in this file are:

`EDOM` If a function has passed an argument not within the function's defined domain, a "domain error" occurs. The value returned by the function is implementation-defined, and `errno` is set to `EDOM`.

ERANGE If a function cannot represent the result as a double, a "range error" occurs. Usually, if a function senses numeric overflow (number too big) or underflow, the function sets errno to ERANGE. The specific value associated with ERANGE is implementation-defined.

Both macros are used with math functions (see math.h). ANSI does not guarantee the UNIX sys_errlist, but has two functions [perror() and strerror()] that can be used to output a similar list.

The number of symbolic constants contained in errno.h will vary among operating systems. You should print the errno.h header file to see which symbolic constants are supported by your compiler.

fcntl.h SYSV

This non-ANSI header file contains #defines for symbolic constants often used with the unbuffered file input/output functions, such as creat(), open(), read(), and write(). Although the ANSI standard discourages the use of these low-level functions (to the extent of not including them in the standard library), they are common in many programs.

These constants are flags that are used when a file is opened, and may be OR'ed together.

O_RDONLY	open for reading only
O_WRONLY	open for writing only
O_RDWR	open for reading or writing
O_APPEND	open for writing at end of file
O_CREAT	create file if it doesn't exist
O_TRUNC	if file exists, truncate the file to a 0 length
O_EXCL	exclusive open

For example,

```
open("tempfile.c", O_WRONLY | O_CREAT | O_EXCL, mode);
```

says to open tempfile.c for writing and, if the file does not already exist, create the file. Use this to open a temporary file, but not overwrite a file with the same name if one already exists.

Also see the fcntl() and open() function descriptions in Chapter 7.

float.h ANSI

This header file is similar to the `limits.h` header file but concerns how floating point is represented by the compiler. Defined in this file are symbolic constants that explain the maximum and minimum floating-point limits, default precision, maximum exponent value, and others. Several constants represent what ANSI deems to be minimally acceptable values. These constants may vary among implementations.

```
#define FLT_RADIX    2
```

Here is the radix of the exponent for floating-point numbers (base 2 in this example). ANSI states that FLT_RADIX is the only macro that is a restricted constant expression in this header file.

```
#define FLT_ROUNDS  Ø
```

How addition rounding is handled: indeterminable (-1), rounds toward 0 (0), rounds toward nearest number (1), rounds toward positive infinity (2), or rounds toward negative infinity (3). Any other value is implementation-defined. A Ø for the constant assumes that the result is chopped.

```
#define FLT_DIG       6
#define DBL_DIG      1Ø
#define LDBL_DIG     1Ø
```

These are the minimal number of base 10 digits of precision in the mantissa for `float`, `double`, and `long double` data types.

```
#define FLT_EPSILON        1E-5
#define DBL_EPSILON        1E-9
#define LDBL_EPSILON       1E-9
```

These values represent the smallest number that can be added to a `float`, `double`, or `long double` data type and change the original value. That is, if a `float x = 1.Ø`, then: `x + FLT_EPSILON != 1.Ø`. If values smaller than epsilon are added to a number, there is no guarantee that the difference is measurable in floating-point representation.

```
#define DBL_MANT_DIG
#define FLT_MANT_DIG
#define LDBL_MANT_DIG
```

These symbolic constants represent the number of digits used in the floating-point mantissa, expressed in the base of FLT_RADIX. If the radix is base 2, these constants represent the number of bits in the mantissa.

```
#define DBL_MAX          1E+37
#define FLT_MAX          1E+37
#define LDBL_MAX         1E+37
```

Here is the maximum finite floating-point number that can be represented.

```
#define DBL_MAX_10_EXP   37
#define FLT_MAX_10_EXP   37
#define LDBL_MAX_10_EXP  37
```

These constants represent the largest integer power by which 10 can be raised and still represent a finite floating-point number—that is, 10E37.

```
#define DBL_MAX_EXP
#define FLT_MAX_EXP
#define LDBL_MAX_EXP
```

These constants represent the largest integer power minus 1 to which FLT_RADIX can be raised and still represent a finite floating-point number.

```
#define DBL_MIN          1E-37
#define FLT_MIN          1E-37
#define LDBL_MIN         1E-37
```

These constants represent the smallest normalized floating-point number.

```
#define DBL_MIN_10_EXP   -37
#define FLT_MIN_10_EXP   -37
#define LDBL_MIN_10_EXP  -37
```

These constants represent the smallest integer power by which 10 can be raised and still represent a normalized floating-point number—that is, 10E-37.

```
#define DBL_MIN_EXP
#define FLT_MIN_EXP
#define LDBL_MIN_EXP
```

These constants represent the smallest integer power minus 1 to which FLT_RADIX can be raised and still represent a finite floating-point number.

All the symbolic constants discussed are implementation-defined, and the values are required minimums.

limits.h ANSI

This header file contains symbolic constants for the limits of each basic data type. For example, INT_MAX may be #defined to be +32767 for one machine, but +2147483647 for another. This header file gives you a convenient place to find the limits of the compiler's data types. The following values are minimal values to be met by a complying ANSI compiler.

```
#define CHAR_BIT    8
#define CHAR_MAX    UCHAR_MAX or SCHAR_MAX
#define CHAR_MIN    SCHAR_MIN or 0
#define INT_MAX     +32767
#define INT_MIN     -32767
#define LONG_MAX    +2147483647
#define LONG_MIN    -2147483647
#define SCHAR_MAX   +127
#define SCHAR_MIN   -127
#define SHRT_MAX    +32767
#define SHRT_MIN    -32767
#define UCHAR_MAX   255U
#define UINT_MAX    65535U
#define ULONG_MAX   4294967295U
#define USHRT_MAX   65535U
```

The strange abbreviations are SCHAR for signed char and SHRT for short int. By looking at several of the names and unsigned constants, you can see that the leading U in the macro names is for unsigned. The compiler recognizes U (or u) appended to the number for an unsigned data type. This is an invention by ANSI.

locale.h ANSI

This header file contains information that sets "locale" and environment information for the system. The feeling is that C does, and will continue to, exist in areas where ASCII is not the standard character set or the decimal point may not be a period (it could be a comma or raised dot elsewhere). The purpose of this header file is to collect in one place these "locale-specific" differences.

The following are the macros defined in this header:

- `LC_ALL` A macro to set all of the area-specific data.
- `LC_COLLATE` A macro to change the collation table for the `strcoll()` and `strxfrm()` functions. This provides a means for ensuring that functions like `strcmp()` and `memcmp()` behave in an expected manner when dealing with non-ASCII character sets and alphabets.
- `LC_CTYPE` A macro to change the translation table used for function calls and macros that are part of `ctype.h`, such as `isalpha()`.
- `LC_NUMERIC` A macro to change the run-time radix character for the whole versus fractional part of the number. This means that a comma could be used between the 3 and the 14 in pi (3,14) in a call to `scanf()`. (In a source file, the radix character remains a period and `3.14`, not `3,14`, must be used regardless of the locale setting.)
- `LC_TIME` A macro that changes the presentation of information by the time functions. See the `time.h` header file.

Each macro may be used as the first argument to a call to the `set-locale()` function, which is the only function listed in the `locale.h` header file.

Of the ANSI headers, `locale.h` will be the most likely to change when the international proposals are considered by X3J11 in late 1987.

malloc.h SYSV

```
malloc()     free()     realloc()     calloc()
mallopt()    mallinfo()
```

See the `stdlib.h` header file for information on `calloc()`, `free()`, `malloc()`, and `realloc()`. The other functions, `mallopt()` and `mal-linfo()`, are not covered in this book.

math.h ANSI

This header file contains either the prototypes or declarations for functions found in the math library. Most return `double` data types.

In addition, this header file contains the macro

`HUGE_VAL`	If a function generates a result that causes numeric overflow, the function returns the value `HUGE_VAL`. (The value's sign is the expected sign of the function.) Most functions that return `HUGE_VAL` also set `errno`.

Note that `HUGE_VAL` has no counterpart. That is, there is no `TINY_VAL` macro. When numeric underflow occurs, most functions simply return zero.

The `math.h` header file includes prototypes for the following functions:

```
acos()      asin()      atan()      atan2()
cos()       sin()       tan()       cosh()
sinh()      tanh()      exp()       frexp()
ldexp()     log()       log10()     modf()
pow()       sqrt()      ceil()      fabs()
floor()     fmod()
```

memory.h SYSV

```
memccpy()   memchr()    memcmp()    memcpy()
memset()
```

See the `string.h` header file for the "mem" functions.

search.h

See the `stdlib.h` header file for `bsearch()`. The remaining functions, the `hsearch()` family, `lsearch()`, and the `tsearch()` family, are not covered in this book.

setjmp.h ANSI

The setjmp.h header file contains prototypes for the setjmp() and longjmp() functions, plus a typedef for jmp_buf. The jmp_buf typedef is an array, capable of storing information necessary to save the calling environment, and is implementation-defined. The purpose of jmp_buf is to save sufficient information to permit the equivalent of a nonlocal, interfunction goto statement. For more information, see the discussion of the setjmp() and longjmp() functions in Chapter 8.

signal.h ANSI/SYSV

This header #defines numerous symbolic constants and macros used to process "signals" or interrupts. The function used to process a signal is the signal() function. The processing of signals or interrupts is implementation-specific, and the extent of signal processing varies among environments.

Several macros, prototypes, and a typedef are defined in this header file.

```
sig_atomic_t
```

This is a typedef in the ANSI proposal for an integral data type whose modification can be completed while asynchronous interrupts occur. This means a sig_atomic_t data type can be modified even in the presence of an interrupt. For example, if you are processing a long and an interrupt occurs, it is unlikely that the long operation will be completed before the interrupt takes control. On the other hand, if the data item is an integer, the operation on the integer can be finished prior to serving the interrupt. The sig_atomic_t type states that data items of this type will have processing completed in the presence of an interrupt.

The following three macros may be used as the second argument of the signal() function.

SIG_DFL	Default processing of signals
SIG_ERR	The request for user-supplied signal processing cannot be honored
SIG_IGN	Ignore signal processing

The following macros evaluate to a positive integral constant expression that is the signal number of the signal condition. Other macros may be present, but the compiler is required to provide only those in the following list.

`SIGABRT`	Abnormal process termination
`SIGFPE`	Some form of error in an arithmetic operation
`SIGILL`	Illegal function image
`SIGINT`	Interactive attention signal
`SIGSEGV`	Illegal storage access
`SIGTERM`	Program termination request

The functions prototyped in the header file include

`signal()` `raise()`

The functions are discussed in Chapter 8.

stdarg.h ANSI
varargs.h SYSV

This header file implements several macros, function prototypes, and data types for processing a variable number of arguments on a function call. These macros are used with `vprintf()` and its relatives. The following are items included in this header file:

`va_list`

This is a `typedef` for an array of objects that hold information for use by the variable argument macros (for example, `va_arg`). The list of macros includes

`va_start()` `va_arg()` `va_end()`

stddef.h ANSI

This header file contains definitions for several variables and macros. It may also contain variable names reserved by the compiler and symbolic constants. What follows is a list of the macros and functions in this header.

NULL

Although NULL is often defined as zero, nothing says that NULL must be zero—it is implementation-specific. Because the null pointer may vary among environments, the ANSI proposal does not state what NULL is, only that it is to be defined in this header file.

`offsetof(struct t, member_id)`

This macro yields an integral constant, which is the number of bytes from the beginning of the structure named `t` to the member of the structure named `member_id`. Use this function to determine the byte-offset of most data types (its behavior on bit-fields is undefined).

Because this functionality is difficult to implement as a macro, the X3J11 proposal has made `offsetof()` an operator to the C language. If the proposal is accepted, `offsetof()` will become a keyword (meaning its use is reserved), and the macro will be struck from `stddef.h`.

`ptrdiff_t`

This is a `typedef` for the signed integral produced by the subtraction of two pointers. This `typedef` is included, like `size_t`, because pointer sizes vary among environments. The `ptr_diff_t` type provides an easy means of coping with these differences.

`size_t`

The `size_t` `typedef` defines a data type large enough to hold the unsigned integral result from the `sizeof` operator. This makes sense because a data item can be larger than what an unsigned `int` can represent. Use the `size_t` `typedef` for objects that use the `sizeof` operator.

stdio.h ANSI

This is probably one of the most-used header files in typical C programs. There are, however, new things in this file, and perhaps one or two things missing compared to older versions. At this time, this file contains a number of `typedef`s and macros, plus prototypes for a large number of input/output-related functions.

`fpos_t`

This `typedef` defines an object capable of storing the numeric position in a stream. Like `size_t` discussed in the `stddef.h` header, different operating systems are capable of different file sizes. The `fpos_t` type can hold any position in the stream.

```
_IOFBF
_IOLBF
_IONBF
```

These three macros may be used for the third (`mode`) argument in `setvbuf()`. The third argument is used to determine how input/output buffering is to be performed. In the example, the macros' interpretations are fully buffered, line buffered, and no buffering. (See the `setvbuf()` function in Chapter 7 for a full description.)

```
BUFSIZ
```

This macro expands to an integral constant expression that is the size of the buffer used by the `setbuf()` function.

```
EOF
```

This macro results in a negative integral expression that indicates end-of-file.

```
FILE
```

This is a data type capable of storing the information necessary to control an input/output stream. If you list this header, you can see that FILE is usually a `typedef` of a structure, whose members work in concert to control the stream.

```
L_tmpnam
```

This is a constant expression that is used to define the size of an array large enough to hold a temporary file name produced by the `tmpnam()` function.

```
OPEN_MAX
```

This results in an integral constant expression that is equal to the minimum number of files which may be open at the same time. (This is similar to NFILES for earlier C compilers.)

```
SEEK_CUR
SEEK_END
SEEK_SET
```

These three macros expand to integer constant expressions that may be used to set the file pointer in an input/output stream and can also be used as the third argument in a call to `fseek()`. Because the third argument in `fseek()` is used to set a position in the stream and it is an integer value, programmers in the past tended to write their own macros for these integers. Where 0 meant beginning of file, you may now use SEEK_SET instead. The other two symbolic constants relate seeking from the current position in the stream (SEEK_CUR) and from the end-of-file (SEEK_END).

TMP_MAX

This macro produces an integral number that equals the minimum number of unique file names `tmpnam()` can produce.

stderr
stdin
stdout

These are objects of type pointer to FILE that are associated with the standard error stream, `stderr`; the standard input stream, `stdin`; and the standard output stream, `stdout`.

Because ANSI states that any required `typedef` or macro will be included in each appropriate header, definitions for NULL and `size_t` will also appear in this file.

Functions prototyped in this header file include the following:

```
clearerr()      fclose()      feof()        ferror()
fflush()        fgetc()       fgetpos()     fgets()
fopen()         fprintf()     fputc()       fputs()
fread()         freopen()     fscanf()      fseek()
fsetpos()       ftell()       fwrite()      getc()
getchar()       gets()        perror()      printf()
putc()          putchar()     puts()        remove()
rename()        rewind()      scanf()       setbuf()
setvbuf()       sprintf()     sscanf()      tmpfile()
tmpnam()        ungetc()      vfprintf()    vprintf()
vsprintf()
```

stdlib.h ANSI

This header file contains a number of utility functions that don't exactly fit any of the previous header files. In a way, it is a catchall header file for functions without a required header file associated with them. It includes a number of functions that have their own header files under SYSV [for example, `calloc()`] and most of the converter functions presented in Chapter 4.

There are several `typedef`s, macros, and prototypes in this header file. The macros include ERANGE and HUGE_VAL (see the `math.h` header file discussion) in addition to

EXIT_FAILURE

This macro is an integral expression given to the `exit()` function to indicate unsuccessful termination to the operating system.

EXIT_SUCCESS

This macro is an integral expression given to the `exit()` function to indicate successful termination to the operating system.

RAND_MAX

This macro generates an integral constant expression that is the maximum value returned from the `rand()` function.

`div_t`

This is a `typedef` for a structure that can hold the quotient and remainder from a call to the `div()` function.

`ldiv_t`

This is the same as `div_t`, except the quotient and remainder from the `ldiv()` function call are `long` integer values.

Because ANSI states that any required `typedef` or macro will be included in each appropriate header, definitions for NULL and `size_t` will also appear in `stdlib.h`.

This header also includes a number of functions that used to be associated with the `malloc.h` [for example, `malloc()`, `free()`, etc.] and the `search.h` [for example, `bsearch()`, `qsort()`, etc.] header files. Functions in this header file include the following:

```
abort()      abs()        atexit()     atof()
atoi()       atol()       bsearch()    calloc()
div()        exit()       free()       getenv()
labs()       ldiv()       malloc()     qsort()
rand()       realloc()    srand()      strtod()
strtol()     strtoul()    system()
```

string.h ANSI

The `string.h` header file contains the prototypes for all "str" functions [for example, `strlen()`, `strcmp()`, `strcat()`, etc.]. Some headers may include `#defines` for str-type functions that replace older functions, such as `strchr()` for `index()`, and `strrchr()` for `rindex()`, which are no longer part of the ANSI standard C library, and in fact, dropped from the System V library.

Because ANSI states that any required `typedef` or macro will be included in each appropriate header, the definition for `size_t` will also appear in this file.

This header file also includes some of the functions [for example, `memcpy()`, `memmove()`, etc.] associated with the `memory.h` header file in SYSV. The following are the ANSI functions:

```
memchr()      memcmp()      memcpy()      memmove()
memset()      strcat()      strchr()      strcmp()
strcoll()     strcpy()      strcspn()     strerror()
strlen()      strncat()     strncmp()     strncpy()
strpbrk()     strrchr()     strspn()      strstr()
strtok()      strxfrm()
```

time.h ANSI

This header file contains macros, `typedefs`, and function prototypes concerned with time. These include the following:

```
clock_t
time_t
```

These two `typedefs` establish an arithmetic type capable of storing time values used in the time functions, both as arguments and return data types.

```
struct tm
```

This is one of the few data items expressed by ANSI in terms of its contents. The structure holds what ANSI refers to as "broken-down time." The `tm` structure must hold these members as a minimum (see table 3.1).

Table 3.1
Members of `tm` Structure

Member Name	Normal Range	Description
`int tm_sec;`	0 - 59	seconds after the minute
`int tm_min;`	0 - 59	minutes after the hour
`int tm_hour;`	0 - 23	hours after midnight
`int tm_mday;`	1 - 31	day of the month
`int tm_mon;`	0 - 11	months since January
`int tm_year;`	---	years since 1900
`int tm_wday;`	0 - 6	days since Sunday
`int tm_yday;`	0 - 365	days since January 1
`int tm_isdst;`	*	is Daylight Savings Time?

* DST in effect if > 0, DST not in effect if == 0, and don't know if < 0

There may be additional members in the `tm` structure.

`CLK_TCK`

This macro is the number of clock ticks (the units returned by the `clock()` function, `clock_t`) per second. Therefore, the value returned from `clock()`, divided by `CLK_TCK`, measures processor time in seconds. (See the `clock()` function discussion in Chapter 9.)

The following are the functions provided in the `time.h` header file:

`asctime()`	`clock()`	`ctime()`	`difftime()`
`gmtime()`	`localtime()`	`mktime()`	`strftime()`
`time()`			

values.h

See the `limits.h` and `float.h` header files.

varargs.h

See the `stdarg.h` header file.

4

Converter Functions

The functions in this chapter are designed to convert string data into numeric form. You will not find the venerable `itoa()` or `ftoa()` functions in either the ANSI or SYSV standard. Rather, both standards prefer that you use `sprintf()` instead. Program 4.1 shows how to do this.

Program 4.1

```
/* sprintf() instead of itoa() */

#include <stdio.h>

int main()
{
      char buff[20];
      int i;

      i = 65;
      sprintf(buff, "%d", i);
      printf("i = %d ASCII i = %s", i, buff);
}
```

The call to `sprintf()` causes the output, produced by the control string and its argument, to be written into `buff[]`, not `stdout`. The `printf()` call shows that the integer value `i` and its ASCII representation are the same. This method will work for the other data types supported by `printf()` family.

Even though `itoa()` and `ftoa()` are gone from both standards, the functionality remains inherent in `sprintf()`.

Function Names

`atoi()` `atol()` `atof()`

Standard Met

ANSI, SYSV

Purpose

To convert string data into numeric values.

Prototypes

```
int atoi(const char *str)
long int atol(const char *str)
double atof(const char *str)
```

Required Header

`#include <stdlib.h>`	ANSI
None provided	SYSV

Usage

```
int atoi(const char *str)
```

The `atoi()` function returns an integer number, which is formed from the contents of the string pointed to by `str`. If `str` contains any leading white space characters (a space, carriage return, new line, form feed, tab, or vertical tab), they are ignored in the conversion. The conversion ends when the null character `\0` or a nondigit character is read. If an integer number cannot be formed from the contents of the string, the return value is indeterminate (although most implementations return a zero). The function does not perform error checking (for example, determining whether the value is within the range of an `int`).

```
long int atol(const char *str)
```

The function returns a long integer value, which is formed from the contents pointed to by `str`. The function operates like `atoi()`: (1) leading white space characters are ignored, (2) conversion ends on reading `\0` or a nondigit character, (3) the return value is indeterminate if a long integer number cannot be formed, and (4) no error checking is performed. The primary difference between this function and `atoi()` is that `atol()` returns a long integer, not an `int`.

```
double atof(const char *str)
```

This function returns a double-precision, floating-point number, which is formed from the contents pointed to by `str`. Leading white space characters are ignored, and the conversion continues until `\0` or a nondigit character is read. The decimal point and sign characters [(+) or (-)] are considered valid conversion characters in the string. The conversion string also may contain the letter `e` or `E`, followed by an optional sign character and an integer value (for example, `2.9E-23`).

ANSI and SYSV state that `atof()` behaves in a manner similar to `strtod()`, except ANSI states that the behavior on errors is different. For SYSV, if overflow is detected, plus or minus `HUGE` is returned, depending on the sign of the argument. On underflow, zero is returned. In both cases, `errno` is set to `ERANGE`. For ANSI, whether `errno` is set on an error is implementation-defined, and if the result cannot be represented (an overflow or underflow condition), the behavior of the function is undefined.

Caution

You may forget to declare what `atol()` and `atof()` return. If an integer is not the same size as a `long` integer (common for many 16-bit implementations), forgetting to declare `atol()` causes the compiler to malform `atol()`'s return value into an `int`. And since few implementations have an integer whose size is the same as a `double` (typically eight bytes), forgetting to declare `atof()` causes the returning `double` data type to be mangled into an `int`.

To avoid this problem, you should include the header file that contains the prototypes for the appropriate functions (such as `stdlib.h`). If your compiler does not support prototyping, you should declare each function that returns a noninteger data type at the top of the file, or create your own header file that declares all of the (non-`int`) functions in your library.

Illustration

```
#include <stdio.h>                /* I/O function header file      */
#include <stdlib.h>               /* Miscellaneous library header  */

#define MAXSTR 50                 /* For a big string              */

int main()
{
     char s1[MAXSTR];              /* Create a working string       */
     void getnumber(char *s);      /* General input function        */

     getnumber(s1);
     printf("Number is %d using atoi().\n", atoi(s1));
     printf("Number is %ld using atol().\n", atol(s1));
     printf("Number is %f using atof().\n", atof(s1));
}

void getnumber(char *s)
{
     printf("Enter a number: ");
     gets(s);
}
```

Program Comment

The function `getnumber()` is a dumb function (that is, without error checking) that asks you to input a number and uses the `gets()` function to fill in the character pointer `s` which is passed to the function. After you enter the number, a series of `printf()`'s print out the number by calls to `atoi()`, `atol()`, and `atof()`.

Note that when a floating-point number is entered, the value is truncated by `atoi()` and `atol()`. That is, `2.9` produces a return value of 2 for both `atoi()` and `atol()`; the function does not round the number.

You may want to enter floating-point values that would produce overflow (a number too large for the compiler to represent) and underflow (a number too small for the compiler to represent), to see how these extremes are treated.

Miscellaneous Comments

Two alternative functions, strtol() and strtod(), are replacing atol() and atof() in the ANSI and SYSV libraries. These two functions are becoming more popular because of greater flexibility and tighter error-checking facilities. Under ANSI, atoi(), atol(), and atof() need not affect the value of errno if a conversion error occurs. The strtol() and strtod() functions guarantee errno is set on an erroneous conversion.

Also note that the atof() function can be affected by the call to setlocale(). If the decimal point character (LC_NUMERIC) is changed through the call to setlocale(), the atof() function uses the appropriate character for the decimal-point.

Function Names

```
strtod()        strtol()        strtoul()
```

Standard Met

`strtod(), strtol(), strtoul()`	ANSI
`strtod(), strtol()`	SYSV

Purpose

To convert string data into numeric values.

Prototypes

```
double strtod(const char *str, char **nptr)
long int strtol(const char *str, char **nptr, int base)
unsigned long int strtoul(const char *str, char **nptr, int base)
```

Required Header

`#include <stdlib.h>`	ANSI
None provided	SYSV

Usage

```
double strtod(const char *str, char **nptr)
```

This function returns a double data type, which is formed by the contents of the string pointed to by `str`. If `str` contains leading white space characters (a space, carriage return, new line, form feed, tab, or vertical tab), they are ignored. The string may also contain a sign character, [(+) or (-)], followed by a string of one or more digits, and an optional decimal point. The decimal point may be followed by an e or E character for scientific notation, which may be followed by an optional sign character, followed by a sequence of one or more digits to form an integer exponent. Therefore, 123e2 is a valid input string. The parsing of `str` stops on the first character inconsistent with a valid `double` data type.

If strtod() is called with the second argument cast to a null pointer [for example, (char **) NULL], the function performs the same as atof().

The pointer pointed to by nprt can assume two values if nprt is nonnull. If a successful conversion takes place or the converted value cannot be represented as a double, the pointer pointed to nptr will be set to point to the character that terminated the scan of str. If the string is empty or does not have the expected form, the pointer pointed to by nptr will point to str.

If a double cannot be formed from the contents of str, the return value from strtod() is zero. If the value causes overflow, ANSI returns HUGE_VAL, whereas SYSV returns HUGE, and both set errno to ERANGE. If underflow is detected, the return value is zero, and errno is set to ERANGE under SYSV. Under the proposed ANSI standard, you cannot be sure that errno is set to ERANGE because it is implementation-defined.

```
long int strtol(const char *str, char **nptr, int base)
```

This function returns a long integer formed from the contents of the string pointed to by str. If str contains leading white space characters (that is, space, carriage return, new line, form feed, tab, or vertical tab), they are ignored in the conversion. The string may contain a sign character [(+) or (-)]. The conversion ends on reading a null character or a character that is not consistent with the base numbering system as determined by the value of the integer argument base.

With one exception, the argument base must fall within the range of 2 through 36. If base is set to zero, the contents of str determines the base used in the conversion. If the string begins with the character digit Ø, the base is octal. If the string begins with Øx or ØX, the base is hexadecimal. If base is zero and the string does not begin with a Ø, Øx, or ØX, the base is assumed to be decimal.

The argument nptr can assume two values: NULL or non-NULL. If nptr is a null pointer, nptr is ignored and strtol() functions the same as atol(). If nptr is not a NULL, nprt assumes one of two values. If a long integer can be formed or the number has the correct form but cannot be represented in a long int, the pointer pointed to by nptr will point to the character that terminated the scan of str. If the string is empty or does not have the proper form, the pointer pointed to by nptr points to str.

If an integer number cannot be formed from the contents of the string, the return value is zero.

The SYSV version of this function does not perform error checking (for example, determine whether the value is within the range of a `long int`).

The ANSI version states that overflow sets the return value to either `LONG_MIN` or `LONG_MAX` (see `limits.h`), as determined by the sign of the value. Also, `errno` is set to the value `ERANGE`.

```
unsigned long strtoul(const char *str, char **nptr, int base)
```

The `strtoul()` function is the same as `strtol()` with the following exceptions: The minus sign is not a valid member of its set, the return value is an unsigned long integer, and overflow returns `ULONG_MAX`.

Caution

Note that the number of arguments for `strtol()` and `strtoul()` differs from that for `strtod()`. A base converter is not part of the `strtod()` function. Also note that `strtoul()` is not part of the SYSV library.

Illustration

```
#include <stdio.h>                      /* Standard header files        */
#include <stdlib.h>                     /* for ANSI                     */

#define MAXSTR 50                       /* For a big string             */

void getnumber(char *s);                /* General input                */
void getbase(char *s, int *ptr);        /* Input for base number        */

int main()
{
     char s1[MAXSTR],                   /* Create a working string      */
          *nptr,                        /* If things go wrong           */
          basestr[MAXSTR];              /* Create base string           */

     int base;                          /* Hold the base value          */
```

```
    getnumber(s1);
    getbase(basestr, &base);

    printf("With an input base of %d the decimal values are:\n\n", base);
    printf("long = %ld [strtol()]\n",
        strtol(s1, &nptr, base) );
    printf("endptr pointer is :%s: for strtol().\n\n\n", nptr);

#ifdef ANSI
    printf("unsigned long = %ld [strtoul()]\n",
        strtol(s1, &nptr, base);
    printf("endptr pointer is :%s: for strtoul().\n\n\n", nptr);
#endif

    printf("The input number in base 10 for floating point becomes:\n\n");
    printf("double = %f [strtod()].\n",
        strtod(s1, &nptr);
    printf("endptr pointer is :%s: for strtod().\n", nptr);
}

void getnumber(char *s)
{
    printf("Enter a number: ");
    gets(s);
}

void getbase(char *basestr, int *base)
{
    int i;

    for (;;) {
        printf("\n\nEnter a number base, either 0 or between 2 and 36: ");
        i = atoi( gets(basestr) );
        if (i < 0 || i == 1 || i > 36) {
            printf("\nBase %d out of range. Must be 0 or 2-36. Try again.");
        } else
            break;
    }
    *base = i;
}
```

Program Comment

Note that we have included the `stdlib.h` header file because it often contains several symbolic constants used in error checking in addition to prototyping. Since we do no range checking on the numbers, we have omitted `limits.h`, which is used to test the return values for errors.

The `#define ANSI` is used to toggle the code that tests `strtoul()`. We do this because SYSV does not support this function.

Once in `main()`, several working variables are defined, plus the declarations for several functions used in the program. Note that we have defined a character pointer named `nptr` for use in the converter functions.

Eventually, the call to `getnumber()` asks you to enter a number that is used by the converter functions. The call to `getbase()` asks you to enter the base for use in the `strtol()` and `strtoul()` (if supported) function calls. Once these functions have been called, the program has the necessary information to exercise the converters.

Let's see what happens with different input values. For example, suppose that you enter a value of `7f` for the number, and a base of `16` (for hexadecimal). You would get the following output [the `strtoul()` values are the same]:

```
long = 127 for strtol()
endptr pointer is :: for strtol().
```

and

```
double = 7.000000 for strtod()
endptr pointer is :f: for strtod().
```

What happened? First, a hexadecimal value of `7f` is 127 in decimal. Because both input characters (that is, `7` and `f`) are within the set of the base given (hexadecimal or base 16), the error pointer points to the null that terminates `str`. Since this is a nonprintable character, nothing appears on the display.

When we call `strtod()` with the same input, the results are different. Because `strtod()` always expects its input expressed in base 10 and the character `f` is not part of the base 10 character set, `strtod()` attempts to form a double from the portion of `str` consistent with the base 10 character set. Because `7` is within the valid character set but `f` is not, `strtod()` returns `7` as the answer and sets the error pointer to point to f as the invalid character in the input. Therefore, the error pointer points to f.

Let's examine the program with the input 10.0e10 and the base set to 10. In this case, the output becomes

```
long = 10 for strtol()
endptr pointer is :.0e10: for strtol().
```

and

```
double = 100000000000.000000 for strtod()
endptr pointer is :: for strtod().
```

The results are somewhat reversed from the prior example. Because a decimal point (.) is not consistent with the valid character set for a long integer, the scan of the input stream stops at the decimal point. As a result, the error pointer is set to point to the decimal point, and the program prints .0e10 for the error pointer. Therefore, only the first two digits, 1 and 0 of str, fall within the character set, so the value returned is 10.

Notice that the strtol() function returns only 0 if no integer value can be formed. If part of the string can be formed into an integer, you will get part of an integer back as the return value.

When strtod() is called with the same input, the proper value is returned as a double because all of the characters in str fall within the character set for a floating-point number.

As a final example, if you enter 8 for the number and set the base to octal (base 8), the program would output:

```
long = 0 for strtol()
endptr pointer is :8: for strtol().
```

and

```
double = 8.000000 for strtod()
endptr pointer is :: for strtod().
```

The return value for strtol() is 0 because 8 is not part of the octal character set (the highest digit character is 7), and the error pointer points to the offending character 8. This is a deviation from earlier behavior from SYSV implementations, which allowed 8 or 9 as octal digits. The result is also different because parsing of the input string fails on the first character; hence, no integer value can be formed, and the return value is zero.

For the `strtod()` function, however, 8 falls within the valid character set, so a floating-point 8 is returned, and the error pointer points to the null terminator of the input string `str`.

Also note that the `strtod()` function can be affected by the call to `setlocale()`. If the decimal-point character (`LC_NUMERIC`) is changed through the call to `setlocale()`, the `strtod()` function uses the appropriate character for the decimal point.

Miscellaneous Comments

The `atol()` and `atof()` functions are being phased out in favor of the `strtol()` and `strtod()` functions in this section.

5

String and Character Operations

Functions that perform operations on either string or character data are discussed in this chapter. Many functions in this section expect the header files `ctype.h` or `string.h` to be `#included` into your program. ANSI and SYSV use these header files in virtually the same manner. The details of these two header files are in Chapter 3.

You will notice that the `const` keyword and `size_t` are used in several function prototypes. The `const` keyword is explained in detail in Chapter 2 on ANSI. The `size_t` typedef is explained in Chapter 3. The original typedef declaration for `size_t` is found in the `stddef.h` header file and is an unsigned integral type large enough to hold the result of the `sizeof` operator. The size of `size_t`, therefore, is implementation-specific but for most compilers will be an `unsigned int`. Since ANSI requires each header file associated with a function which returns this typedef to defined `size_t`, We do not necessarily state that `stddef.h` is a required header file; however, for the purposes of good programming style, any function that returns a data type defined as a type specifier should `#include <stddef.h>`.

We suggest that you list out `ctype.h`, `stddef.h`, and `string.h` for use as you read this chapter.

Function Names

```
isalnum()     isalpha()     isascii()     iscntrl()
isdigit()     isgraph()     islower()     isprint()
ispunct()     isspace()     isupper()     isxdigit()
```

Standard Met

ANSI, SYSV

Purpose

To test the attributes of the character passed as the function argument.

Prototypes

Normally, there are no prototypes because these routines are implemented as macros. The macros are defined in the `ctype.h` header file. Since ANSI states that a macro will be accompanied by an equivalent function, the prototypes for those functions are also shown here.

```
int isalnum(int c)
int isalpha(int c)
int isascii(int c)
int iscntrl(int c)
int isdigit(int c)
int isgraph(int c)
int islower(int c)
int isprint(int c)
int ispunct(int c)
int isspace(int c)
int isupper(int c)
int isxdigit(int c)
```

Required Header

```
#include <ctype.h>
```
ANSI/SYSV

Usage

Normally, these routines are macros defined in the `ctype.h` header file. In each macro, the integer argument is tested to see whether that argument passes or fails the test being performed. (See Chapter 3 for a way to call a function instead of the macro.)

All the functions return logical true (that is, nonzero) if the argument matches the function's argument description. If the argument does not agree with the description, logical false (that is, zero) is the returned value.

All functions in this section except `isdigit()`, `isspace()`, and `isxdigit()` are affected by the character-mapping impact of the `locale.h` header file. In our examples, I have assumed the ASCII character set. The results from these programs may be different if a different locale is in force when the the function is used. (See the `locale.h` header file discussion in Chapter 3.)

```
int isalnum(int c)
```

Is the argument an alphanumeric character? The argument is not case-sensitive.

```
int isalpha(int c)
```

Is the argument an upper- or lowercase letter?

```
int isascii(int c)              /* SYSV only */
```

Is the argument in the ASCII character set? The domain is decimal 0 through 127.

```
int iscntrl(int c)
```

Is the argument a control character? The domain is decimal 0 through 32, and decimal 127 (the delete character) in the ASCII character set.

```
int isdigit(int c)
```

Is the argument a digit 0 through 9? The domain is decimal 48 through 57 in the ASCII character set.

```
int isgraph(int c)
```

Is the argument printable? The space character (' ') is not considered a printing character in this instance.

```
int islower(int c)
```

Is the argument a lowercase letter?

```
int isprint(int c)
```

This function is the same as `isgraph()`, but the space is considered a printable character.

```
int ispunct(int c)
```

Is the argument a punctuation mark? If the argument is a punctuation mark, the argument cannot be a space nor return logical true for `isalnum()`. Although the ANSI document does not say, `iscntrl()` cannot return logical true for a punctuation character.

```
int isspace(int c)
```

Is the argument a tab (9 decimal), new line (10 decimal), vertical tab (11 decimal), form feed (12 decimal), carriage return (13 decimal), or a space (32 decimal)?

```
int isupper(int c)
```

Is the argument an uppercase letter?

```
int isxdigit(int c)
```

Is the argument a hexadecimal digit? Valid hex digits are 0 through 9, A through F, and a through f.

For the previous macros or functions, if the test on the argument is logical true, the value returned will be nonzero. If the test on the argument fails, the return value is zero. The return value is undefined if the argument does not fall within the domain of the function.

Illustration

```
/*
                              is*()
*/

#include <stdio.h>
#include <stdlib.h>
#include <ctype.h>                   /* Header for is* functions          */

int main()
{
     int c;
     void dotest(int);
```

```
    printf("\nEnter character for test: ");
    c = getchar();              /* Input single char                */
    printf("%c     (%d decimal,  %x hex, %o octal)\n", c, c, c, c);
    dotest(c);
}

/*
                                  dotest()
*/

void dotest(int c)
{
    void dospace(void);

    printf("\n   Character is an:                  Character is not an:     \n");
    printf("-----------------------------------------------------------\n");

    if ( isalpha(c) == 0)
        dospace();                  /* Do if function is false          */
    printf("   isalpha()\n");

    if ( isupper(c) == 0)
        dospace();
    printf("   isupper()\n");

    if ( islower(c) == 0)
        dospace();
    printf("   islower()\n");

    if ( isdigit(c) == 0)
        dospace();
    printf("   isdigit()\n");

    if ( isxdigit(c) == 0)
        dospace();
    printf("   isxdigit()\n");

    if ( isalnum(c) == 0)
        dospace();
    printf("   isalnum()\n");
```

```
     if ( isspace(c) == 0)
          dospace();
     printf("     isspace()\n");

     if ( ispunct(c) == 0)
          dospace();
     printf("     ispunct()\n");

     if ( isprint(c) == 0)
          dospace();
     printf("     isprint()\n");

     if ( isgraph(c) == 0)
          dospace();
     printf("     isgraph()\n");

     if ( iscntrl(c) == 0)
          dospace();
     printf("     iscntrl()\n");

#ifdef SYSV                              /* Forget it if not SYSV */
     if ( isascii(c) == 0)
          dospace();
     printf("     isascii()\n");
#endif
}

/*
                                        dospace()
*/

void dospace(void)
{
     printf("                    ");
     /*           twenty spaces           */
}
```

Program Comment

The routines that are used to test the character entered by the user are macros, not functions. Since the definitions for the macros are in the `ctype.h` header file, we must `#include` that header file in the program. The example does not `#define SYSV`; the final test for `isascii()`, therefore, will not be compiled into the program unless you add a `#define` for `SYSV`. (You can also do this from the command line with `-dSYSV` or `-DSYSV`.)

After the character is entered, its value is displayed in decimal, hexadecimal, and octal. The program then calls `dotest()`. The `dotest()` function prints a header and then tests the character for its attributes by exercising each of the `is*()` macros. In each case, if the test fails (that is, the macro returns a zero for logical false), the function `dospace()` is called. The `dospace()` function prints out 40 spaces, so the name of the macro that just failed is printed under the "`Character is not an:`" heading in the program. If the character passes the macro's test, no call to `dospace()` is made, and the macro name appears under the "`Character is an:`" heading.

The way the program works is best illustrated by a sample program run. If you enter the character `a` from the keyboard, the output becomes

```
Enter character for test: a     (97 decimal,  61 hex,  141 octal)

        Character is an:              Character is not an:
        ------------------------------------------------------------
        isalpha()
                                              isupper()
        islower()
                                              isdigit()
        isxdigit()
        isalnum()
                                              isspace()
                                              ispunct()
        isprint()
        isgraph()
                                              iscntrl()
```

The program run was generated with a compiler that uses the ASCII character set.

Miscellaneous Comments

See the comments in Chapter 3 about how a function can be forced to override a macro definition that is in scope.

Function Names

`tolower()` `toupper()`

Standard Met

ANSI, SYSV

Purpose

Converts characters between lower- and uppercase.

Prototypes

```
int tolower(int letter)
int toupper(int letter)
```

Required Header

`#include <ctype.h>` ANSI/SYSV

Usage

```
int tolower(int letter)
```

This function returns the lowercase equivalent of `letter`. If `letter` is not an uppercase letter, `letter` is returned unchanged.

```
int toupper(int letter)
```

This function returns the uppercase equivalent of `letter`. If `letter` is not a lowercase letter, `letter` is returned unchanged.

Caution

Earlier versions of these functions that had a leading underscore character [for example, `_tolower()`] are being phased out. This is consistent with the convention of not using a leading underscore in variable and function names.

Illustration

```
/*
                              tolower(), toupper()
*/

#include <stdio.h>              /* Standard header file          */
#include <stdlib.h>
#include <ctype.h>              /* Header file for functions     */

void pause(void),
     dotuplo(const char letter),
     start1(char *s1);

int main()
{
     char c;

     start1(&c);
     dotuplo(c);                  /* Do converters                  */
}

/*
                                  start1()
*/

void start1(char *s1)
{
     char buff[10];

     printf("Enter a character to test: ");
     gets(buff);
     *s1 = buff[0];
}

/*
                                  dotuplo()
*/

void dotuplo(const char letter)
{
```

```
        printf("\nOriginal character is: = %c\n", letter);
        printf("toupper(%c) = %c\n", letter, toupper(letter) );
        printf("tolower(%c) = %c\n", letter, tolower(letter) );
        pause();
}

/*
                                    pause()
*/

void pause(void)
{
        printf("\n\nPress RETURN or ENTER to continue: ");
        getchar();
}
```

Program Comment

The program begins with the usual header files, including `ctype.h`. The call to `start1()` asks you to enter a letter, and the function `dotuplo()` calls the `tolower()` and `toupper()` functions with the letter you entered. The program then shows the value returned from the calls.

Miscellaneous Comments

None.

Function Names

`memcpy()` `memmove()` `strcpy()` `strncpy()`

Standard Met

ANSI, SYSV

Purpose

Functions to copy characters.

Prototypes

```
void *memcpy(void *str1, const void *str2, size_t num)
void *memmove(void *str1, const void *str2, size_t num)
char *strcpy(char *str1, const char *str2)
char *strncpy(char *str1, const char *str2, size_t num)
```

Required Header

`#include <string.h>`	ANSI/SYSV
`#include <memory.h>`	SYSV for `memcpy()` only

Usage

```
void *memcpy(void *str1, const void *str2, size_t num)
```

This function copies `num` characters from whatever is pointed to by `str2` to whatever is pointed to by `str1`. The function returns a pointer to `str1`. The `memcpy()` function does not necessarily copy correctly when the two areas overlap.

Note the use of `void` pointers in this function. These pointers allow the function to be used with data types other than character strings. Because these two pointers (`str1` and `str2`) are void pointers and are prototyped as `char` pointers, they can point to any data item without drawing an error message.

```
void *memmove(void *str1, const void *str2, size_t num)
```

The memmove() function works the same as memcpy(), except memmove() guarantees that the function will work properly even if the data items overlap. The memcpy() function might be somewhat faster than memmove() because checking for overlap is not part of memcpy(). The function returns str1.

```
char *strcpy(char *str1, const char *str2)
```

This function copies the string at str2 into the character array at str1, including the null character in str2. Interesting things may happen if the null character is missing from str2 because a null character terminates the copy. If the strings overlap, strcpy() will produce unpredictable results.

```
char *strncpy(char *str1, const char *str2, size_t num)
```

This function copies num characters from the string pointed to by str2 into the character array pointed to by str1. If the string length of str2 is less than the value of num, enough null characters are copied to bring the total length to num. If the length of str2 is num or more characters, no null character is appended to str1. The function returns a pointer to str1.

Caution

Some versions of the strncpy() function automatically append a null character to the end of the copied string. Both the ANSI and SYSV specifications state that a null character is appended to the string only if the length of str2 is less than num.

Illustration

```
/*
                memcpy(), memmove(), strcpy(), strncpy()
*/

#include <stdio.h>              /* Standard header file          */
#include <stdlib.h>
#include <stddef.h>             /* Need for size_t               */
#include <string.h>             /* Header file for strings       */
#ifdef SYSV
     #include <memory.h>        /* Need for SYSV                 */
#endif
```

```
#define MAXSTR 50                  /* For a big string                */

void start(char *str1),
     showem(const char *str1),
     pause(void),
     docpy(const char *str1),
     domemcopy(const char *str1);

int main()
{
     char s1[MAXSTR];                /* Create two working strings    */

     start(s1);                      /* Fill in the two strings       */

     showem(s1);                     /* Show how they are at first    */

     docpy(s1);                      /* Do copy and ncopy             */
     domemcopy(s1);                  /* Do memcopy() and memmove()    */
}

/*
                              start()
*/

void start(char *s1)
{
     printf("Enter a string of 20 or so characters: ");
     gets(s1);
}

/*
                              showem()
*/

void showem(const char *s1)
{
     printf("\nOriginal s1 = %s\n", s1);
}

/*
                              pause()
*/
```

```
void pause(void)
{
     printf("\nPress RETURN or ENTER to continue: ");
     getchar();
}

/*
                                docpy()
*/

void docpy(const char *s1)
{
     char buff[MAXSTR + 1], temp[10], *ptr;
     size_t num;
                                 /* Do strcpy() first              */
     printf("Illustrating strcpy() and strncpy()\n");
     printf("\nThe original string s1 is %s\n\n", s1);
     ptr = strcpy(buff, s1);
     printf("\n  The new string buff is:  %s1\n", buff);
     printf("  The return pointer points to:  %s\n", ptr);
     pause();

                                 /* Now do strncpy()               */

     printf("\n\nHow many characters should be copied: ");
     num = (size_t) atoi(gets(temp));

     if (num) {
          ptr = strncpy(buff, s1, num);
     }

     buff[num] = '\0';                          /* Because no null is appended   */
     printf("\n\n  The copy of %d characters from s1 is:  %s\n", num, buff);
     printf("\n  The return pointer points to: %s\n", ptr);
     pause();
}

/*
                    domemcopy()
*/

void domemcopy(const char *s1)
{
```

```
     char m1[MAXSTR + 1], m2[MAXSTR + 1];
     size_t i, len;

     printf("\n\nFor memcpy():\n");
     i = strlen(s1) / 2;

     len = (i != 0) ? i : strlen(s1);

     memcpy(m1, s1, len);                          /* Do memcpy() */
     m1[len + 1] = '\0';
     printf("   m1 = %s\n", m1);
     pause();

#ifndef SYSV
     printf("\nFinally for memmove()\n");
     memmove(&m1[1], &m1[0], strlen(m1) );        /* Do memmove() */
     printf("m1 = %s\n", m1);
#endif
}
```

Program Comment

The program begins with the normal include for `stdio.h` and several other overhead header files. The `string.h` header file contains either the prototypes or the declarations for the string functions. The define for `MAXSTR` sets the maximum string size for several character arrays.

The `start()` function asks you to enter a string for use by the subsequent function calls. The `showem()` function prints the entered string. The call to `docpy()` copies the string into `buff`, and prints the string. It also shows that the return value in `ptr` points to the string, too.

The call to `domemcpy()` determines half of the string length (if it's at least three characters long), calls `memcpy()`, and displays the result. The call to `memmove()` copies the string at `m1[]` in such a way that overlapping does occur. Because `memmove()` guards against overwriting however, the copy still works as expected (that is, it duplicates the first character in `m1[]`).

To use this program under SYSV, add `-dSYSV` or `-DSYSV` to the command line. This will force the compiler to include the lines demonstrating `memmove()`.

Miscellaneous Comments

None.

Function Names

`strcat()` `strncat()`

Standard Met

ANSI, SYSV

Purpose

Functions to concatenate one string onto another.

Prototypes

```
char *strcat(char *s1, const char *s2)
char *strncat(char *s1, const char *s2, size_t num)
```

Required Header

`#include <string.h>` ANSI/SYSV

Usage

```
char *strcat(char *s1, const char *s2)
```

This function concatenates the string pointed to by s2 onto the end of the string pointed to by s1. The result is a new string that is s1 + s2 + \Ø. The first character of the string s2 overwrites the null character at the end of s1. The function returns a pointer to s1.

```
char *strncat(char *s1, const char *s2, size_t at_most)
```

This function is similar to strcat(), except only at_most characters are appended to s1. The null character is not part of the at_most count. If the string length of s2 is less than the value in at_most, the length of s2 determines the number of characters added onto s1. The first character in s2 overwrites the null termination character in s1. The resulting string will always have a null added at the end.

The function returns a pointer, which points to the beginning of the resulting string s1.

Caution

None.

Illustration

```
/*
                                strcat(), strncat()
*/

#include <stdio.h>                  /* Standard header file          */
#include <stdlib.h>
#include <stddef.h>                 /* Need for size_t               */
#include <string.h>                 /* Header file for strings       */

#define MAXSTR 50                   /* For a big string              */

void start(char *s1, char *s2),
     showem(const char *s1, const char *s2),
     docat(const char *s1, const char *s2);
     pause(void);

int main()
{
     char s1[MAXSTR], s2[MAXSTR];  /* Create two working strings  */

     start(s1, s2);                 /* Fill in the two strings       */

     showem(s1, s2);                /* Show how they are at first    */

                                    /* Show string...                */

     docat(s1, s2);                 /*             concatenation     */
}

/*
                                    start()
*/

void start(char *s1, char *s2)
{
```

```
    printf("Enter a string of 10 or so characters: ");
    gets(s1);
    printf("\nEnter a second string of about 10 characters: ");
    gets(s2);
}

/*
                        showem()
*/

void showem(const char *s1, const char *s2)
{
    printf("\nOriginal s1 = %s\n", s1);
    printf("\nOriginal s2 = %s\n", s2);
}

/*
                        docat()
*/

void docat(const char *s1, const char *s2)
{
    char buff[MAXSTR * 2 + 1];          /* Make one big enough for all  */
    char temp[10];
    size_t len, n;

    showem(s1, s2, "strcat() and strncat()");  /* Show them first     */
    strcpy(buff, s1);                   /* Copy so they don't change    */
    strcat(buff, s2);                   /* Append s1 to s2              */

    printf("\nAfter simple string concatenation:\n");
    printf("\n      s1 = %s\n      s2 = %s\n", buff, s2);
    pause();

                        /* Do strncat() */

    printf("\nHow many characters to append onto s1 from s2? ");
    n = (size_t) atoi(gets(temp));
    if (n) {
        strcpy(buff, s1);                           /* recopy it */
    }
    strncat(buff, s2, n);
    printf("\nAfter concatenating %d more characters onto s1 from s2\n", n);
    printf("\n      s1 = %s\n", buff);
```

```
        len = strlen(s2);

        if (n > len) {
              printf("\nOnly %d chars were appended, not the %d you wanted", len, n);
              printf("\nbecause there are only %d characters in s2", len);
        }
        pause();
}

/*
                                    pause()
*/

void pause(void)
{
        printf("\n\n  Press RETURN or ENTER to continue: ");
        getchar();
}
```

Program Comment

The program begins by including the necessary header files for use in the program. In `main()`, two working character arrays are defined to hold the strings. The call to `start()` fills in these strings with your input, and `showem()` displays what you entered.

Next, `docat()` is called to show string concatenation for `strcat()` and `strncat()`. The first thing we do is copy the original `s1` string into a temporary buffer named `buff[]`. A call to `strcat()` with `buff[]` as the first argument, and `s2` as the second, concatenates the two strings into one long string, which is then displayed.

The second part of `docat()` uses `strncat()` to concatenate at most `n` characters from `s2` onto `s1`. The call to `strncat()` then adds at most `n` characters from `s2` onto `s1`. The last part of the `docat()` function shows that, if you request more characters to be concatenated (`n`) than there are in the string (`len`), only `len` characters will be added onto the string. The result is then displayed.

Miscellaneous Comments

None.

Function Names

`memcmp()` `strcmp()` `strncmp()` `strcoll()` `strxfrm()`

Standard Met

ANSI, SYSV

Purpose

Functions that compare character strings.

Prototypes

```
int memcmp(const void *s1, const void *s2, size_t at_most)
int strcmp(const char *s1, const char *s2)
int strcoll(const char *s1, const char *s2)
int strncmp(const char *s1, const char *s2, size_t at_most)
size_t strxfrm(char *s1, const char *s2, size_t big)
```

Required Header

`#include <string.h>`	ANSI, SYSV
`#include <memory.h>`	SYSV for `memcmp()`

Usage

```
int memcmp(const void *s1, const void *s2, size_t at_most)
```

This function compares the first `at_most` characters pointed to by `s2` with the item pointed to by `s1`. The function returns a value greater than, equal to, or less than zero, according to whether the item pointed to by `s1` is greater than, equal to, or less than the item pointed to by `s2`. The ANSI and SYSV functions are compatible, except that the SYSV version expects the `memory.h` header file to be included in the program.

```
int strcmp(const char *s1, const char *s2)
```

This function compares two strings pointed to by `s1` and `s2`. The return value is calculated by subtracting the value of the characters found in s2 from s1. Therefore: if s1 = "Jim Adams" and s2 = "Jim Baker", the comparison stops on 'A' in s1 and 'B' in s2, and the value returned will be negative. If the contents of strings s1 and s2 were reversed, the value returned would be positive. If the strings s1 and s2 are identical, the value returned is 0. Therefore, the return value will be less than, equal to, or greater than 0, depending on the result of the comparison.

```
int strcoll(const char *s1, const char *s2)
```

This function behaves like `strcmp()`, except that `strcoll()` compares the two strings in the underlying character set, which may or may not be ASCII. The function is equivalent to:

```
strxfrm(t1, s1, length1);
strxfrm(t2, s2, length2);
result = strcmp(t1, t2);
```

`strcoll()` is useful when only one or two comparisons will be performed on the strings. If further comparisons are needed, `strxform()` should be used to produce the collated strings, then comparisons should be performed.

For more information, see `strxfrm()` in this section.

```
int strncmp(const char *s1, const char *s2, size_t at_most)
```

This function behaves like `strcmp()`, except that `strncmp()` compares only `at_most` characters from the string pointed to by s1, relative to the string pointed to by s2. The value returned is determined in the same manner as `strcmp()`.

There is no guarantee that comparing 'a' to 'b' returns a -1. You can only be sure that this comparison returns a value less than 0.

```
size_t strxfrm(char *s1, const char *s2, size_t at_most)      /* ANSI */
```

This function is probably most useful for writing code where the underlying character set may change in the future. In essence, this function is used so that subsequent calls to `memcmp()` or `strcmp()` produce the proper collating sequence independent of different character sets (for example, comparisons using the German alphabet set instead of the American alphabet set).

This function, therefore, translates the string pointed to by s2 and places the result into s1. Because foreign character sets may require up to four bytes per character for proper collating (for example, the German B may map to "ss" in the United States), the resulting size of the transformed string s1 may be at most four times as large as the input string s2. Variable at_most sets the limit as to how large the transformed string s1 may be, including the null termination character.

Although the ANSI standard does not say, there is no guarantee that the transformed string s1 is useful for any purpose other than collating. In other words, the resulting string held in s1 may not even be printable, which implies the only null character in the string is the terminating null. The string s1 is guaranteed to work properly with strcmp() and memcmp().

The return value from strxfrm() is the length of the transformed string s1, exclusive of the null termination character. If the transformation of s2 fails because of insufficient space, zero is returned, and the contents of s1 are indeterminate.

This function does not appear in SYSV.

Caution

The values returned from the comparison functions are stated relative to zero and are not absolute values. Tests on the return values should be stated relative to 0. If value is returned from strcmp(), the fragment:

```
if (value == -1)
```

may not function correctly. The test:

```
if (value < 0)
```

correctly tests value.

Some code assumes that a comparison of the letters 'i' and 'j' will generate a -1 (which is true for ASCII characters). For the EBCDIC character set, the comparison result would be -8 ('i' is an 89 hexadecimal. 'j' is a 91 hexadecimal). The specification only states the result will be less than, greater than, or equal to zero.

Illustration

```
/*
                memcmp(), strcmp(), strncmp(), strcoll(),
                strxfrm()
*/
```

```
#include <stdio.h>              /* Standard header file          */
#include <stdlib.h>
#include <stddef.h>             /* Need for size_t               */
#include <string.h>             /* Header file for strings       */

#define MAXSTR 50               /* For a big string              */

void pause(void);
void result(int num);

int main()
{
     char s1[MAXSTR], s2[MAXSTR];  /* Create two working strings  */
     void docmp(const void *s1, const void *s2),
          dostrxfrm(const char *s1),
          dostrcoll(const char *s1, const char *s2),
          start(char *s1, char *s2);

     start(s1, s2);              /* Fill in the two strings       */

                                 /*             comparison        */
     docmp(s1, s2);
#ifdef ANSI
     dostrxfrm(s1);
     dostrcol(s1);
#endif

}

/*
                              start()
*/

void start(char *s1, char *s2)
{
     printf("Enter a string of 10 or so characters: ");
     gets(s1);
     printf("\nEnter a second string of about 10 characters: ");
     gets(s2);
}

/*
                              pause()
*/
```

```
void pause(void)
{
     printf("\n\n  Press RETURN or ENTER to continue: ");
     getchar();
}

/*
                              docmp()
*/

void docmp(const void *s1, const void *s2)
{
     char temp[10];
     int flag;
     size_t num;

                                   /* Do strcmp() first              */

     printf("\nThe result of strcmp() and strncmp() is:\n\n");

     flag = strcmp(s1, s2);        /* Get return value        */

     result(flag);
                                   /* Now do strncmp()               */

     printf("\n\nHow many characters for comparison: ");

     num = (size_t) atoi(gets(temp));

     flag = strncmp(s1, s2, num);
     result(flag);

     printf("\n\nThe same test using memcmp() is:\n\n");
     flag = memcmp(s1, s2, num);
     result(flag);
}

#ifdef ANSI
/*
                              dostrxfrm()
*/
```

```
void dostrxfrm(const char *s1)
{
     char destin[ (MAXSTR s* 2) + 1];
     size_t big;

     big = strcoll(destin, s1, (size_t) MAXSTR * 2);
     printf("The strcoll() collated array did");
     if (big == Ø)
          printf("n't");
     printf(" fit.\n");
     pause();
}

/*
                              dostrcol()
*/

void dostrcol(const char *s1, const char *s2)
{
     int flag;

     printf("\nThe result of strcoll() is:\n\n");

     flag = strcoll(s1, s2);            /* Get return value        */

     result(flag);

     pause();
}
#endif

/*
                              result()
*/

void result(int num)
{
     printf("\nComparing the two strings shows that the strings");
     printf("\nare ");
     if (num != Ø)
          printf(" not ");
```

```
        printf("the same.");

        pause();
}
```

Program Comment

The program includes several headers files that are needed for the program to work. If you are running under SYSV, you will also need to `#include` the `memory.h` header file. Strings used in the program are entered by the call to `start()`.

The `docmp()` call first tests `strcmp()`, using the two strings you entered. The call to `result()` prints a message that states whether the strings are the same. You then enter a number, whose value is used as the third argument to `strncmp()`. Again, the `result()` function tells whether they are the same. Control then passes back to `main()`.

The call to `dostrcoll()` is essentially identical to the call to `dostrcmp()`. The call to `dostrxfrm()` does a test of the `strcoll()` function, using the return value to determine whether the function executed properly. The code will not include the calls to either function unless the macro `ANSI` is defined.

Miscellaneous Comments

See `locale.h` and `set_locale()`.

Function Names

`memchr()` `strchr()` `strcspn()` `strpbrk()` `strrchr()` `strspn()` `strstr()` `strtok()`

Standard Met

ANSI, SYSV

`strstr()` ANSI only

Purpose

Functions to perform character and string comparisons.

Prototypes

```
void *memchr(const void *s1, int letter, size_t num)
char *strchr(const char *s1, int c)
size_t strcspn(const char *s1, const char *s2)
char *strpbrk(const char *s1, const char *s2)
char *strrchr(const char *s1, int c)
size_t strspn(const char *s1, const char *s2)
char *strstr(const char *s1, const char *s2)        /* ANSI only */
char *strtok(char *s1, const char *s2)
```

Required Header

```
#include <string.h>
#include <memory.h>        SYSV only
```

Usage

```
void *memchr(const void *s1, int letter, size_t num)
```

The `memchr()` function searches the data item pointed to by `s1` for the first occurrence of `letter` in the initial `num` characters. If `letter` is found, the function returns a pointer to character. If `letter` is not found, `memchr()` returns a null pointer.

```
char *strchr(const char *s1, int c)
```

The function searches string s1 from left to right for a match on the character held in c and returns a pointer to the first match found. If no match is found, the function will return a NULL pointer.

```
size_t strcspn(const char *s1, const char *s2)
```

This function compares the characters in s1 with the characters in s2 and returns the number of nonmatches before the first match. That is, if s1 = "look" and s2 = "peek", the function would return a value of 3, because 3 is the number of nonmatched character comparisons that occurred before the match on 'k' was found on the fourth character. Notice that all characters in s2 are compared against each character in s1. A comparison of "lopsided" and "peek" yields 2 with the comparison ending at the 'p' in "lopsided." The null terminator is not considered part of s2.

```
char *strpbrk(const char *s1, const char *s2)
```

This function searches the string pointed to by s1 for the first occurrence of any character in the string pointed to by s2. The function returns a pointer to the first occurrence if a match is found, or a null pointer if no character in s2 is found in s1. For example, if s1 = "Bonnie" and s2 "Jerome", the return pointer would point to the 'o' in "Bonnie". This also means that a %s on the return pointer would yield "onnie" in the example.

```
char *strrchr(const char *s1, int c)
```

The string pointed to by s1 is searched for a match on the character held in c (after c is converted to a char). The function returns a pointer to the last match on c in the string. Because the null character is considered part of the string, c could be a null character. If no match is found, a null pointer is returned. This behavior is only slightly different from strchr() as strrchr() finds the last occurrence of the character and strchr() finds the first occurrence.

```
size_t strspn(const char *s1, const char *s2)
```

This function returns the length of the initial segment in the string pointed to by s1 which matches any character in the string pointed to by s2. If s1 = "Jennie" and s2 = "kneejerk", the function would return the value 4, because 4 is the number of matched characters that occurred before the conflict with the 'i' in s1, which does not appear in s2.

```
char *strstr(const char *s1, const char *s2) /* ANSI only */
```

This function searches the string pointed to by s1 for the first occurrence of the sequence of characters in the string pointed to by s2. The null termination character is not considered in the search. If the search is successful, the function returns a pointer to the located string in the string pointed to by s1. If the search fails, a null pointer is returned. For example, if s1 points to "when in the course", and s2 points to "the course", the function will return a pointer to "the course" in the string pointed to by s1.

```
char *strtok(char *s1, const char *s2)
```

This function searches the string pointed to by s1 for tokens separated by characters pointed to by s2. A token is a sequence of one or more characters; in essence, a string or substring. Each token is separated by a delimiter, a character from the set of one or more characters (s2). Delimiters separate the tokens.

On the first call to strtok(), s1 is passed as a pointer to the string being searched, and s2 is passed as the pointer to the string which contains the delimiter(s) to be used in the search. The first call to strtok() searches for the first character in s1 NOT found in the delimiter string pointed to by s2. If this first call to strtok() fails to find a character that is not a delimiter, there are no tokens in s1, and a null pointer is returned.

If a match exists between the Ds1 and a character in s2, a null character is written into the string s1 following the token. The null character overwrites the delimiting character in s1, although this behavior is not stated. The function then returns a pointer to the first character of the token.

If a subsequent call is made and a null character pointer is given for s1, strtok() continues the search of s1 where it left off from the previous call.

The search string s2 can be changed between calls, allowing strtok() to continue parsing the same string, using a different set of delimiters.

When the search for additional tokens fails or s1 is completely searched, a null pointer is returned. The code fragment shows what is returned from strtok() on a series of calls.

```
static char s1[] = "__Jones, Sam:123 Main St.";
char *ptr;
```

```
ptr = strtok(s1, "_,");
printf("%s\n", ptr);                    /* Prints "Jones" */

ptr = strtok( (char *) NULL, ",:");
printf("%s\n", ptr);                    /* Prints " Sam" */

ptr = strtok( (char *) NULL, ":.");
printf("%s\n", ptr);                    /* Prints "123 Main St" */

ptr = strtok( (char *) NULL, ".");
```

The first call sets the pointer to J, because J is the first character not in the delimiter set. The function keeps looking at the characters until it finds another delimiter. Because a comma is a delimiter, a null is written into the string, and the pointer (pointing to J) is returned.

On the second call, we start with a null character pointer, which means that we want to pick up where we left off. Because the comma and the colon characters are now the delimiters, the token is "`Sam`". The return pointer is set to the blank space, and the null is written where the colon appeared in the string.

On the third call (again with a null pointer for the first argument), we pick up where we left off and print "123 `Main` St". Again, the period in "`St`" is eaten by the null termination character. If we leave the colon out of the third call, the printed string would be "`:123 Main St`".

Finally, because the fourth call begins where the period is, only the null terminator is left in the string; a null pointer, therefore, is returned, and nothing is displayed.

Caution

The description of `strtok()` states that a null is written into the original string `s1` if a match on a set of delimiters is found. This means that the original string may be altered during the call to `strtok()`.

Some implementations of the `strtok()` function appear to copy the string into a static character array on the first call, leaving the original `s1` string unchanged. Relying on the original `s1` being unchanged after successful calls to `strtok()` may cause portability problems later. To be safe, copy the string with `strcpy()` prior to the call(s) to `strtok()` and restore the original string by a final `strcpy()` after all calls to `strtok()` have been made.

Illustration

```
/*
                memchr(), strchr(), strcspn(), strpbrk(),
                strrchr(), strspn(), strstr(), strtok()
*/

#include <stdio.h>                  /* Standard header file         */
#include <stddef.h>
#include <stdlib.h>
#include <string.h>                 /* Header file for strings      */

#ifdef SYSV
     #include <memory.h>            /* Needed for SYSV              */
#endif

#define MAXSTR 50                   /* For a big string             */

void pause(void),
     start(char *s1, char *s2),
     showem(char *s1, char *s2),
     dochr(char *s1),
     dobrk(const char *s1, const char *s2),
     dospn(const char *s1, const char *s2),
     dostrtok(char *s1),
     dostrstr(const char *s1, const char *s2),
     domemchr(const void *s1);

int main()
{
     char s1[MAXSTR], s2[MAXSTR];    /* Create two working strings   */

     start(s1, s2);                  /* Fill in the two strings      */

     showem(s1, s2);                 /* Show how they are at first   */

                                     /* Show string...               */
     dochr(s1);                      /*             search           */
                                     /*             bi-string search */
```

```
     dobrk(s1, s2);
     domemchr(s1);                    /*            memory search      */
                                      /*            match length       */
     dospn(s1, s2);
                                      /*            tokens             */
     dostrtok(s1);
                                      /*            string-in-string   */
     dostrstr( s1, s2);
}

/*
                            start()
*/

void start(char *s1, char *s2)
{
     printf("Enter a string of 10 or so characters: ");
     gets(s1);
     printf("\nEnter a second string of about 10 characters: ");
     gets(s2);
}

/*
                            showem()
*/

void showem(const char *s1, const char *s2)
{
     printf("\nOriginal s1 = %s", s1);
     printf("\nOriginal s2 = %s\n", s2);
}

/*
                            pause()
*/

void pause(void)
{
printf("\n\n  Press RETURN or ENTER to continue: ");
getchar();
}
```

```
/*
                                dochr()
*/

void dochr(const char *s1)
{
     char *ptr;
     int c;

     printf("\nDo strchr()\n");
     printf("The original string is %s\n", s1);
     printf("\nFor which character would you like to search: ");
     c = getchar();
                                   /* Do strchr() */
     ptr = strchr(s1, c);
     printf("\nThe first match yields a pointer to: %s", ptr);

                                   /* Do strrchr() */
     printf("\nDo strrchr()\n");
     ptr = strrchr(s1, c);
     printf("\nThe last match yields a pointer to: %s", ptr);
     pause();
}

/*
                                dobrk()
*/

void dobrk(const char *s1, const char *s2)
{
     char *ptr;

     printf("\nDo strpbrk()\n");
     ptr = strpbrk(s1, s2);

     printf("\nThe first place where letters match is at: %s\n", ptr);
     pause();
}

/*
                                domemchr()
*/
```

```
void domemchr(const void *s1)
{
     char buff[MAXSTR], ptr;
     int c;
     size_t num;

     printf("\nDo memchr()\n");
     printf("\nEnter which letter to search for: ");
     gets(buff);
     c = buff[0];
     printf("\nEnter max chars to examine: ");
     num = (size_t) atoi(gets(buff));

     ptr = (char *) memchr(s1, c, num);
     if (ptr)
          printf("\nThe match occurs at %s\n", ptr);
     else
          printf("\nThere was no match\n");
     pause();
}

/*
                              dospn()
*/

void dospn(const char *s1, const char *s2)
{
     printf("\nDo strspn()\n");
     printf("\nThe number of character matches is %d", strspn(s1, s2));
     pause();

     printf("\n\nFor strcspn():\n");
     printf("\nThe number of non-character matches is %d", strcspn(s1, s2));
     pause();
}

/*
                              dostrtok()
*/

void dostrtok(const char *s1)
{
     char temp[20], *ptr;
```

```
     printf("Enter a string of delimiters for search (max of 15): ");
     gets(temp);

     printf("\nLooking in s1 (= %s) for delimiters from %s\n",
                                                      s1, temp);
     ptr = strtok(s1, temp);

     while (ptr) {
          printf("\nThe token is: %s", ptr);
          ptr = strtok( (char *) 0, temp);
     }
     pause();
}

/*
                                   dostrstr()
*/

void dostrstr(const char *s1, const char *s2)
{
     char *ptr;

     printf("\nDo strstr().\n\n");
     ptr = strstr(s1, s2);
     if (ptr)
          printf("\nThe match occurs at %s\n", ptr);
     else
          printf("\nNo match found.\n");

     pause();
}
```

Program Comment

The program begins with several `#includes` for necessary header files. The `memory.h` must also be included if the program is used with a SYSV library.

The program first asks you to enter two strings, which are placed into `s1` and `s2`. The `showem()` function prints these on the display.

The call to `dochr()` passes `s1` to the function and asks you to enter the character for which you want to search. The call to `strchr()`

passes s1 and the letter just entered to strchr() and returns a pointer to where a match is found. The printf() displays the string, beginning with the character located. If no match is found, ptr will be a null pointer, and nothing is printed. The call to strrchr() behaves in a similar fashion, except that it displays the last occurrence of where a match is found. Nothing is printed if no match is found.

The call to dobrk() receives s1 and s2 from main() and calls strpbrk() to see whether any characters in s2 are found also in s1. If a match is found, ptr is used to display the first match. If no characters match, nothing is printed, and control returns to main().

The domemchr() asks you to enter a letter to search for and the maximum number of characters to search. If a match is found, ptr will point to the match, and the string is displayed. If no match is found, ptr is a null pointer, and a message is displayed stating no match was found.

The dospn() function calls strspn() with s1 and s2 to see how many characters in s1 match those in s2. The value returned may be 0 or more characters. The call to strcspn() does the reverse of strspn() and shows how many characters in s1 are not found in s2. The value may also be 0 or more characters.

The dostrtok() function asks you to enter a set of delimiters to be used in the strtok() call. This means that we are searching for tokens in s1, using the delimiters you just entered into temp[]. If you enter a blank space for the delimiters and nothing else, for example, the dostrtok() function will print out the words in the string. You may want to run the program several times with different data in s1 and different delimiter strings to see how the function works.

The final call is to dostrstr(), which searches s1 for the character sequence pointed to by s2. This amounts to searching a "big" string (s1) for a smaller string (s2). If a match is found, ptr is used to show the match; otherwise, the null pointer in ptr will cause the "no match" message to be displayed.

Miscellaneous Comments

The strstr() function is not part of the SYSV specification.

Function Names

`memset()` `strlen()` `strerror()`

Standard Met

ANSI, SYSV

Purpose

Miscellaneous functions for character setting, determining a string's length, and generating string-related error messages.

Prototypes

```
char *strerror(int error)                    /* ANSI only */
size_t strlen(const char *s1)
void *memset(void *s, int letter, size_t num)
```

Required Headers

```
#include <string.h>       ANSI
#include <memory.h>       SYSV for memset()
```

Usage

```
void *memset(void *s, int letter, size_t num)
```

This function produces `num` copies of `letter` in the data item pointed to by `s`. The function returns `s`. Under ANSI, `letter` is converted to an `unsigned char`.

If this function is used under SYSV, the `memory.h` header file must be `#include`d in the program.

```
char *strerror(int error)                    /* ANSI only */
```

This function returns a pointer to an error message whose contents are mapped by `error`. Therefore, you could use `puts()` or `printf()` to display what the return pointer points to. The contents of the error messages and the potential values for `error` are implementation-defined.

Although the ANSI standard does not say, the messages are likely held in `sys_errlist[]`, and the index passed in `error` is similar to that of `errno`. Further, since the returned pointer points to a fixed set of messages, the prototype should be considered `const char *strerror(int error)`.

```
size_t strlen(const char *s1)
```

The function returns the number of characters starting with `s1` and ending with the null character. The null character is not included in the count. A good way to surprise yourself is to forget to null-terminate `s1`.

Caution

The `strerror()` function is not part of SYSV.

Illustration

```
/*
                    memset(), strlen(), strerror()
*/

#include <stdio.h>              /* Standard header file          */
#include <stdlib.h>
#include <stddef.h>
#include <string.h>             /* Header file for strings       */

#ifdef SYSV
     #include <memory.h>        /* Need for SYSV                 */
#endif

#define MAXSTR 50               /* For a big string              */
#define MAXERR 5                /* Number of error messages????  */

void pause(void),
     showit(const char *s1),
     start1(char *s1),
     dolen(const char *s1),
     domemset(void),
     doerror(void);
```

```
int main()
{
     char s1[MAXSTR];             /* Create working string   */
                                  /* Fill it in              */
     start1(s1);
     showit( (const char *) s1); /* Show how it looks       */
                                  /* Show string...          */
     dolen(s1);                   /*           length        */
     doerror();                   /*           error         */
     domemset();                  /*           set memory    */
}

/*
                              start1()
*/

void start1(char *s1)
{
     printf("Enter a string of 10 or so characters: ");
     gets(s1);
}

/*
                              showit()
*/

void showit(const char *s1)
{
     printf("\nOriginal s1 = %s\n", s1);
}

/*
                              dolen()
*/

void dolen(const char *s1)
{
     printf("\n\nDo strlen()\n");
     printf("\n     length of s1 = %u", (unsigned) strlen(s1) );
     pause();
}
```

```
/*
                                doerror()
*/

void doerror(void)
{
     int i;                          /* Change MAXERR above for number */
                                     /* of internal error messages     */
     for (i = 0; i < MAXERR; i++) {
          printf("error number %d: %s\n", i, strerror(i) );
     }
}

/*
                                domemset()
*/

void domemset(void)
{
     char buff[MAXSTR];
     int c;
     void *ptr;

     printf("Which letter should be copied: ");
     gets(buff);
     c = (int) buff[0];
     ptr = memset(buff, c, (size_t) MAXSTR - 1);
     buff[MAXSTR - 1] = '\0';
     printf("\nThe area in memory looks like:\n%s", (char *) ptr);
     pause();
}

/*
                                pause()
*/

void pause(void)
{
     printf("\n\n  Press RETURN or ENTER to continue: ");
     getchar();
}
```

Program Comment

There are no surprises. The usual header files are #included into the program (stddef.h is needed for the size_t typdef). The call to start1() asks you to enter a string, and dolen() finds the string's length.

The domemset() function asks you to enter a letter, which is then copied MAXSTR -1 times into the string. We add a null termination character so that we can print buff as a string.

The doerror() calls strerror() MAXERR times to see what is stored in those messages. The number of messages available for your strerror() should be stated in the documentation for the standard library that comes with your compiler. You might want to change MAXERR to reflect your version of strerror().

Miscellaneous Comments

Compare the messages from strerror() with those held in sys_errlist[] to see whether they are the same. Also, note that the return value from strlen() is cast to an unsigned integral type. The reason is that strlen() returns a size_t data type, which does not have a direct conversion character in printf().

6
Math Functions

This chapter presents functions prototyped in the ANSI `math.h` header. In addition, we have included the `rand()` and `srand()` functions in this chapter, rather than the miscellaneous utilities section, Chapter 8. The `rand()` function is the only function that returns a data type other than `double`.

ANSI versus SYSV

The most notable difference between the ANSI and SYSV math functions is the way error conditions are processed. Under SYSV most trigonometric functions call a default `matherr()` function used for displaying an error message. ANSI, however, does not define `matherr()`, and programmers must devise their own methods for coping with error conditions.

Most of the function arguments for trigonometric functions are expressed in radians.

The following example illustrates a simple use of the SYSV `matherr()` function.

```
#include <stdio.h>
#include <stdlib.h>
#include <math.h>                /* Need for matherr() */
#include <errno.h>

#ifndef errno
     extern int errno;
#endif
```

```
int main()
{
     int flag;
     double x;

     x = acos(3.0);                /* Force an error */
}

int matherr(struct exception *e)
{
     char *type = "";

     switch(e->type) {
          case DOMAIN:
               type = "Domain";
               break;
          case SING:
               type = "Singularity";
               break;
          case OVERFLOW:
               type = "Overflow";
               break;
          case UNDERFLOW:
               type = "Underflow";
               break;
          case TLOSS:
               type = "Total loss";
               break;
          case PLOSS:
               type = "Partial loss";
               break;
     }
     if (strlen(type) > 1) {
        printf("%s error: %s %f %g %g", type, e->name,
                                e->arg1, e->arg2, e->retval);
        return 1;
     } else
        return 0;
}
```

In `main()`, `acos()` is called with an invalid argument, which generates a domain error. In `matherr()`, a switch is used on the type of error that was sensed (`e->type`), and a string is set based upon the type of error sensed. The printf() displays the values that have been set. The members of type struct exception include the following:

e->type	the type of error detected (for example, DOMAIN)
e->name	the name of the function causing the problem [for example, acos()]
e->arg1	the first argument used in the offending function (for example, 3.Ø)
e->arg2	the second argument used in the offending function [there isn't one for acos()]
e->retval	the value returned from the offending call (for example, the previous table shows acos() returns 0 on error)

When the sample program above is run, the call to printf() displays:

```
Domain error: acos 3.ØØØØØ Ø Ø
```

Therefore, the printf() tells us (variable names are in parentheses): we have a DOMAIN error (type) in acos() (e->name) with an argument value of 3.Ø (e->arg1), the second argument for acos() was Ø (e->arg2 is zero because there is no second argument), and the return value from the acos() call was Ø (e->retval), which is the function's error condition return value.

Whenever the result of an ANSI math function produces a result that cannot be represented as a double, a range error occurs. If the result is too large, an overflow range error exists, and the return value is HUGE_VAL with the sign being the correct value of the function. The variable errno is set to ERANGE. If the result is too small to properly represent, an underflow range error exists, and the function returns the value zero. On underflow, the value of errno is implementation-defined.

Function Name

`acos()`

Standard Met

ANSI, SYSV

Purpose

Determine an arccosine.

Prototypes

```
double acos(double rads)
```

Required Header

`#include <math.h>` ANSI/SYSV

Usage

```
double acos(double rads)
```

The function returns the arccosine of the argument `rads` expressed in radians. The return value is within the range 0 to pi. If the argument value for `rads` is not within the range of -1.0 to +1.0, `errno` is set to `EDOM`, and the return value is implementation-defined.

Caution

SYSV handles error values a little differently. If you do not supply your own `matherr()` function, default error processing occurs. In the case of the `acos()` function, SYSV states that a message (relating to `EDOM`) is printed (presumably on `stderr`), and 0 is returned.

Illustration

```
/*
                                        acos()
*/

#include <stdio.h>
#include <stdlib.h>
#include <stddef.h>
#include <math.h>
#include <errno.h>

int main()
{
     char buff[20];
     int i;
     double x, y;

     for (;;) {
          printf("\nEnter a value in radians (-1 to +1): ");
          x = strtod( gets(buff), (char **) NULL );
          errno = 0;
          y = acos(x);
          i = errno;
          printf("The arccosine of %f is %f\n", x, y);
          if (errno = i)
               perror("Error detected");
          else
               break;
     }
}
```

Program Comment

The program `#includes` the necessary header files and asks you to enter a value expressed in radians. The call to `strtod()` converts the input and stores the double in `x`. Variable `errno` is cleared, `acos()` is called, and `x` is used as `acos()`'s argument.

Because `acos()` may generate an error for the value of `x`, we assign the value of `errno` to `i` and print the result returned from `acos()`. If an error did occur in `acos()`, you can see the implementation-defined value passed back from the `acos()` function.

If `i` is nonzero, an error occurred, and we call `perror()`. The `perror()` function prints out the argument passed to it, a semicolon, and then the error message associated with the value held in `errno`. [The assignment of `i` into `errno` in the `if` test is to guard against the possibility of `printf()` modifying `errno`.]

If no error is detected, the `break` statement is executed, and the program ends.

Miscellaneous Comments

You may want to consult the `perror()` function.

The most common error with any math function is forgetting to declare that the function returns a double data type. You can eliminate this problem if you `#include` the `math.h` header file.

Function Name

```
asin()
```

Standard Met

ANSI, SYSV

Purpose

Determine an arcsine.

Prototypes

```
double asin(double rads)
```

Required Header

`#include <math.h>` ANSI/SYSV

Usage

```
double asin(double rads)
```

This function returns the arcsine of the argument `rads` expressed in radians. The return value is within the range -pi/2.0 to +pi/2.0. If the argument value for `rads` is not within the range of -1.0 to +1.0, `errno` is set to `EDOM`, and the return value is implementation-defined.

Caution

SYSV handles error values a little differently. If you do not supply your own `matherr()` function, default error processing occurs. In the case of the `asin()` function, SYSV states that a message (relating to `EDOM`) is printed (presumably on `stderr`), and 0 is returned.

Illustration

```
/*
                              asin()
*/

#include <stdio.h>
#include <stdlib.h>
#include <stddef.h>
#include <math.h>
#include <errno.h>

int main()
{
     char buff[20];
     int i;
     double x, y;

     for (;;) {
          printf("\nEnter a value in radians (-1 to +1): ");
          x = strtod( gets(buff), (char **) NULL );
          errno = 0;
          y = asin(x);
          i = errno;
          printf("The arcsine of %f is %f\n", x, y);
          if (i)
               perror("Error detected");
          else
               break;
     }
}
```

Program Comment

The program `#include`s the necessary header files and asks you to enter a value expressed in radians. The call to `strtod()` converts the input and stores the double in `x`. Variable `errno` is cleared, `asin()` is called, and `x` is used as `asin()`'s argument.

Because `asin()` may generate an error for the value of `x`, we assign the value of `errno` to `i` and print the result returned from `asin()`. If an error did occur in `asin()`, you can see the implementation-defined value passed back from the `asin()` function.

If `i` is nonzero, an error occurred, and we call `perror()`. The `perror()` function prints out the argument passed to it, a semicolon, and then the error message associated with the value held in `errno`. [The assignment of `i` into `errno` in the `if` test is to guard against the possibility of `printf()` modifying `errno`.]

If no error is detected, the `break` statement is executed, and the program ends.

Miscellaneous Comments

You should read the discussion on the `perror()` function.

The most common error with any math function is forgetting to declare that the function returns a double data type. You can eliminate this problem if you `#include` the `math.h` header file.

Function Name

`atan()`

Standard Met

ANSI, SYSV

Purpose

Determine an arctangent.

Prototypes

```
double atan(double rads)
```

Required Header

`#include <math.h>` ANSI/SYSV

Usage

```
double atan(double rads)
```

This function returns the arctangent of the argument `rads` expressed in radians. The return value from `atan()` is within the range -pi/2.0 to +pi/2.0.

Caution

None.

Illustration

```
/*
                                        atan()
*/

#include <stdio.h>
#include <stdlib.h>
#include <math.h>

int main()
{
     char buff[20];
     double x;

     printf("\nEnter a value in radians: ");
     x = strtod( gets(buff), (char **) NULL );
     printf("The arctangent of %f is %f\n", x, atan(x));
}
```

Program Comment

The program `#includes` the necessary header files and asks you to enter a value expressed in radians. The call to `strtod()` converts the input and stores the `double` in `x`. Because neither ANSI nor SYSV does error checking on `atan()`, we simply call the function and display the results.

Miscellaneous Comments

The most common error with any math function is forgetting to declare that the function returns a double data type. You can eliminate this problem if you `#include` the `math.h` header file.

Function Name

`atan2()`

Standard Met

ANSI, SYSV

Purpose

Determine the arctangent of y/x.

Prototypes

```
double atan2(double y, double x)
```

Required Header

`#include <math.h>` ANSI/SYSV

Usage

```
double atan2(double y, double x)
```

The function returns the arctangent of `y/x` expressed in radians. The quadrant is determined by the sign of the two arguments, and the return value is within the range of -pi to pi. If the value for both arguments is zero, `errno` is set to `EDOM`, and the return value is implementation-defined.

Caution

SYSV handles error values a little differently. If you do not supply your own `matherr()` function, default error processing occurs. In the case of the `atan2()` function, SYSV states that a message (for example, relating to `EDOM`) is printed (presumably on `stderr`), and 0 is the return value.

Illustration

```
/*
                                    atan2()
*/

#include <stdio.h>
#include <stdlib.h>
#include <stddef.h>
#include <math.h>
#include <errno.h>

int main()
{
     char buff[20];
     int i;
     double atn, x, y;

     for (;;) {
          printf("\nEnter a value for x: ");
          x = strtod( gets(buff), (char **) NULL );
          printf("\nEnter a value for y: ");
          y = strtod( gets(buff), (char **) NULL );
          errno = 0;
          atn = atan2(y, x);
          i = errno;
          printf("The arctangent of %f / %f is %f\n", x, y, atn);
          if (i)
               perror("Error detected");
          else
               break;
     }
}
```

Program Comment

The program `#includes` the necessary header files and asks you to enter two values by calls to `gets()` and `strtod()`. After the value for `y` is determined, variable `errno` is cleared, `atan2()` is called, and `x` and `y` are used as arguments.

Because `atan2()` may generate an error if `x` and `y` are zero, we assign the value of `errno` to `i` and print the result returned from atan2(). If an error did occur in atan2(), you can see the implementation-defined value passed back from the atan2() function.

If i is nonzero, an error occurred, and we call perror(). The perror() function prints out the argument passed to it, a semicolon, and then the error message associated with the value held in errno. [The assignment of i into errno in the if test is to guard against the possibility of printf() modifying errno.]

If no error is detected, the break statement is executed, and the program ends.

Miscellaneous Comments

You may want to consult the perror() function.

The most common error with any math function is forgetting to declare that the function returns a double data type. You can eliminate this problem if you #include the math.h header file.

Function Name

`ceil()`

Standard Met

ANSI, SYSV

Purpose

Determine the smallest integer number.

Prototypes

```
double ceil(double value)
```

Required Header

`#include <math.h>` ANSI/SYSV

Usage

```
double ceil(double value)
```

The function returns the smallest integer number that is not smaller than `value`. If `value` is 4.2, `ceil()` would return 5. If `value` is -4.2, `ceil()` returns -4. No error checking is done on the value.

Caution

None.

Illustration

```
/*
                                              ceil()
*/

#include <stdio.h>
#include <stdlib.h>
#include <stddef.h>
#include <math.h>

int main()
{
     char buff[20];
     double x, y;

     printf("\nEnter a value: ");
     x = strtod( gets(buff), (char **) NULL );
     y = ceil(x);
     printf("The smallest integer value of %f is %f\n", x, y);
}
```

Program Comment

The program `#includes` the necessary header files and asks you to enter a value. The call to `strtod()` converts the input and stores the double in `x`. The `ceil()` function is called, `x` is used as `ceil()`'s argument, and the result is displayed.

Miscellaneous Comments

Note that the function has the effect of rounding up on any fractional value if `value` is positive, and rounding down if `value` is negative.

The most common error with any math function is forgetting to declare that the function returns a double data type. You can eliminate this problem if you `#include` the `math.h` header file.

Function Name

`cos()`

Standard Met

ANSI, SYSV

Purpose

Determine a cosine.

Prototypes

```
double cos(double rads)
```

Required Header

`#include <math.h>` ANSI/SYSV

Usage

```
double cos(double rads)
```

The function returns the cosine of the argument `rads`, which is expressed in radians. The ANSI specification states that large values for `rads` may produce a result that has no significance.

Caution

SYSV differentiates between a partial loss (PLOSS) and total (TLOSS) of significance of the result and sets `errno` to ERANGE if either case is sensed. If you do not supply your own `matherr()` function, default error processing occurs. In the case of the `cos()` function, SYSV states that a message relating to a range error be displayed (presumably on `stderr`) and a value of 0 returned when TLOSS is sensed. For a partial loss, as much as possible of the value is returned and no error message is displayed.

Illustration

```
/*
                                        cos()
*/

#include <stdio.h>
#include <stdlib.h>
#include <stddef.h>
#include <math.h>
#include <errno.h>

int main()
{
     char buff[20];
     int i;
     double x, y;

     for (;;) {
          printf("\nEnter a value in radians: ");
          x = strtod( gets(buff), (char **) NULL );
          errno = 0;
          y = cos(x);
          i = errno;
          printf("The cosine of %f is %f\n", x, y);
          if (i)
               perror("Error detected");
          else
               break;
     }
}
```

Program Comment

The program `#includes` the necessary header files and asks you to enter a value expressed in radians. The call to `strtod()` converts the input and stores the double in `x`. Variable `errno` is cleared, `cos()` is called, and `x` is used as `cos()`'s argument.

Because `cos()` may generate an ERANGE error associated with large values for `x`, we assign the value of `errno` to `i` and then print the result returned from `cos()`. If an error did occur in `cos()`, you can see the implementation-defined value passed back from the `cos()` function.

If `i` is nonzero, an error occurred and we call `perror()` to print out an error message. The error message is the quoted string in `perror()`, followed by a predetermined error message associated with the value held in `errno`. [The assignment of `i` into `errno` in the `if` test is to guard against the possibility of `printf()` modifying `errno`.]

If no error is detected, the `break` statement is executed, and the program ends.

Miscellaneous Comments

You may want to consult the `perror()` function.

The most common error with any math function is forgetting to declare that the function returns a double data type. You can eliminate this problem if you `#include` the `math.h` header file.

Function Name

`cosh()`

Standard Met

ANSI, SYSV

Purpose

Determine a hyperbolic cosine.

Prototypes

```
double cosh(double rads)
```

Required Header

`#include <math.h>` ANSI/SYSV

Usage

```
double cosh(double rads)
```

The function returns the hyperbolic cosine of the argument `rads`, which is expressed in radians. The ANSI specification states that large values for `rads` may produce range (ERANGE) errors (overflow), for which the function returns HUGE_VAL.

Caution

SYSV handles the error differently. If you do not supply your own `matherr()` function, default error processing occurs. In the case of the `cosh()` function, SYSV states that a message (relating to ERANGE) is printed (presumably on `stderr`), and the return value is +HUGE.

Illustration

```
/*
                                                cosh()
*/

#include <stdio.h>
#include <stdlib.h>
#include <stddef.h>
#include <math.h>
#include <errno.h>

int main()
{
     char buff[20];
     int i;
     double x, y;

     for (;;) {
          printf("\nEnter a value in radians: ");
          x = strtod( gets(buff), (char **) NULL );
          errno = 0;
          y = cosh(x);
          i = errno;
          printf("The hyperbolic cosine of %f is %f\n", x, y);
          if (i)
               perror("Error detected");
          else
               break;
     }
}
```

Program Comment

The program `#includes` the necessary header files and asks you to enter a value expressed in radians. The call to `strtod()` converts the input and stores the double in `x`. Variable `errno` is cleared, `cosh()` is called, and `x` is used as `cosh()`'s argument.

Because `cosh()` may generate an ERANGE (overflow) error associated with large values for `x`, we assign the value of `errno` to `i` and then print the result returned from `cosh()`. If an error did occur in cosh(), you can see the implementation-defined value passed back from the cosh() function. (The value is HUGE in SYSV.)

If i is nonzero, an error occurred and we call perror() to print out an error message. The error message is the quoted string in perror(), followed by a predetermined error message associated with the value held in errno. (The assignment of i into errno in the if test is to guard against the possibility of printf() modifying errno.)

If no error is detected, the break statement is executed, and the program ends.

Miscellaneous Comments

You may want to consult the perror() function.

The most common error with any math function is forgetting to declare that the function returns a double data type. You can eliminate this problem if you #include the math.h header file.

Function Name

`exp()`

Standard Met

ANSI, SYSV

Purpose

Determine an exponential function.

Prototypes

```
double exp(double val)
```

Required Header

`#include <math.h>` ANSI/SYSV

Usage

```
double exp(double val)
```

The function returns the value of `e` raised to the `val` power. The ANSI specification states that large values for `val` may produce a range error (ERANGE) and return HUGE_VAL on overflow or 0 on underflow.

Caution

SYSV handles the range errors differently. If you do not supply your own `matherr()` function, default error processing occurs. In the case of the `exp()` function, no message is printed and the return value is either +HUGE (overflow) or 0 (underflow).

Illustration

```
/*
                                        exp()
*/

#include <stdio.h>
#include <stdlib.h>
#include <stddef.h>
#include <math.h>
#include <errno.h>

int main()
{
     char buff[20];
     int i;
     double x, y;

     for (;;) {
          printf("\nEnter a value for the exponent: ");
          x = strtod( gets(buff), (char **) NULL );
          errno = 0;
          y = exp(x);
          i = errno;
          printf("The value e raised to the %f power is %f\n", x, y);
          if (i)
               perror("Error detected");
          else
               break;
     }
}
```

Program Comment

The program #includes the necessary header files and asks you to enter a value. The call to strtod() converts the input and stores the double in x. Variable errno is cleared, exp() is called, and x is used as exp()'s argument.

Because exp() may generate an ERANGE error associated with large values for x, we assign the value of errno to i and then print the result returned from exp(). If an error did occur in exp(), you can see the implementation-defined value passed back from the `exp()` function.

If `i` is nonzero, an error occurred and we call `perror()` to print out an error message. The error message is the quoted string in `perror()`, followed by a predetermined error message associated with the value held in `errno`. [The assignment of `i` into `errno` in the `if` test is to guard against the possibility of `printf()` modifying `errno`.]

If no error is detected, the `break` statement is executed, and the program ends.

Miscellaneous Comments

You may want to consult the `perror()` function. Also note that the return value is different for overflow and underflow error conditions.

The most common error with any math function is forgetting to declare that the function returns a double data type. You can eliminate this problem if you `#include` the `math.h` header file.

Function Name

`fabs()`

Standard Met

ANSI, SYSV

Purpose

Determine the absolute value of a floating-point number.

Prototypes

```
double fabs(double value)
```

Required Header

`#include <math.h>` ANSI/SYSV

Usage

```
double fabs(double value)
```

The function returns the absolute value of the argument `value`. No error checking is done by either ANSI or SYSV.

Caution

None.

Illustration

```
/*
                                              fabs()
*/

#include <stdio.h>
#include <stdlib.h>
#include <stddef.h>
#include <math.h>

int main()
{
     char buff[20];
     double x, y;

     printf("\nEnter a positive or negative value: ");
     x = strtod( gets(buff), (char **) NULL );
     y = fabs(x);
     printf("The absolute value of %f is %f\n", x, y);
}
```

Program Comment

The program `#includes` the necessary header files and asks you to enter a value. The call to `strtod()` converts the input and stores the double in `x`. The function `fabs()` uses `x` as an argument, returns the absolute value, and assigns the value into `y`. The return value is then displayed.

Miscellaneous Comments

The most common error with any math function is forgetting to declare that the function returns a double data type. You can eliminate this problem if you `#include` the `math.h` header file.

Function Name

`floor()`

Standard Met

ANSI, SYSV

Purpose

Determine the largest integer number.

Prototypes

```
double floor(double value)
```

Required Header

`#include <math.h>` ANSI/SYSV

Usage

```
double floor(double value)
```

The function returns the largest integer number that is not larger than `value`. If `value` is 4.2, `floor()` would return 4. If `value` is -4.2, `floor()` returns -5. No error checking is done on the value.

Caution

None.

Illustration

```
/*
                                        floor()
*/

#include <stdio.h>
#include <stdlib.h>
#include <stddef.h>
#include <math.h>

int main()
{
     char buff[20];
     double x, y;

     printf("\nEnter a value: ");
     x = strtod( gets(buff), (char **) NULL );
     y = floor(x);
     printf("The largest integer value of %f is %f\n", x, y);
}
```

Program Comment

The program `#include`s the necessary header files and asks you to enter a value. The call to `strtod()` converts the input and stores the double in `x`. The `floor()` function uses `x` as an argument, and `printf()` displays the result.

Miscellaneous Comments

Note that the function has the effect of rounding down on any fractional value if `value` is positive, and rounding up if `value` is negative.

The most common error with any math function is forgetting to declare that the function returns a double data type. You can eliminate this problem if you `#include` the `math.h` header file.

Function Name

`fmod()`

Standard Met

ANSI, SYSV

Purpose

Determine a floating-point remainder.

Prototypes

```
double fmod(double x, double y)
```

Required Header

`#include <math.h>` ANSI/SYSV

Usage

```
double fmod(double x, double y)
```

The function returns the floating-point remainder of `x/y`. If `y` is zero, the function returns 0. If `y` is not zero, the value returned has the same sign as `x` and satisfies the equation `x = i * y + fmod(x, y)` for some integer value `i`, and the absolute value of the result from `fmod()` is less than the absolute value of `y`.

If the result of `x/y` cannot be represented, a range error occurs. On overflow, plus or minus `HUGE_VAL` is returned, based upon the correct sign for the arguments, and `errno` is set to `ERANGE`. On underflow, 0 is returned, but the setting of `errno` to `ERANGE` is implementation-defined.

Caution

Under SYSV, if `y` is zero, an overflow error occurs, but the specification does not state how it is handled.

Illustration

```
/*
                                              fmod()
*/

#include <stdio.h>
#include <stdlib.h>
#include <stddef.h>
#include <math.h>

int main()
{
     char buff[20];
     double x, y, z;

     printf("\nEnter a value for x: ");
     x = strtod( gets(buff), (char **) NULL );
     printf("\nEnter a value for y: ");
     y = strtod( gets(buff), (char **) NULL );
     z = fmod(x, y);
     printf("The fmod() of %f / %f is %f\n", x, y, z);
}
```

Program Comment

The program `#includes` the necessary header files and asks you to enter a value. The call to `strtod()` converts the two input values and stores them in `x` and `y`. The `fmod()` function uses `x` and `y` as arguments. The call to `printf()` displays the floating-point remainder.

Miscellaneous Comments

The most common error with any math function is forgetting to declare that the function returns a double data type. You can eliminate this problem if you `#include` the `math.h` header file.

Function Name

`frexp()`

Standard Met

ANSI, SYSV

Purpose

Decompose a floating-point value into a normal fraction and exponent power of 2.

Prototypes

```
double frexp(double val, int *exponent)
```

Required Header

`#include <math.h>` ANSI/SYSV

Usage

```
double frexp(double val, int *exponent)
```

The function decomposes a floating-point number into a normalized fraction as an integral power of 2. If a number is nonzero, it may be expressed as a power of 2 in the form:

`val` = fraction * 2 ^ `exponent`

where:

`val` - the floating-point number

fraction - the normalized fraction that is the mantissa. The domain of the fraction is:
0.5 <= fraction <= 1.0

`exponent` - the exponent by which 2 is raised. That is, "2 ^ `exponent`" is read: "Two raised to the exponent power."

The function returns the normalized fraction and writes the exponent by indirection. If the floating-point value is zero, both the return value and the exponent are zero. Neither ANSI nor SYSV performs error checking.

Caution

None.

Illustration

```
/*
                                        frexp()
*/

#include <stdio.h>
#include <stdlib.h>
#include <stddef.h>
#include <math.h>
#include <errno.h>

int main()
{
     char buff[20];
     int i, expon;
     double x, mantissa;

     for (;;) {
          printf("\nEnter a number: ");
          x = strtod( gets(buff), (char **) NULL );
          errno = 0;
          mantissa = frexp(x, &expon);
          i = errno;
          printf("The value %f may be expressed as:\n\n", x);
          printf("    %f * 2 ^ %d\n\n", mantissa, expon);
          if (i)
               perror("Error detected");
          else
               break;
     }
}
```

Program Comment

The program #includes the necessary header files and asks you to enter a value. The call to strtod() converts the input and stores the double in x. Variable errno is cleared, and frexp() is called, with x as the first argument and a pointer-to-int as the second argument (for holding the exponent).

Even though frexp() states that there is no error checking, we have left errno and i in the program if an implementation does provide error checking. If i is nonzero, an error occurred, and we call perror() to print out an error message. The error message is the quoted string in perror(), followed by a predetermined error message associated with the value held in errno. [The assignment of i into errno in the if test is to guard against the possibility of printf() modifying errno.]

If no error is detected, the break statement is executed, and the program ends.

Miscellaneous Comments

You may want to consult the perror() function.

The most common error with any math function is forgetting to declare that the function returns a double data type. You can eliminate this problem if you #include the math.h header file.

Function Name

`ldexp()`

Standard Met

ANSI, SYSV

Purpose

Return a value equal to a number raised to a power of 2.

Prototypes

```
double ldexp(double val, int exponent)
```

Required Header

`#include <math.h>` ANSI/SYSV

Usage

```
double ldexp(double val, int exponent)
```

The function returns a floating-point number that is the result of multiplying another floating-point number (`val`) by 2 raised to the `exponent` value. This function is similar to the `frexp()` function "in reverse."

If an overflow occurs, the function returns plus or minus HUGE_VAL (according to the correct sign for the return value for the function), and `errno` is set to ERANGE (range error). On underflow, the function returns 0 and the setting of `errno` to ERANGE is implementation-defined.

Caution

SYSV, under a range error, returns plus or minus HUGE (according to the sign of `val`).

Illustration

```
/*
                                          ldexp()
*/

#include <stdio.h>
#include <stdlib.h>
#include <stddef.h>
#include <math.h>

int main()
{
     char buff[20];
     int expon;
     double x, mantissa;

     printf("\nEnter a number for mantissa: ");
     mantissa = strtod( gets(buff), (char **) NULL );
     printf("\nEnter a number for exponent: ");
     expon = atoi( gets(buff) );
     x = ldexp(mantissa, expon);
     printf("\n%f = %f * 2 ^ %d\n\n", x, mantissa, expon);
}
```

Program Comment

The program #includes the necessary header files and asks you to enter two values: one for the mantissa and one for the exponent. The call to strtod() converts the input and stores the double in mantissa. The call to atoi() converts its argument to an integer and stores it in expon. The call to ldexp() assigns the return value into x, the printf() displays the results, and the program ends.

Miscellaneous Comments

The most common error with any math function is forgetting to declare that the function returns a double data type. You can eliminate this problem if you #include the math.h header file.

Function Name

`log()`

Standard Met

ANSI, SYSV

Purpose

Determine a natural logarithm.

Prototypes

```
double log(double value)
```

Required Header

```
#include <math.h>          ANSI/SYSV
```

Usage

```
double log(double value)
```

The function returns the natural logarithm of the argument `value`. If the argument is negative, a domain error (EDOM) occurs, and the return value is implementation-defined. If the argument is negative, a range error (ERANGE) occurs.

Caution

SYSV handles error values a little differently. If you do not supply your own `matherr()` function, default error processing occurs. In the case of the `log()` function, SYSV states that a message [relating to EDOM if `value` is negative, or SING (singularity error) if `value` is 0] is printed (presumably on `stderr`), and -HUGE is returned.

Illustration

```
/*
                                        log()
*/

#include <stdio.h>
#include <stdlib.h>
#include <stddef.h>
#include <math.h>
#include <errno.h>

int main()
{
     char buff[20];
     int i;
     double x, y;

     for (;;) {
          printf("\nEnter a value: ");
          x = strtod( gets(buff), (char **) NULL );
          errno = 0;
          y = log(x);
          i = errno;
          printf("The natural log of %f is %f\n", x, y);
          if (i)
               perror("Error detected");
          else
               break;
     }
}
```

Program Comment

The program `#include`s the necessary header files and asks you to enter a value. The call to `strtod()` converts the input and stores the double in `x`. Variable `errno` is cleared, `log()` is called, and `x` is used as `log()`'s argument.

Because `log()` may generate an error for the value of `x`, we assign the value of `errno` to `i` and print the result returned from `log()`. If an error did occur in `log()`, you can see the implementation-defined value passed back from the `log()` function.

If `i` is nonzero, an error occurred, and we call `perror()`. The `perror()` function prints out the argument passed to it, a semicolon, and then the error message associated with the value held in `errno`. [The assignment of `i` into `errno` in the `if` test is to guard against the possibility of `printf()` modifying `errno`.]

If no error is detected, the `break` statement is executed, and the program ends.

Miscellaneous Comments

You may want to consult the `perror()` function.

The most common error with any math function is forgetting to declare that the function returns a double data type. You can eliminate this problem if you `#include` the `math.h` header file.

Function Name

`log10()`

Standard Met

ANSI, SYSV

Purpose

Determine a base-10 logarithm.

Prototypes

```
double log10(double value)
```

Required Header

`#include <math.h>` ANSI/SYSV

Usage

```
double log10(double value)
```

The function returns the base-10 logarithm of the argument `value`. If the argument is negative, a domain error (`EDOM`) occurs, and the return value of `error` is implementation-defined. A range error occurs if the argument is zero.

Caution

SYSV handles errors differently. Default error processing occurs if you do not supply your own `matherr()` function for SYSV error values. In the case of the `log10()` function, SYSV states that a message [relating to `EDOM` if `value` is negative, or `SING` (singularity error) if `value` is 0] is printed (presumably on `stderr`), and `-HUGE` is returned.

Illustration

```
/*
                                        log10()
*/

#include <stdio.h>
#include <stdlib.h>
#include <stddef.h>
#include <math.h>
#include <errno.h>

int main()
{
     char buff[20];
     int i;
     double x, y;

     for (;;) {
          printf("\nEnter a value: ");
          x = strtod( gets(buff), (char **) NULL );
          errno = 0;
          y = log10(x);
          i = errno;
          printf("The base-ten log of %f is %f\n", x, y);
          if (i)
               perror("Error detected");
          else
               break;
     }
}
```

Program Comment

The program `#includes` the necessary header files and asks you to enter a value. The call to `strtod()` converts the input and stores the double in `x`. Variable `errno` is cleared, `log10()` is called, and `x` is used as `log10()`'s argument.

Because `log10()` may generate an error for the value of `x`, we assign the value of `errno` to `i` and print the result returned from `log10()`. If an error did occur in `log10()`, you can see the implementation-defined value passed back from the `log10()` function.

If `i` is nonzero, an error occurred, and we call `perror()`. The `perror()` function prints out the argument passed to it, a semicolon, and then the error message associated with the value held in `errno`. [The assignment of `i` into `errno` in the `if` test is to guard against the possibility of `printf()` modifying `errno`.]

If no error is detected, the `break` statement is executed, and the program ends.

Miscellaneous Comments

You may want to consult the `perror()` function.

The most common error with any math function is forgetting to declare that the function returns a double data type. You can eliminate this problem if you `#include` the `math.h` header file.

Function Name

`modf()`

Standard Met

ANSI

Purpose

Decompose floating-point number into fractional and integral parts.

Prototypes

```
double modf(double x, double *y)
```

Required Header

```
#include <math.h>          ANSI
```

Usage

```
double modf(double x, double *y)
```

The function returns the fractional part of the floating-point number `x`. Variable `y` is passed as a pointer and is filled in by `modf()` with the integral part of `x`. If, for example, pi is passed as `x`, the return value from `modf()` is .14159, and `y` would contain 3.0.

There is no error checking.

Caution

This function is not part of SYSV at the present time.

Illustration

```
/*
                                    modf()
*/

#include <stdio.h>
#include <stdlib.h>
#include <stddef.h>
#include <math.h>

int main()
{
     char buff[20];
     double x, y, z;

     printf("\nEnter a value: ");
     x = strtod( gets(buff), (char **) NULL );
     z = modf(x, &y);
     printf("The value %g breaks into", x);
     printf(" %g for the fraction and %g for the exponent.\n", z, y);
}
```

Program Comment

The program `#includes` the necessary header files and asks you to enter a value. The call to `strtod()` converts the value you input and stores the value in `x`. The `modf()` function is called, with `x` and a pointer to `y` as arguments. The return value from `modf()` is stored in `z`, and all three values are then displayed.

Miscellaneous Comments

The most common error with any math function is forgetting to declare that the function returns a double data type. You can eliminate this problem if you `#include` the `math.h` header file.

Function Name

`pow()`

Standard Met

ANSI, SYSV

Purpose

Determine the value of a number raised to a power.

Prototypes

```
double pow(double x, double y)
```

Required Header

`#include <math.h>` ANSI/SYSV

Usage

```
double pow(double x, double y)
```

The function returns the value of x raised to the y power. If the x argument is negative and y is not an integer value, a domain (EDOM) error occurs. A domain error may also occur if x is zero and y is equal to or less than zero. It is also possible to have a range error (ERANGE) from overflow. The return value on a domain error is implementation-defined. The return value on a range error is HUGE_VAL.

Caution

SYSV handles errors differently. If you do not supply your own `matherr()` function, the possible error values produce default error processing. For the `pow()` function, SYSV states that a message is printed (presumably on `stderr`) for an EDOM error only when the value is negative and the exponent is noninteger. If overflow occurs (ERANGE), plus or minus HUGE is returned, depending on the signs of the arguments.

Illustration

```
/*
                                    pow()
*/

#include <stdio.h>
#include <stdlib.h>
#include <stddef.h>
#include <math.h>
#include <errno.h>

int main()
{
     char buff[20];
     int i;
     double x, y, z;

     for (;;) {
          printf("\nEnter a value: ");
          x = strtod( gets(buff), (char **) NULL );
          printf("\nEnter a power: ");
          y = strtod( gets(buff), (char **) NULL );
          errno = 0;
          z = pow(x, y);
          i = errno;
          printf("%f is %f raised to the %f power\n", z, x y);
          if (i)
               perror("Error detected");
          else
               break;
     }
}
```

Program Comment

The program #includes the necessary header files and asks you to enter two values. The call to strtod() converts both values and stores them in `x` and `y`. Variable `errno` is cleared, and `pow()` then uses `x` and `y` as arguments.

Because `pow()` may generate an `EDOM` or `ERANGE` error, we assign the value of `errno` to `i` and print the result returned from `pow()`. If an error did occur in `pow()`, you can see the implementation-defined value passed back from the `pow()` function.

If `i` is nonzero, an error occurred, and we call `perror()`. The `perror()` function prints out the argument passed to it, a semicolon, and then the error message associated with the value held in `errno`. [The assignment of `i` into `errno` in the `if` test is to guard against the possibility of `printf()` modifying `errno`.]

If no error is detected, the `break` statement is executed, and the program ends.

Miscellaneous Comments

You may want to consult the `perror()` function.

The most common error with any math function is forgetting to declare that the function returns a double data type. You can eliminate this problem if you `#include` the `math.h` header file.

Function Name

`rand()` `srand()`

Standard Met

ANSI, SYSV

Purpose

Generate a sequence of pseudo-random numbers between 0 and RAND_MAX.

Prototypes

```
int rand(void)
void srand(unsigned int seed)
```

Required Header

#include <stdlib.h>	ANSI
None provided	SYSV

Usage

```
int rand(void)
```

The `rand()` function returns an integer, pseudo-random number with the domain 0 to RAND_MAX. (RAND_MAX is #defined in stdlib.h.) ANSI states that RAND_MAX shall not be less than 32,767 whereas SYSV states that the domain for the values shall be 0 to 32,767.

```
void srand(unsigned int seed)
```

The `srand()` is used to generate a new sequence of pseudo-random numbers for subsequent calls to `rand()`. If `srand()` is never called, `rand()` will always produce the same sequence of pseudo-random numbers because there is a default seed value. If `srand()` is called with varying `seed` values prior to the call to `rand()`, the sequence of pseudo-random numbers will vary. No value is returned from `srand()`.

Caution

Programs developed under ANSI specifications may have larger values from `rand()` than do programs under SYSV.

Illustration

```
/*
                                        rand(), srand()
*/

#include <stdio.h>
#include <stdlib.h>

int main()
{
     unsigned int i;

     for (i = 0; i < 20; i++) {
          printf("%d ", rand() );
     }

     printf("\n\n");

     srand(i);

     for (i = 0; i < 20; i++) {
          printf("%d ", rand() );
     }
}

/*
ANSI and SYSV publish the following code for rand() and
srand() for testing these functions in different
environments, while producing the same sequence of pseudo-
random numbers.
*/
```

```
static unsigned long next = 1;
int rand(void)
{
     next = next * 1103515245 + 12345;
     return (unsigned int)(next/65536) % 32768;

}

void srand(unsigned int seed)
{
     next = seed;
}
```

Program Comment

The program begins with the required header files and then calls `rand()` without first calling `srand()`. The sequence of 20 numbers is the "naked" sequence produced by `rand()` without using a `seed`. (See the static definition of `next` in the program example.)

The program then calls `srand()`, using the value of `i` for the seed. Because `srand()` assigns `seed` to `next`, the calculation in `rand()` is affected. You should be able to convince yourself, however, that the sequence will still repeat each time the program is run. If a more "random" sequence is needed, something "outside" the program is going to have to influence the value of `seed` (for example, a value entered by you or some form of hardware-determined value).

Miscellaneous Comments

The function `rand()` is the only function in this chapter that returns an integer value.

Function Name

`sin()`

Standard Met

ANSI, SYSV

Purpose

Determine a sine.

Prototypes

```
double sin(double rads)
```

Required Header

`#include <math.h>` ANSI/SYSV

Usage

```
double sin(double rads)
```

The function returns the sine of the argument `rads`, which is expressed in radians. The ANSI specification states that large values for `rads` may produce a result which has no significance.

Caution

SYSV differentiates between a partial loss of significance (PLOSS) and a total loss of significance (TLOSS) when the argument (`rads`) is far from 0. `errno` is set to ERANGE on either condition.

If you do not supply your own `matherr()` function, default error processing occurs. In the case of the `sin()` function, SYSV states that, for a TLOSS condition, a message relating to TLOSS is printed (presumably on `stderr`), and the return value is 0. Default processing for a partial loss is that a PLOSS error is generated, no message is printed, and as much as possible of the value is returned by the function.

Illustration

```
/*
                                        sin()
*/

#include <stdio.h>
#include <stdlib.h>
#include <stddef.h>
#include <math.h>
#include <errno.h>

int main()
{
     char buff[20];
     int i;
     double x, y;

     for (;;) {
          printf("\nEnter a value in radians: ");
          x = strtod( gets(buff), (char **) NULL );
          errno = 0;
          y = sin(x);
          i = errno;
          printf("The sine of %f is %f\n", x, y);
          if (i)
               perror("Error detected");
          else
               break;
     }
}
```

Program Comment

The program `#includes` the necessary header files and asks you to enter a value expressed in radians. The call to `strtod()` converts the input and stores the double in `x`. Variable `errno` is cleared, `sin()` is called, and `x` is used as `sin()`'s argument.

Because `sin()` may generate an `ERANGE` error associated with large values for `x`, we assign the value of `errno` to `i` and then print the result returned from `sin()`. If an error did occur in `sin()`, you can see the implementation-defined value passed back from the `sin()` function.

If `i` is nonzero, an error occurred and we call `perror()` to print out an error message. The error message is the quoted string in `perror()`, followed by a predetermined error message associated with the value held in `errno`. [The assignment of `i` into `errno` in the `if` test is to guard against the possibility of `printf()` modifying `errno`.]

If no error is detected, the `break` statement is executed and the program ends.

Miscellaneous Comments

You may want to consult the `perror()` function.

The most common error with any math function is forgetting to declare that the function returns a double data type. You can eliminate this problem if you `#include` the `math.h` header file.

Function Name

`sinh()`

Standard Met

ANSI, SYSV

Purpose

Determine a hyperbolic sine.

Prototypes

```
double sinh(double rads)
```

Required Header

`#include <math.h>` ANSI/SYSV

Usage

```
double sinh(double rads)
```

The function returns the hyperbolic sine of the argument `rads`, which is expressed in radians. The ANSI specification states that large values for `rads` may produce range errors (`ERANGE`) for overflow, and the function returns `+/HUGE_VAL` according to the correct sign for the function's return value.

Caution

SYSV handles the error differently. If you do not supply your own `matherr()` function, default error processing occurs. In the case of the `sinh()` function, SYSV states that a message (relating to `ERANGE`) is printed (presumably on `stderr`), and the return value is plus or minus `HUGE`, depending on the return value's sign.

Illustration

```
/*
                                        sinh()
*/

#include <stdio.h>
#include <stdlib.h>
#include <stddef.h>
#include <math.h>
#include <errno.h>

int main()
{
     char buff[20];
     int i;
     double x, y;

     for (;;) {
          printf("\nEnter a value in radians: ");
          x = strtod( gets(buff), (char **) NULL );
          errno = 0;
          y = sinh(x);
          i = errno;
          printf("The hyperbolic sine of %f is %f\n", x, y);
          if (i)
               perror("Error detected");
          else
               break;
     }
}
```

Program Comment

The program `#includes` the necessary header files and asks you to enter a value expressed in radians. The call to `strtod()` converts the input and stores the double in `x`. Variable `errno` is cleared, and `sinh()` then uses `x` as an argument.

Because `sinh()` may generate an `ERANGE` (overflow) error associated with large values for `x`, we assign the value of `errno` to `i` and then print the result returned from `sinh()`. If an error did occur in `sinh()`, you can see the implementation-defined value passed back from the `sinh()` function. (The value can be plus or minus HUGE in SYSV.)

If `i` is nonzero, an error occurred and we call `perror()` to print out an error message. The error message is the quoted string in `perror()`, followed by a predetermined error message associated with the value held in `errno`. [The assignment of `i` into `errno` in the `if` test is to guard against the possibility of `printf()` modifying `errno`.]

If no error is detected, the `break` statement is executed, and the program ends.

Miscellaneous Comments

You may want to consult the `perror()` function.

The most common error with any math function is forgetting to declare that the function returns a double data type. You can eliminate this problem if you `#include` the `math.h` header file.

Function Name

`sqrt()`

Standard Met

ANSI, SYSV

Purpose

Determine the square root of a value.

Prototypes

```
double sqrt(double value)
```

Required Header

`#include <math.h>` ANSI/SYSV

Usage

```
double sqrt(double value)
```

The function returns the square root of the argument `value`. If the argument is negative, a domain error (EDOM) occurs. The return value on error is implementation-defined.

Caution

Under SYSV a negative argument also produces a domain error (EDOM). If you do not supply your own `matherr()` function, default error processing occurs. In the case of the `sqrt()` function, SYSV states that a message (relating to EDOM) is printed (presumably on `stderr`), and 0 is returned.

Illustration

```
/*
                                        sqrt()
*/

#include <stdio.h>
#include <stdlib.h>
#include <stddef.h>
#include <math.h>
#include <errno.h>

int main()
{
     char buff[20];
     int i;
     double x, y;

     for (;;) {
          printf("\nEnter a value: ");
          x = strtod( gets(buff), (char **) NULL );
          errno = 0;
          y = sqrt(x);
          i = errno;
          printf("The square root of %f is %f\n", x, y);
          if (i)
               perror("Error detected");
          else
               break;
     }
}
```

Program Comment

The program `#includes` the necessary header files and asks you to enter a value. The call to `strtod()` converts the input and stores the double in `x`. Variable `errno` is cleared, `sqrt()` is called, and `x` is used as `sqrt()`'s argument.

Because `sqrt()` may generate an `EDOM` error for the value of `x`, we assign the value of `errno` to `i` and print the result returned from `sqrt()`. If an error did occur in `sqrt()`, you can see the implementation-defined value passed back from the `sqrt()` function.

If `i` is nonzero, an error occurred and we call `perror()`. The `perror()` function prints out the argument passed to it, a colon, and then the error message associated with the value held in `errno`. [The assignment of `i` into `errno` in the `if` test is to guard against the possibility of `printf()` modifying `errno`.]

If no error is detected, the `break` statement is executed, and the program ends.

Miscellaneous Comments

You may want to consult the `perror()` function.

The most common error with any math function is forgetting to declare that the function returns a double data type. You can eliminate this problem if you `#include` the `math.h` header file.

Function Name

`tan()`

Standard Met

ANSI, SYSV

Purpose

Determine a tangent.

Prototypes

```
double tan(double rads)
```

Required Header

`#include <math.h>` ANSI/SYSV

Usage

```
double tan(double rads)
```

The function returns the tangent of the argument `rads`, which is expressed in radians. The ANSI specification states that large values for `rads` may produce a result which has no significance.

Caution

SYSV differentiates between a partial loss of significance (PLOSS) and a total loss of significance (TLOSS) when the argument (`rads`) is far from 0. `errno` is set to ERANGE on either condition.

If you do not supply your own `matherr()` function, default error processing occurs. In the case of the `sin()` function, SYSV states that, for a TLOSS condition, a message relating to TLOSS is printed (presumably on `stderr`) and the return value is 0. Default processing for a partial loss is that a PLOSS error is generated, no message is printed, and as much as possible of the value is returned by the function.

Illustration

```
/*
                                            tan()
*/

#include <stdio.h>
#include <stdlib.h>
#include <stddef.h>
#include <math.h>
#include <errno.h>

int main()
{
     char buff[20];
     int i;
     double x, y;

     for (;;) {
          printf("\nEnter a value in radians: ");
          x = strtod( gets(buff), (char **) NULL );
          errno = 0;
          y = tan(x);
          i = errno;
          printf("The tangent of %f is %f\n", x, y);
          if (i)
               perror("Error detected");
          else
               break;
     }
}
```

Program Comment

The program `#includes` the necessary header files and asks you to enter a value expressed in radians. The call to `strtod()` converts the input and stores the double in `x`. Variable `errno` is cleared, `tan()` is called, and `x` is used as `tan()`'s argument.

Because `tan()` may generate an ERANGE error associated with large values for `x`, we assign the value of `errno` to `i` and then print the result returned from `tan()`. If an error did occur in `tan()`, you can see the implementation-defined value passed back from the tan() function.

If i is nonzero, an error occurred and we call perror() to print out an error message. The error message is the quoted string in perror(), followed by a predetermined error message associated with the value held in errno. [The assignment of i into errno in the if test is to guard against the possibility of printf() modifying errno.]

If no error is detected, the break statement is executed, and the program ends.

Miscellaneous Comments

You may want to consult the perror() function.

The most common error with any math function is forgetting to declare that the function returns a double data type. You can eliminate this problem if you #include the math.h header file.

Function Name

`tanh()`

Standard Met

ANSI, SYSV

Purpose

Determine a hyperbolic tangent.

Prototypes

```
double tanh(double rads)
```

Required Header

```
#include <math.h>          ANSI
#include <math.h>          SYSV
```

Usage

```
double tanh(double rads)
```

The function returns the hyperbolic tangent of the argument `rads`, which is expressed in radians. No error checking is done in either ANSI or SYSV.

Caution

None.

Illustration

```
/*
                                             tanh()
*/

#include <stdio.h>
#include <stdlib.h>
#include <stddef.h>
#include <math.h>

int main()
{
     char buff[20];
     double x;

     printf("\nEnter a value in radians: ");
     x = strtod( gets(buff), (char **) NULL );
     printf("The hyperbolic tangent of %f is %f\n", x, tanh(x) );
}
```

Program Comment

The program `#includes` the necessary header files and asks you to enter a value expressed in radians. The call to `strtod()` converts the input and stores the double in `x`. Variable `errno` is cleared, and `tanh()` is called using `x` as an argument. No error checking is performed on the value determined by `tanh()`.

Miscellaneous Comments

The most common error with any math function is forgetting to declare that the function returns a double data type. You can eliminate this problem if you `#include` the `math.h` header file.

7 Input/Output Functions

In this chapter, we present those functions concerned with input and output tasks.

As you read through this section, you will notice that the proposed ANSI standard does not provide for low-level input/output functions [for example, `open()`, `close()`, `read()`, `write()`, etc.]. Even though they are not part of the standard, we have included these functions in this chapter because much existing code uses low-level input/output functions. You would be prudent to try to use the high-level input/output functions [for example, `fopen()`, `fclose()`, `fread()`, `fwrite()`, etc.] whenever possible in case compiler manufacturers drop the low-level functions in the future.

UNIX versus Other Operating Systems

Although the C language and library is highly portable, the C library must interact with the operating system, and operating systems are different. The differences, and perplexing problems in writing portable programs, are evident when performing input and output.

The major problems come from operating systems that use a multicharacter end-of-line sequence and operating systems that have a record-oriented file structure.

UNIX, the founding basis of the C library, is different from some operating systems. One difference is the end-of-line character. UNIX uses a single end-of-line character, the line feed (`0x10`). Many other operating systems use a two-character sequence within a text file, usually a carriage return (0x0d) followed by a line feed (0x10). To make this difference almost transparent, compiler writers use the '\n' newline escape character within C programs to represent the end-of-line sequence, regardless of how many characters actually terminate a line.

Hence, there is a difference between files that contain binary information and files that contain text. Text files on operating systems that use a multicharacter end-of-line sequence require translation. On input, the end-of-line sequence is converted to the single '\n' character. On output, the newline character is expanded to the appropriate multicharacter sequence.

Because UNIX does not require translations to the newline sequence, UNIX does not treat binary files differently from text files. However, other operating systems see a difference between these two types of files and cause newline sequence translations.

An offshoot of this problem is console input/output. UNIX isolates newline translations into the device driver for a peripheral, but allows user control over these translations. Other operating systems force the library to perform the newline translation. There is no portable method to enable or disable newline translations other than opening a file in an explicit binary or text mode [shown in the discussion of `fopen()` later in this chapter].

The other problem is that some operating systems do not use the stream model for files. UNIX and several operating systems act as if a file is one contiguous structure, without gaps and with a single beginning boundary and a single ending boundary. Record-oriented operating systems, such as IBM®'s OS/370 and its derivatives, and Hewlett-Packard®'s MPE operating system, use a model in which each file is comprised of a number of individual records of a fixed length.

These models clash when storing information of varying lengths in a file. The record-oriented operating systems may pad text files with some character [usually a '\0' or space (0x20)] to fill out records.

ANSI C enforces the stream model for binary and text files. However, ANSI also recognizes the logical appearance of a file by a program may be different than the underlying physical use of the file. The astonishment comes when using `fseek()` and `ftell()` on a text file. Because newline translations or record padding may take place, the return value of `ftell()` may not yield the true physical position within a file. The value of `ftell()` is only meaningful when used as an argument to `fseek()` and when moving from the beginning of the file. For any other use of `fseek()`, the physical distance moved may be different than the number of characters requested. Also, random movement in any direction onto an end-of-line sequence (for example, the carriage return in a carriage return-line feed combination) has no predictable result.

You must use caution if you want to write maximumly portable programs that use any input/output. If you are writing for a single operating system, you can ignore the inherent differences. However, if your program will be used in a variety of operating system environments, assume all files, unless explicitly opened in a binary mode, are treated as text files and that end-of-line translations will take place.

Function Name

`chdir()`

Standard Met

SYSV only

Purpose

To change the directory for the current process.

Prototypes

```
int chdir(char *directory)
```

Required Header

None provided. SYSV

Usage

```
int chdir(char *directory)
```

The `chdir()` function causes the directory pointed to by `directory` to become the current working directory for all subsequent processes. The value returned from the call to `chdir()` is 0 if the call is successful or -1 if there is an error. If an error is detected, the current working directory is not changed. See the Caution section for possible error values.

Caution

Although a required header is not specified, you can detect certain types of errors by reading the value of `errno`:

EACCES	When access is denied to the directory
ENOENT	When the directory does not exist or cannot be found

`ENOTDIR`	When all or part of the directory name is not a directory

If you want to have access to these symbolic constants, you should `#include` the `errno.h` header file in your program.

Illustration

```
/*
                                    chdir()
*/

#include <stdio.h>
#include <stdlib.h>

#define MAXPATH 64

void dochdir(void), doend(void);
                                   /* These are for errno processing */
extern char *sys_errlist[];
extern int errno;

int main()
{
     dochdir();                    /* Test chdir()              */
     doend();
}

/*
                                   dochdir()
*/

void dochdir(void)
{
     char *oldpath, *newpath, buff[MAXPATH];

                                   /* Find out where we are now */

     getcwd(oldpath, MAXPATH);
     printf("The old path name is: %s\n", oldpath);
```

```
        printf("Enter a new path name: ");
        gets(buff);

        if (chdir(buff) != 0) {
             printf("Error in chdir(): error %d -- %s\n", errno, sys_errlist[errno]);
             exit(1);
        }
                                    /* Show that we are someplace else */

        getcwd(newpath, MAXPATH);
        printf("The new path name is: %s\n", newpath);

        chdir(oldpath);             /* Put us back where we were */
}

/*
                                        doend()
*/

void doend(void)
{
        printf("\nPress RETURN to continue: ");
        while (getchar() != '\n')
             ;
}
```

Program Comment

The program begins with two #include statements to include required header files and then calls dochdir(). In dochdir(), we call getcwd() to get the current working directory (cwd). We won't discuss getcwd() here; it returns a pointer that points to a string which represents the cwd. The call to printf() then displays the cwd.

You then type in a new cwd via the call to gets(). The call to chdir() passes the directory path you just entered and attempts to make cwd the path. If a nonzero value is returned from chdir(), an error message is printed. In this example, we print out the error number held in errno and the number's interpretation in sys_errlist[] so that you have some idea of why the call to chdir() failed.

If the call to `chdir()` was successful, we print out the new `cwd`. The program then makes one final call to `chdir()`, using the old path name so that you end in the same `cwd` as that in which you began when the program started.

Miscellaneous Comments

None.

Function Names

`clearerr()`, `feof()`, `ferror()`, `fileno()`

Standard Met

`clearerr()`, `feof()`, `ferror()`	ANSI/SYSV
`fileno()`	SYSV only

Purpose

To determine whether a stream has an error, is at the end of file, or gets a file description associated with a FILE pointer.

Prototypes

The functions presented in this section should be implemented as macros, so prototypes are inappropriate. If the functions were implemented as functions, the following would be the prototypes:

```
void clearerr(FILE *fp)
int feof(FILE *fp)
int ferror(FILE *fp)
int fileno(FILE *fp)
```

Required Header

```
#include <stdio.h>          ANSI/SYSV
```

Usage

```
void clearerr(FILE *fp)
```

The `clearerr()` macro call causes the error and EOF flags associated with the stream pointed to by `fp` to be cleared. Note that `clearerr()` returns a void data type.

```
int feof(FILE *fp)
```

The `feof()` macro is used to determine whether the EOF flag associated with the stream pointed to by `fp` has been set. If EOF is detected, feof() will return a nonzero value. If EOF is not detected, feof() returns 0.

```
int ferror(FILE *fp)
```

If an error condition exists for the stream associated with the stream pointed to by fp from a read or write operation, ferror() returns a nonzero value. The ferror() macro returns 0 if no error condition exists.

```
int fileno(FILE *fp)
```

The macro fileno() returns the file descriptor for the stream associated with the FILE pointer fp. Use this macro to use low-level functions on a file opened with the high-level functions.

Caution

None.

Illustration

```
/*
                    clearerr(), feof(), ferror(), fileno()
*/

#include <stdio.h>
#include <string.h>
#include <stdlib.h>

#define MAXSTR 200

FILE *fpin, *fpout;                          /* I/O FILE pointers        */

void dofor(void), dofow(void), dotest(void), doend(void);

int main()
{
     dotest();                               /* Test putc()              */
     doend();
}
```

```
void dotest(void)
{
     char string[MAXSTR];
     int   i;

     strcpy(string, "\nWrite a test string to a disk file.\n");

     dofow();                          /* Open a test file        */

     for (i = Ø; string[i]; i++)       /* Write to it             */
          putc(string[i], fpout);
          fclose(fpout);               /* Close it                */

     dofor();                          /* Reopen it               */
     printf("\nThe file descriptor from fpin = %d\n", fileno(fpin) );

     while((i = getc(fpin)) != EOF)    /* Read and show the file  */
          putchar(i);
     printf("  ferror() = %d\n", ferror(fpin) );
     printf("    feof() = %d\n", feof(fpin) );
     printf("\nNow we call clearerr().\n", clearerr(fpin));
     printf("\n    feof() = %d\n", feof(fpin) );
     fclose(fpin);                     /* Close it again          */
}

void dofow(void)
{
     if ((fpout = fopen("filename.xxx", "w")) == (FILE *) NULL) {
          printf("Cannot open test file for writing.\n");
          exit(1);
     }
}

void dofor(void)
{
     if ((fpin = fopen("filename.xxx", "r")) == (FILE *) NULL) {
          printf("Cannot open test file for reading.\n");
          exit(1);
     }
}
```

```
void doend(void)
{
     printf("\nPress RETURN to continue: ");
     while (getchar() != '\n')
          ;
}
```

Program Comment

The program begins with several `#includes` for necessary header files and defines several working variables. Once inside `main()`, we call `dotest()` to perform the various calls being tested.

The `dotest()` function first copies a string constant into the `string` buffer. Having done that, the program calls `dofow()` to open a file for writing. On the assumption that the file is opened successfully, the program writes the string to the data file by calls to `putc()` and then closes the file by the call to `fclose()`. The `dofor()` call reopens the test data file. At this point in the program, we call `fileno()` and use `printf()` to show the file descriptor (`fd`) associated with the open test file. (You must define the macro SYSV for this example to be compiled into the program.) Next, we write the contents of the file to `stdout` by calls to `putchar()`. Notice that the file is not closed after we have sensed EOF by the call to `getc()`.

The program now calls `ferror()` and `feof()` as part of the `printf()` call to show their return values. In most cases, we would expect `ferror()` to have a zero (that is, no error) value. The call to `feof()`, however, should produce some nonzero value because the EOF flag should be set by the previous call to `getc()`. If `feof()` did return a nonzero value, the call to `clearerr()` should reset the EOF and error flags to zero. The final `printf()` should show `feof()` to return a zero value. If you want, you could put in a second call to `ferror()` to see whether its value has also been reset if the first call showed an error condition.

Miscellaneous Comments

The UNIX System V and ANSI specifications tend to avoid low-level file input/output in applications programming. This trend suggests that programmers have less need to use the `fileno()` and other unbuffered function calls.

Function Name

`close()`

Standard Met

SYSV only

Purpose

Releases the file descriptor associated with a file.

Prototypes

```
int close(int fd)
```

Required Header

None provided. SYSV

Usage

```
int close(int fd)
```

The `close()` function closes the file associated with the file descriptor `fd`. The `close()` function returns 0 if no error occurred or -1 if an error is detected. If the `close()` function does fail, `errno` will be set to:

EBADF	The file descriptor was not valid [for example, trying to `close()` a file that was not open].

Caution

To use `errno`, `perror()`, or both, you must supply `#include errno.h` in your program. (See the example.)

Illustration

```
/*
                                        close()
*/

#include <stdio.h>
#include <stdlib.h>
#include <fcntl.h>
#include <string.h>

#define MAXSTR    200
#define PMODE  0666     /* NOTE: Op system specific value */
                        /* Use 0 for MS-DOS               */

int fdin, fdout;

void doclose(void), doow(void), dor(void), doend(void);

extern int errno;               /* Need for error processing  */

int main()
{
     doclose();
     doend();
}

void doclose(void)
{
     char string[MAXSTR], buff[MAXSTR];
     int big, done;
     void doc(int fd);

     strcpy(string, "This tests the close() function.\n");

     doow();                            /* Open a test file        */

     big = strlen(string) + 1;          /* Also keep the null      */

     if ((done = write(fdout, string, big)) == -1 || done != big) {
          printf("Error writing string to file.\n");
          exit(1);
     }
```

```
    doc(fdout);                             /* Close it              */

    dor();                                  /* Reopen it             */

    if ((done = read(fdin, buff, big)) == -1 || (done != big) ) {
        printf("Error reading string from file.\n");
        exit(1);
    }
    doc(fdin);                              /* Close it again        */

    printf("\nstring = %s\n", buff);
}

void doc(int fd)                            /* The real file close   */
{
    if (close(fd) == -1) {
        perror("Close failure");
        exit(1);
    }
}

void doow(void)
{
    if ((fdout = open("filename.xxx", O_WRONLY | O_CREAT, PMODE)) == -1) {
        printf("Cannot open test file for writing.\n");
        exit(1);
    }
}

void dor(void)
{
    if ((fdin = open("filename.xxx", O_RDONLY)) == -1) {
        printf("Cannot open test file for reading.\n");
        exit(1);
    }
}

void doend(void)
{
    printf("\nPress RETURN to continue: ");
    getchar();
}
```

Program Comment

The normal header files are #included into the program as well as string.h, fcntl.h, and errno.h. The file control header file (fcntl.h) contains a number of symbolic constants, as illustrated in the doow() and dor() functions. The errno.h header file comes into play in the doc() function when perror() is used. (See the discussion of header files in Chapter 2.)

The doclose() function begins by copying a string constant into string and calls doow() to open the file for writing. Although the symbolic constants are defined elsewhere, O_WRONLY | O_CREAT are similar to flags that tell what to do when the file is opened and what type of access is permitted. In this example, we are saying that if the file does not exist, create the file and then open it for the write-only mode of access. If the open fails, an error message is printed.

If the file is successfully opened, the contents of string are written to the file. The file is closed by the call to doc(). If an error occurs during the close() function call, perror() is used (with errno) to display the appropriate error message.

The call to dor() reopens the file for reading (that is, O_RDONLY). The contents of the file are read into buff (to keep string separate from buff) and displayed. We again call doc() to close the file after it has been read. We then print the contents of buff, which will be the same as the string constant held in string.

Miscellaneous Comments

If you would like to force an error to see how perror() works, try calling doc() after doend() in main(), using some number too large for the file descriptor argument, such as 10 or higher.

Function Name

`creat()`

Standard Met

SYSV only

Purpose

To create a new file or rewrite an existing file.

Prototypes

```
int creat(const char *fname, int mode)
```

Required Header

None provided. SYSV

Usage

```
int creat(const char *fname, int mode)
```

The `creat()` function uses the name pointed to by `fname` to create a new file if the file does not already exist, or rewrites the existing file if the file does exist. If `creat()` is rewriting an existing file, the file is truncated to a zero-length file, and the file's original `mode` is left unchanged.

The values permissible for `mode` are operating-system specific. User and group identifications have no meaning in some environments (for example, MS-DOS) but are an integral part of other operating systems (for example, UNIX). As a result, no generic meaning is assigned to specific values for `mode`. You must consult your library documentation to determine the required values for `mode`.

The `creat()` function returns a nonnegative file descriptor for the created file if the file was created successfully. If an error is detected, `creat()` returns -1, and `errno` will be set to one of the following possible values:

ENOTDIR	Part of path name is not a directory.
ENOENT	Part of path name does not exist.
EACESS	Access permission is denied.
EROFS	Read-only file system
ETXTBSY	Shared text file and tried to execute it
EISDIR	The file is a directory name.
EMFILE	Maximum number of files is already open.
ENOSPC	Directory is full.
ENFILE	Full file table

You would normally include errno.h.

Caution

ANSI does not provide this function and would prefer the use of fopen().

Illustration

```
/*
                                     creat()
*/

#include <stdio.h>
#include <stdlib.h>
#include <fcntl.h>                  /* SYSV only */
#include <string.h>

#define MAXSTR        200
#define PMODE 0                     /* NOTE: Op system specific value */
                                    /* 0666 for UNIX, 0 for MS-DOS    */

int fdin, fdout;
void doc(int fd);
void doclose(void), doow(void), dor(void), dowrite(void), doend(void);

int main()
{
   dowrite();
   doend();
}
```

```
void doow(void)
{
     if ((fdout = creat("filename.xxx", PMODE)) == -1) {
          printf("Cannot create test file for writing.\n");
          perror("The precise problem is");
          exit(1);
     }
}

void dowrite(void)
{
     char string[MAXSTR], buff[MAXSTR];
     int big, done;

     strcpy(string, "Test the creat() function.\n");

     doow();                              /* Open a test file        */

     big = strlen(string) + 1;            /* Also keep the null      */

     if ((done = write(fdout, string, big)) == -1 || done != big) {
          printf("Error writing string to file.\n");
          exit(1);
     }

     doc(fdout);                          /* Close it                */

     dor();                               /* Reopen it               */

     if ((done = read(fdin, buff, big)) == -1) {
          printf("Error reading string from file.\n");
          exit(1);
     }

     doc(fdin);                           /* Close it again          */

     printf("\nstring = %s\n", buff);
}
```

```
void doc(int fd)                           /* The real file close      */
{
     if (close(fd) == -1) {
          perror("Close failure");
          exit(1);
     }
}

void dor(void)
{
     if ((fdin = open("filename.xxx", O_RDONLY)) == -1) {
          printf("Cannot open test file for reading.\n");
          exit(1);
     }
}

void doend(void)
{
     printf("\nPress RETURN to continue: ");
     while (getchar() != '\n')
          ;
}
```

Program Comment

The program `#includes` quite a few header files, some of which are specific to SYSV. The `fcntl.h` header is needed to process properly the symbolic constant (for example, `O_RDONLY`) used to `open()` the file in the example.

The call to `doow()` [that is, do `open()` for write] attempts to `creat()` a file for reading and writing. The mode for which the file is opened is operating-system specific and has been `#defined` for the host environment. If the file cannot be created, an error message is given, and the program ends by a call to `exit()`. We use the call to `perror()` to see a more precise statement of the nature of the error.

The call to `dowrite()` writes a string to the file we just created, closes the file, reopens it, reads it, and then prints out the string to the display device.

Miscellaneous Comments

Notice that the test for a successful create is against -1, not NULL or zero. Also keep in mind that ANSI is steering programmers away from the low-level input/output functions in favor of high-level functions [that is, the "f" functions like `fopen()`, `fread()`, etc.].

Function Names

`fclose()` `fflush()`

Standard Met

ANSI, SYSV

Purpose

These functions close the file or flush the file's buffer.

Prototypes

```
int fclose(FILE *fp)
int fflush(FILE *fp)
```

Required Header

`#include <stdio.h>` ANSI/SYSV

Usage

```
int fclose(FILE *fp)
```

The `fclose()` function causes the contents of the buffer associated with FILE pointer `fp` to be written out. Any unread data from the file is discarded. The stream is then closed, and `fp` is unlinked from the stream. If an associated buffer was automatically allocated, the buffer is deallocated. The return value from `fclose()` is zero if no error occurred. If an error is detected, `fclose()` returns nonzero for ANSI and EOF for SYSV. If an `exit()` is called in a program before an `fclose()` is called, the `exit()` will do an `fclose()` on all open files.

```
int fflush(FILE *fp)
```

The `fflush()` function causes the contents of the buffer associated with FILE pointer `fp` to be written to the `fp`'s stream, but the stream is not closed. The return value from `fflush()` is zero if no error occurred, or nonzero for ANSI and EOF for SYSV if an error is detected.

Caution

Note that ANSI and SYSV react differently on error. ANSI states that a nonzero value is returned on error. SYSV stipulates that EOF is returned on error.

Illustration

```
/*
                              fclose(), fflush()
*/

#include <stdio.h>
#include <string.h>
#include <stdlib.h>

#define MAXSTR 200

FILE *fpin, *fpout;                    /* I/O FILE pointers       */

void dofor(void), dofow(void), doflu(void), doend(void);

int main()
{
     doflu();                          /* Test putc()             */
     doend();
}

void doflu(void)
{
     char string[MAXSTR];
     int   i;

     strcpy(string, "\nWrite some characters to a file.\n");

     dofow();                          /* Open a test file        */

     printf("Before putc() calls.\n");
     doend();

     for (i = 0; string[i]; i++)       /* Write to it             */
          putc(string[i], fpout);
```

```
    printf("The putc() calls are done--still no disk activity.\n");
    printf("Now the drive light may or may not activate during fflush().\n");
    doend();

    if (fflush(fpout) == EOF) {
         printf("Error in writing to file.\n");
         exit(1);
    }

    printf("After the fflush() and ready for the fclose().\n");
    doend();

    fclose(fpout);                     /* Close it                */

    dofor();                           /* Reopen it               */

    while((i = getc(fpin)) != EOF)     /* Read and show the file  */
         putchar(i);
    fclose(fpin);                      /* Close it again          */

}

void dofow(void)
{
    if ((fpout = fopen("filename.xxx", "w")) == (FILE *) NULL) {
         printf("Cannot open test file for writing.\n");
         exit(1);
    }
}

void dofor(void)
{
    if ((fpin = fopen("filename.xxx", "r")) == (FILE *) NULL) {
         printf("Cannot open test file for reading.\n");
         exit(1);
    }
}

void doend(void)
{
    printf("\nPress RETURN to continue: ");
    while (getchar() != '\n')
         ;
}
```

Program Comment

The program starts with several `#includes` for header files that are needed in the program, followed by the definition of several FILE pointers. The `doflu()` call causes a string to be copied into the `string` variable. Function `dofow()` opens a file for writing, and a `for` loop uses calls to `putc()` to write the contents of `string` to the file. Because we are writing a relatively small amount of data, the `putc()` calls most likely will not fill the buffer for the `fpout` file. Therefore, if you have your system where you can see it, the drive light will not be activated by the calls to `putc()`. (If you are working on a large system or a network, it may be difficult to see the drive light come on. Short of a phone call to the system's room, this example won't be informative.)

Next we call `fflush()` to flush the contents of the buffer that was written to by the calls to `putc()`. The `fflush()` moves the contents of the buffer you control in your program to the buffer controlled by the operating system. If the operating system's buffer can hold the data without overflowing, the operating system probably won't activate the drive either. Everything may work properly to this point, and the drive light will still not come on.

When we call `fclose()`, however, we tell the operating system that we are through using this file, so write the contents of the buffer to disk before closing the file. Now you should see some drive light activity.

The `dofor()` call reopens the file for reading, and the `getc()` calls get the data from the disk file. The `putchar()` call displays the contents of `string` on `stdout`, and the program ends.

Miscellaneous Comments

The call to `fflush()` prior to `fclose()` is usually not necessary because `fclose()` flushes the contents of the buffer to the disk anyway. There may be instances where you have written data to the buffer, but because the buffer was not filled, the data has not yet been written to disk. If you want to do some extensive processing before closing the file and wish to ensure the data is written to disk (in case Murphy strikes), use a call to `fflush()`.

Function Names

`fgetpos()`   `fsetpos()`

Standard Met

ANSI

Purpose

To get and set a file position.

Prototypes

```
int fgetpos(FILE *fp, fpos_t *pos)
int fsetpos(FILE *fp, fpos_t *pos)
```

Required Header

`#include <stdio.h>`   ANSI

Usage

```
int fgetpos(FILE *fp, fpos_t *pos)
```

The `fgetpos()` function saves the present file pointer value associated with FILE pointer `fp` in variable `pos`. This value may later be used in a call to `fsetpos()` to restore the file pointer to its position at the time `fgetpos()` was called. That is, `fgetpos()` marks the current position in the file. A subsequent call to `fsetpos()` restores that same position, probably after other file operations have moved the file pointer.

The `fgetpos()` returns zero if the call is successful, and nonzero on failure. If failure occurs, `errno` is set to some implementation-defined, nonzero value.

```
int fsetpos(FILE *fp, fpos_t *pos)
```

The `fsetpos()` function uses the value held in `pos` to restore the file pointer associated with FILE `fp`. The value held in `pos` should be set by a previous call to `fgetpos()`. If the end-of-file indicator associated with fp is set, the call to fsetpos() clears the indicator. The fsetpos() also cancels any effect caused by an ungetc() call (only one pushback by ungetc() is guaranteed), and the subsequent operation on the file can be whatever mode was allowed at the time the file was opened (for example, read, write, append, etc.).

If fsetpos() is successful, the function returns zero. If fsetpos() fails, nonzero is returned, and errno is set to an implementation-defined nonzero value.

Caution

These functions are not provided in SYSV.

Illustration

```
/*
                              fgetpos(), fsetpos()
*/

#include <stdio.h>
#include <stdlib.h>

int fgetpos(FILE *stream, fpos_t *pos);
int fsetpos(FILE *stream, fpos_t *pos);

int   main()
{
      FILE   *fp;
      fpos_t pos;
      int i;

      if ((fp = fopen("filename.xxx", "r")) == (FILE *) NULL) {
            puts("Error in opening file.");
            exit(1);
      }

      while((i = getc(fp)) != '\n')
            ;

      fgetpos(fp, &pos);
```

```
        while ((i = getc(fp)) != '\n')
             putchar(i);

        fsetpos(fp, &pos);

        puts("\nRead it again\n");

        while((i = getc(fp)) != '\n')
             putchar(i);

        fclose(fp);
}
```

Program Comment

The program #includes the required files but does not #include stddef.h, which might be needed if error processing with errno is desired. The program then uses an #ifdef to trigger declarations for the functions being tested if a SYSV library is being used.

We then attempt to fopen() a file named filename.xxx for reading. On the assumption that such a file exists, the calls to getc() in the while loop reads the file a character at a time until the first newline character ('\n') is read. Next, a call to fgetpos() finds the current position of the file pointer associated with the file (that is, fp) and stores that position in variable pos.

The program then continues to read the file, again searching for a newline character. If another newline is read, the while loop terminates, and the call to fsetpos() is made to restore the file pointer value that was recorded in pos on the call to fgetpos().

After returning from fsetpos(), a final while loop displays the line of text to verify that the file pointer position is the same position that was set earlier. The program then closes the file and terminates.

Miscellaneous Comments

Note how pos is defined to be of type fpos_t. This approach ensures that pos can hold a value at least as big as the largest file size supported by the host system.

Function Names

`fopen()` `freopen()` `fdopen()`

Standard Met

`fopen(), freopen()`	ANSI/SYSV
`fdopen()`	SYSV only

Purpose

Functions to open an input/output stream.

Prototypes

```
FILE *fdopen(int fd, char *mode)
FILE *fopen(char *filename, char *mode)
FILE *freopen(char *filename, char *mode, FILE *fp)
```

Required Header

`#include <stdio.h>` ANSI/SYSV

Usage

```
FILE *fdopen(int fd, char *mode)
```

The function `fdopen()` returns a FILE pointer from an open file whose file descriptor is `fd`.

The function's purpose is to obtain a FILE pointer, usable with other high-level functions [such as `gets()`, `printf()`, etc.], from a file which was originally `open()`ed.

If you try to `fdopen()` a file in a mode other than the mode in which the file was originally opened, undefined results may occur. If the call to `fdopen()` is successful, a FILE pointer is returned. If you attempt to call `fdopen()` for a file that is not open or pass a `mode` that is not valid, a NULL pointer is returned, which indicates an error. The permissible values for `mode` are presented later in this section. (See the `errno.h` header file discussion.)

```
FILE *fopen(char *filename, char *mode)
```

The `fopen()` function opens the file pointed to by `filename` in the mode specified by `mode` and returns a FILE pointer if the opening is successful. If the file cannot be opened, if an invalid value for `mode` is given, or if no more streams are available, a NULL pointer is returned to indicate an error. (See the `errno.h` header file discussion.)

```
FILE *freopen(char *filename, char *mode, FILE *fp)
```

The `freopen()` function changes the stream currently associated with FILE pointer `fp` to the file pointed to by `filename` and closes the original stream associated with `fp`. If the call cannot open the file associated with `filename` or if an invalid argument is used for `mode`, a NULL pointer is returned. The original stream associated with `fp` is closed regardless of the result of opening the file `filename`, and a failure to close the original file is ignored.

The following are valid `mode` values:

`"r"`	Opens a file for reading. The stream is at beginning-of-file (BOF).
`"w"`	Opens a file for writing. If the file already exists, it is truncated to zero length. If the file does not exist, it is created.
`"a"`	Opens a file for writing (appending) at the end of-file. If the file does not exist, it is created.
`"r+"`	Opens a file for reading-writing (that is, updating). The stream is opened at BOF. Opening in this mode, followed by statements that write to the file, will overwrite whatever was in the file.
`"w+"`	Performs the same as `w` except that you can also read the file.
`"a+"`	Opens or creates a file for updating. Any writing to the file will be at the end-of-file. Use this mode to read as well as write the file.
`"rb"`	Opens a binary file for reading.

"wb"	Opens a binary file for writing. If the file does not exist, it is created. If it does exist, it is truncated to zero length.
"ab"	Open a binary file if it exists (or create the file if it does not exist) for writing at end-of file.
"rb+"	Open a binary file for updating. The file can be read or written. "r+b" is also legal.
"wb+"	Create a binary file for updating if the file does not exist, or truncate to zero length if the file does exist. "w+b" is also legal.
"ab+"	Open a binary file if it does exist (or create the file if it does not exist) in the append mode (that is, writing to the end-of-file). "a+b" is also legal.

NOTE: As discussed at the beginning of this chapter, the "binary" mode ("b") is used to turn off any conversion processing that might be done by the host system. The "+" character indicates that input and output operations may be done on the file.

Caution

Although not stated in the specification, common practice is that, after a file is opened, the stream is left at the beginning-of-file. After the file is accessed, the stream position is set to the location in the file dictated by the mode value.

Illustration

```
/*
                                fdopen(), fopen(), freopen()
*/

#include <stdio.h>
#include <fcntl.h>                /* SYSV only, does not exist
                                     for ANSI              */
#include <stdlib.h>

int fdin;
```

```
FILE *fpin, *fpout;

void dofdop(void), dofor(void), dofre(void), doop(void);

int main()
{
     printf("The fp for stdout is %p in hex.\n", stdout);

     dofor();              /* Try to open a file which doesn't exist  */
                           /* Now give an error message               */

     dofre();              /* Now reopen stdout as filename.xxx       */

     printf("The fp for stdout is %p in hex.\n", stdout);
     printf("This will be sent to the disk file.\n");
     printf("It will not appear on the screen.\n");
     doend();

     fclose(stdout);

     doop();               /* Use fprintf() and stderr so we can see it */

     fprintf(stderr, "fdin is %x in hex.\n", fdin);
     dofdop();
     fprintf(stderr, "fpin is now egual to %x in hex.\n", fpin);
     doend();
}

void dofor(void)                          /* Do straight fopen() for no file */
{
     if ((fpin = fopen("filename.xxx", "r")) == (FILE *) NULL) {
          fprintf(stderr, "Cannot open test file for reading.\n");
     }
}

void dofre(void)                            /* Do an freopen() */
{
     if ((freopen("filename.xxx", "w", stdout)) == (FILE *) NULL) {
          fprintf(stderr, "Cannot reopen test file for writing.\n");
     }
}
```

```
void doop(void)                          /* Do an fd open()        */
{
     if ((fdin = open("filename.xxx", O_RDONLY)) == -1) {
          fprintf(stderr, "Cannot open() test file for O_RDONLY.\n");
     }
}

void dofdop(void)                        /* Do an fdopen()         */
{
     if ((fpin = fdopen(fdin, "r")) == (FILE *) NULL) {
          fprintf(stderr, "Cannot open test file for reading.\n");
     }
}

void doend(void)
{
     fprintf(stderr, "\nPress RETURN to continue: ");
     while (getchar() != '\n')
          ;
}
```

Program Comment

The `fcntl.h` header file is `#included` along with the other header files because of the call to the `open()` function. After defining several variables, the program begins by a call to `dofor()`, which attempts to open a test file named `filename.xxx`. If this file does not exist and we are attempting to open the file in the `r` mode, an error message should be issued.

Next, the program calls `dofre()`, which reopens the standard output stream `stdout` as `filename.xxx`. Any output that would normally appear on `stdout` [for example, a `printf()` to the screen] ends up being written to `filename.xxx`. If you print out the contents of `filename.xxx` after the program is run, you will see in the file the three `printf()` messages from `main()`. Because `stdout` is closed after the call to `dofre()`, we use `fprintf()` with the `stderr` stream to print the remaining messages to the screen.

The call to `doop()` does an `open()` call in the read-only mode and assigns a file descriptor to `fdin`. The subsequent call to `dofdop()` is used to call `fdopen()` to assign a FILE pointer to the file that was associated with a `fdin` file descriptor. We then print out the `fpin` FILE pointer and end the program.

Miscellaneous Comments

Because the standard output stream may be closed in this program, the `doend()` function also calls `fprintf()` using the `stderr` output stream instead of `stdout`.

Function Names

`fprintf()` `printf()` `sprintf()`

Standard Met

ANSI, SYSV

Purpose

These are general purpose functions for doing formatted output.

Prototypes

```
int fprint(FILE *fp, const char *control, ...)
int printf(const char *control, ...)
int sprintf(char *str, const char *control, ...)
```

Required Header

`#include <stdio.h>` ANSI/SYSV

Usage

```
int fprintf(FILE *fp, const char *control, ...)
```

The `fprintf()` function works the same as `printf()`, except that output is sent to the stream pointed to by the FILE pointer `fp`.

```
int printf(const char *control, ...)
```

The `printf()` function is used for formatted output. The control string (that is, `char *control`) determines what and how the output is written. The control string may contain: (1) special conversion characters (which are explained next), (2) escape sequences, and (3) normal text that is simply written to the output stream. Escape sequences are preceded with a backslash followed by a character. (The escape sequences are given in table 7.1.)

Conversion Options

Any conversion to be performed by one of the format functions is preceded by a percent sign (%). After the conversion character is detected in the control string, several options may be specified.

```
% [flags] [width] [precision] [modifier] [type]
```

Flags

blank	Replace with a blank the first character of a signed conversion. [See the plus sign (+).]
-	Says that the output will be left-justified within whatever width specifier might be given.
+	Says that a signed conversion will always have the sign displayed. The value of the sign may be positive or negative.
#	Indicates that the output is to be displayed in some alternative form.
o	Forces an increase in the precision so that the first digit is a zero.
x or X	Prepends 0x or 0X to the result.
e, E, f	Always uses a decimal point in the result.
g or G	Always uses a decimal point and keeps trailing zeros in the result.

Width

If a digit string follows the conversion character (for example, the 20 in %20s), the string specifies the minimum width to be used in displaying the data item. If the output is smaller than the width specifier, the result is right-justified. If the result exceeds the width specifier, the result is printed. Therefore, a width specifier does not "chop" a result.

Precision

A precision specification is indicated by a period followed by a digit string. This conversion option may be used with the data types:

integral	The minimum number of digits to appear in the result. If the result is smaller than the precision, the result is padded with zeros.
`e, f`	The number of digits to appear after a decimal point. If a 0 is specified, no decimal point is displayed.
`g, G`	The maximum number of significant digits. Precision defaults to six significant digits.
`s`	The maximum number of characters to be displayed.

* (Asterisk)

The asterisk has special meaning after a conversion character. The asterisk may be used to indicate that a variable will follow which tells either the width, the precision, or both. For example:

`printf("%*s", width, str)`	Means that `width` gives the field width for the string `str`.
`printf("%*.*f, w, p, x)`	Means to use a field width of size `w` with a precision of size `p` to print the result of variable `x`.
`printf("%.*f", p, x)`	Means to use the precision given by `p` to display the result of `x`.

Modifier

`l` The letter `l` (ell) or L may be used as a modifier for the integral data types. Valid uses of the `l`:

`ld`	Long decimal number
`lo`	Long octal number
`lu`	Long unsigned number
`lx, lX`	Long hexadecimal number

The l modifier may be used with only the conversion character for the data types shown here. The l is ignored when used with any other data types.

Note that an l or uppercase L may be used with e, E, f, g, or G to denote a long double data type. This use is not supported in SYSV.

Type

The following list describes the conversions that can be done with the formatted output functions. If a conversion character is followed by something other than the conversions in this list, the conversion performed is unspecified.

c
: Displays a character.

d, i
: Converts the result to a signed decimal value.

f
: Displays a float or double data type as a decimal result. If the precision specifier (discussed previously) is omitted, there will be six digits displayed after the decimal point.

e, E
: Displays a float or double data type in scientific notation of:

  [optional sign]x.xxxe[+ or -]xx

  The optional sign may be a minus sign for a negative result. If no precision argument is given, the result will be six digits. The exponent will be two or more digits, as required by the result.

g, G
: Selects e or f specification based on the range of the exponent. An uppercase G means to use E if exponential form is required. If the exponent of the number is greater than or equal to -4 and the exponent is less than or equal to the precision, printing occurs as though %wf (w = width). The precision is the default precision. Otherwise, the number is printed as %we or %wE depending on whether g or G was used.

	Trailing zeros are suppressed, and decimal point is used only if it is followed by a digit.

```
x = 3.14 * 1000;
y = 3.14 / 100000;

printf("%10.2g\n", x);
printf("%10.2g\n", y);
printf("%10.3g\n", x);
printf("%10.3g\n", y);
printf("%10g\n", x / 1000);
```

outputs:

```
3.140000e03
3.140000e-05
      3140
3.140000e-05
      3.14
```

Note that precision cannot be changed with the g specification.

g, G	Displays a `float` or `double` data type in the `e` or `f` format (or style E if `G` was specified). The format style selected depends on the result. Scientific notation (`e` format) is used if the exponent is less than -4 or greater than the precision used (six digits unless the precision specifier is used). If no digit appears to the right of the decimal point, the decimal point is not printed. Trailing zeros also are suppressed.
n	The argument is a pointer to integer. The value written into this integer is the number of characters written to the output stream thus far. (Any null termination characters are not included in the count.) This option is not part of SYSV. The return value from `printf()` does not include this conversion in `printf()`'s total count.
o	Displays the result in `unsigned` octal (base 8) notation.

p Displays a pointer. The exact form this output assumes is a sequence of printable characters that is implementation-specific. For example, on an MS-DOS machine, the form may be `xxxx:XXXX` in which `xxxx` is a hexadecimal number for the segment address, followed by a colon, followed by XXXX, which is the offset address in hexadecimal. On other machines, the output may be a sequence of digits representing a memory address. Consult your documentation for the exact format expected.

This option is not part of SYSV.

s Displays the characters in a character array until the null character ('\Ø') is read. The `%s` conversion recognizes a width and a precision specification of the form:

```
% width . precision s
```

where `width` is the minimum field to use; `precision` is the maximum field to use; and `s` is the string conversion character.

If a precision field is given (for example, `%.2Øs`) a maximum of that many characters are displayed. If the null character is read before "`precision`" characters are read, the display terminates on reading the null character. The following list shows some alternatives for the width and precision specifications:

`%2Øs`	Prints 20 characters or `strlen()`, whichever is longer (pad with blanks).
`%.2Øs`	Prints 20 characters or `strlen()`, whichever is smaller (no padding).
`%2Ø.2Øs`	Print exactly 20 characters [pads if `strlen()` less than 20 or truncates at 20 characters if `strlen()` greater than 20].

u	Displays the result in unsigned decimal notation.
x, X	Displays the result in unsigned hexadecimal (base 16) notation. [If x is used, displayed letters are lowercase (abcdef). If X is used, displayed characters are uppercase (ABCDEF).]

Because of the significance of both the conversion character (%) and the lead-in character for an escape sequence (\), to print these characters, you must use:

```
printf("%%") To print a percent sign
printf("\\") To print a backslash
```

The interpretations for the escape sequences are given in table 7.1.

```
int sprintf(char *str, const char *control, ...)
```

The `sprintf()` function behaves the same as `printf()`, except that output is written to the character array pointed to by `str` and has a null character appended to the output. You must ensure that the character string to receive the output is large enough for the output and the null character.

All three functions return the number of characters that have been sent to the output stream if no error occurred. If an error is sensed, -1 is the return value.

Caution

None.

Table 7.1
Escape Sequences

`\a`	Generates an audible or visible alarm
`\b`	Backspace. This causes the next output position to be one position before the current output position.
`\f`	Formfeed. This causes the next output position to be at the start of the next page.
`\n`	Newline. This causes the next output position to be on the next (new) line starting in the first column.
`\r`	Carriage return. This causes the next output position to be in the first column of the current line.
`\t`	Horizontal tab. This causes the next output position to be x characters to the right of the current output position. The number of characters associated with a tab space (that is, x) is not fixed and may vary between environments and implementations.
`\v`	Vertical tab. This causes the next output position to be at the next vertical tab position. As with the horizontal tab, the specification is not fixed and may vary.

Illustration

```
/*
            This program demonstrates the use of printf().
*/

#include <stdio.h>
```

```
int main()
{
                                        /* create some variables */
    char *p = "Hello world",
         c = 'A';
    int i;
    unsigned u;
    long l;
    unsigned long ul;
    double d;

    printf("\nString printouts using [] to show the field\n\n");

    printf("[%s]\n", p);
    printf("[%20s]\n", p);
    printf("[%-20s]\n", p);
    printf("[%20.3s]\n", p);
    printf("[%-20.3s]\n", p);

    printf("\nCharacter printouts using [] to show fields\n\n");

    printf("[%c]\n", c);
    printf("[%20c]\n", c);
    printf("[%-20c]\n", c);
    printf("[%20.3c]\n", c);
    printf("[%-20.3c]\n", c);

    printf("\nInteger printouts using [] to show fields\n\n");

    for(i = -5; i <= 5; i += 5) {
        u = (unsigned) i;
        printf("%% [%d] [%o] [%x] [%u]\n", i, i, i, u);
        printf("%%010 (old style) [%010d] [%010x] [%010u]\n", i, i, i, u);
        printf("%%- [%-d] [%-o] [%-x] [%-u]\n", i, i, i, u);
        printf("%%C [%D] [%O] [%X] [%U]\n", i, i, i, u);
        printf("%%10 [%10d] [%10o] [%10x] [%10u]\n", i, i, i, u);
        printf("%%10.3 [%10.3d] [%10.3o] [%10.3x] [%10.3u]\n", i, i, i, u);
        printf("%%+ [%+d] [%+o] [%+x] [%+u]\n", i, i, i, u);
        printf("%%# [%#d] [%#o] [%#x] [%#u]\n", i, i, i, u);
        printf("%%  [% d] [% o] [% x] [% u]\n\n", i, i, i, u);
    }
```

```
    printf("\nLong printouts using [] to show fields\n\n");

    for(l = -5l; l <= 5l; l += 5L) {
        ul = (unsigned long) l;
        printf("%% [%ld] [%lo] [%lx] [%lu]\n", l, l, l, ul);
        printf("%%- [%-ld] [%-lo] [%-lx] [%-lu]\n", l, l, l, ul);
        printf("%%C [%lD] [%lO] [%lX] [%lU]\n", l, l, l, ul);
        printf("%%10 [%10ld] [%10lo] [%10lx] [%10lu]\n", l, l, l, ul);
        printf("%%10.3 [%10.3ld] [%10.3lo] [%10.3lx] [%10.3lu]\n", l, l, l, ul);
        printf("%%+ [%+ld] [%+lo] [%+lx] [%+lu]\n", l, l, l, ul);
        printf("%%# [%#ld] [%#lo] [%#lx] [%#lu]\n", l, l, l, ul);
        printf("%%  [% ld] [% lo] [% lx] [% lu]\n\n", l, l, l, ul);
    }

    printf("\nDouble printouts using [] to show fields\n\n");

    for(d = -3.14159; d <= 3.14159; d += 3.14159) {
        printf("%% [%g] [%f] [%e]\n", d, d, d);
        printf("%%C [%G] [%F] [%E]\n", d, d, d);
        printf("%%- [%-g] [%-f] [%-e]\n", d, d, d);
        printf("%%# [%#g] [%#f] [%#e]\n", d, d, d);
        printf("%%  [% g] [% f] [% e]\n", d, d, d);
        printf("%%10.2 [%10.2g] [%10.2f] [%10.2e]\n", d, d, d);
        printf("%%-10.2 [%-10.2g] [%-10.2f] [%-10.2e]\n", d, d, d);
        printf("%%10.2 / 10000.0 [%10.2g] [%10.2f] [%10.2e]\n\n",
                d / 10000.0, d / 10000.0, d / 10000.0);
    }

    printf("\nShow %*, %n, and %p\n");

    i = 10;
    d = 3.14;

    printf("\nwith precision specifier: d = %*.*f\n", i, i - 7, d);
    printf("\nwith n specifier: d = %f%n\n", d, &i);
    printf("\ni now equals %d\n", i);
    printf("\nthe address of i is %p\n", &i);
}
```

Program Comment

The program is designed to exercise most of the `printf()` options. A few of the lines are worth showing because the options are not often used.

In the first section which tests the string variable p, the lines:

```
printf("[%20.3s]\n", p);
printf("[%-20.3s]\n", p);
```

produce the following output:

```
[                 Hel]
[Hel                 ]
```

respectively. You can use the width and precision options (separated by a decimal point) with string data.

The `for` loop in the line used to test various integer values

```
printf("%%C [%D] [%O] [%X] [%U]\n", i, i, i, u);
```

produced:

```
%C [D] [O] [FFFB] [U]
```

as output for the first iteration of the `for` loop. This illustrates that uppercase C, D, O, and U are not necessarily recognized as conversion characters by `printf()`. Only the hexadecimal conversion character may be expressed in uppercase form. (Had a lowercase x been used, the hex value would have been displayed in lowercase letters, or fffb.)

Miscellaneous Comments

The lowercase l (ell) is difficult to spot in some situations because the l looks much like the digit 1. To illustrate, consider the line from the program that tests the `long` data type:

```
for(l = -5l; l <= 5l; l += 5L) {
```

A quick glance might seem to indicate that the loop runs from -51 to plus 51 (that is, fifty-one). The use of the uppercase L makes it easier to see that a long data type is being used. You, however, do not have this choice with `printf()` under SYSV; only the lowercase l may be used as a conversion modifier. ANSI allows both upper and lowercase L in `printf()`.

In the example to illustrate the precision specifier, i is assigned a value of 10, which causes printf() to read variable i and use i's value to print out the value of d. Therefore, with i equal to 10 in the example above, "%*.*f" is the same as "%10.3f".

The next printf() displays a message and then the value of d. The conversion %n causes the count of the number of characters displayed thus far by the printf() to be written into variable i. (The return value from printf() is the number of characters written.) Because we need a pointer to write this value, we use the "address of" operator (&) to write the character count into variable i. The next printf() shows the new value for i.

The final example shows how %p might be used. In this case, we use it to display the address of variable i. The output that is displayed is implementation-specific. On MS-DOS machines using segment addressing, a "small model" pointer (for example, a 16-bit value) may be displayed as a number. A "large model" pointer (that is, a 32-bit value) might show a segment address, a colon, and an offset (for example, B000:0100).

Many pre-SYSV libraries supplied a function named itoa() (that is, integer to ASCII) that was used to convert a decimal integer into a string. That function does not appear in the new specification, nor was it replaced with a new function [a la strtod() or strtol()]. If you want to convert an integer to a string, sprintf() will be used. (An example of using sprintf() for an integer-to-ASCII converter appears at the beginning of Chapter 3.) An example:

```
/* Replace itoa() with sprintf() */

#include <stdio.h>

int main()
{
      char buff[20];
      unsigned int i = 62345;

      sprintf(buff, "%u", i);
      printf("buff = %s   i = %u\n", buff, i);
}
```

The program places the ASCII equivalence of i and writes the characters into buff rather than to the screen.

The fprintf() functions the same as printf(), only the output is sent to a file rather than the screen.

Function Names

`fputc()` `putc()` `putchar()` `putw()`

Standard Met

`fputc()`, `putc()`, `putchar()`	ANSI
`putw()`	SYSV only

Purpose

To put a character or word to a specified output device.

Prototypes

Both `putc()` and `putchar()` are implemented as macros; therefore they have no prototype. If they are implemented as functions rather than macros, the following are the prototypes:

```
int putc(int letter, FILE *fp)
int putchar(int letter)
int fputc(int letter, FILE *fp)
int putw(int word, FILE *fp)
```

Required Header

`#include <stdio.h>` ANSI/SYSV

Usage

```
int fputc(int letter, FILE *fp)
```

This function behaves the same as `putc()`, explained below, except that `fputc()` is a function rather than a macro.

```
int putc(int letter, FILE *fp)
```

This macro writes a single character `letter` to the output device associated with FILE pointer `fp`. The macro returns `letter` if the function is successful, or `EOF` if an error occurred.

```
int putchar(int letter)
```

This macro writes a single character `letter` to `stdout`. The `putchar()` macro calls `putc()` with the FILE pointer being `stdout`. If the write is successful, the character written (that is, `letter`) is returned, but `EOF` is returned on error.

```
int putw(int word, FILE *fp)
```

This function writes `word` to the output stream associated with the FILE pointer `fp`. The size of `word` is whatever an integer is on the host machine and, hence, is machine dependent. If the write is successful, a 0 is returned. Any nonzero value indicates an error.

Note that `putw()` is not part of the ANSI standard library.

Caution

As stated elsewhere, using an operator on an argument that is part of a macro can cause surprises. Therefore, you should not attempt to do any operation on the arguments to `putc()` or `putchar()`.

Illustration

```
/*
                    fputc(), putc(), putchar(), putw()
*/

#include <stdio.h>
#include <string.h>
#include <stdlib.h>

#define MAXSTR 200

FILE *fpin, *fpout;                         /* I/O FILE pointers        */

int dick = 30,
    jane = 25;

void dofor(void), dofow(void), doputc(void),
     doend(void), doputw(void), dofputc(void);
```

```
int main()
{
     doputc();                              /* Test putc()          */
     doend();
     dofputc();                             /* Test fputc()         */
     doputw();                              /* Test putw()          */
}

void doputc(void)
{
     char string[MAXSTR];
     int   i;

     strcpy(string, "\nDick and Jane's ages are 30 and 25.\n");

     dofow();                               /* Open a test file     */

     for (i = 0; string[i]; i++)            /* Write to it          */
          putc(string[i], fpout);
     fclose(fpout);                         /* Close it             */

     dofor();                               /* Reopen it            */

     while((i = getc(fpin)) != EOF)         /* Read and show the file */
          putchar(i);
     fclose(fpin);                          /* Close it again       */
}

void doputw(void)
{
     char buff[MAXSTR];
     int   eflag, i;

     putw(dick, fpout);
     putw(jane, fpout);
     fclose(fpout);                         /* Close it             */

     dofor();                               /* Reopen it            */

     if (fgets(buff, MAXSTR, fpin) != (char *) NULL) {
          printf("%s ", buff);
     } else
          printf("Error reading the string");
```

```
    eflag = 0;
    while((i = getw(fpin)) != EOF || ((eflag = ferror(fpin)) == 0) ) {
         if (eflag)
              printf("Error reading file.\n");
         else {
              eflag = 0;
              printf("%d ", i);
         }
    }
    fclose(fpin);
}

void dofputc(void)
{
    char string[50];
    int  i;

    strcpy(string, "Dick and Jane's ages are: \n");

    dofow();                          /* Open a test file       */

    for (i = 0; string[i]; i++) {     /* We want the null, too  */
         fputc(string[i], fpout);
    }
}

void dofow(void)
{
    if ((fpout = fopen("filename.xxx", "w")) == (FILE *) NULL) {
         printf("Cannot open test file for writing.\n");
         exit(1);
    }
}

void dofor(void)
{
    if ((fpin = fopen("filename.xxx", "r")) == (FILE *) NULL) {
         printf("Cannot open test file for reading.\n");
         exit(1);
    }
}
```

```
void doend(void)
{
     printf("\nPress RETURN to continue: ");
     while (getchar() != '\n')
          ;
}
```

Program Comment

The program begins with several #include statements for required header files and defines two FILE pointers. The doputc() function copies a test string into string and uses calls to putc() to write the string to a disk file. The doputc() function then reopens the file, reads it using getc(), and displays the contents of the file by calls to putchar().

The dofputc() is almost identical to doputc(), except that fputc() rather than putc() is used to write the file. Note also that the file is not closed after the string is written to the file.

The doputw() call uses the putw() function to write out three integer values. The last value written is -1, which often is the same value as EOF. We use the call to ferror() in conjunction with the test on EOF when we read the file so that we don't terminate reading the file before we actually read EOF. This "double test" is necessary because the translation of EOF is a valid integer and may be contained as an integer in the file.

To illustrate why this is necessary, try running the program again, but instead of:

```
while ((i = getw(fpin)) != EOF || (ferror(fpin) == 0) )
```

replace it with:

```
while ((i = getw(fpin)) != EOF)
```

and see what happens. Because test has the value of -1, a simple test for EOF will terminate reading the file before true EOF is read.

Because putw() is not available under ANSI, you must define the macro in SYSV to compile the parts of the program which use this function.

Miscellaneous Comments

Because macros result in in-line code, they should be somewhat quicker than function calls. To see how much this difference is, you might write a copy program that uses `putc()` and `fputc()` and time the difference. Except for large files, the differences will be minor (but worth investigating).

Function Names

`fputs()` `puts()`

Standard Met

ANSI, SYSV

Purpose

Functions to write strings.

Prototypes

```
int fputs(char *str, FILE *fp)
int puts(char *str)
```

Required Header

```
#include <stdio.h>
```

Usage

```
int fputs(char *str, FILE *fp)
```

This function writes the string pointed to by `str` to the output device associated with FILE pointer `fp`. An assumption for the `fputs()` function is that the string is properly terminated with the null character ('\Ø'). Note, however, that the `fputs()` function does not write the null character to the output device. For ANSI, `fputs()` returns zero if successful and nonzero on error. Under SYSV, the return value from `fputs()` is the number of characters written (excluding the null termination character) or EOF on error.

```
int puts(char *str)
```

This function writes the string pointed to by `str` to the standard output device (that is, `stdout`). After the null-terminated string is written, `puts()` adds a newline character. For ANSI, `puts()` returns zero if successful and a nonzero value on error. Under SYSV, the return value from `puts()` is the number of characters written to `stdout` or EOF on error.

Caution

ANSI and SYSV differ on the return values from these functions. Generally, ANSI returns zero if a successful call is made and non-zero if an error was detected. SYSV, on the other hand, returns a count of the characters written to `stdout` on success or `EOF` on error.

Illustration

```
/*
                                    fputs(), puts()
*/

#include <stdio.h>
#include <stdlib.h>
#include <string.h>

#define MAXSTR    200

FILE *fpin, *fpout;

void doputs(void), doend(void), dofputs(void);
void dofow(void), dofor(void);

int main()
{
     doputs();
     doend();
     dofputs();
     doend();
}

void dofputs(void)
{
     char buff[MAXSTR];
     int i;

     strcpy(buff, "There is no newline added here.");
     dofow();

     fputs(buff, fpout);             /* Write the string out */
     fclose(fpout);
```

```
        dofor();
        while ((i = getc(fpin)) != EOF)
                putc(i, stdout);
}

void doputs(void)
{
        puts("Note how the newline is added even though we didn't do it.");
}

void dofow(void)
{
        if ((fpout = fopen("filename.xxx", "w")) == (FILE *) NULL) {
                printf("Cannot open test file for writing.\n");
                exit(1);
        }
}

void dofor(void)
{
        if ((fpin = fopen("filename.xxx", "r")) == (FILE *) NULL) {
                printf("Cannot open test file for reading.\n");
                exit(1);
        }
}

void doend(void)
{
        printf("\nPress RETURN to continue: ");
        while (getchar() != '\n')
                ;
}
```

Program Comment

After the necessary header files are #included and the FILE pointers are defined, the first call is to doputs(). The doputs() function writes the string to the standard output device (stdout). Note that puts() adds a newline to whatever is contained in the string.

The call to dofputs() copies a string into a character array (buff) and calls dofow() to open the file. The call to fputs() then writes the string to disk, and `fclose()` then closes the file. The `dofor()` call reopens the file, and a `while` loop is used to display the contents of the file by calls to `putc()` using `stdout` as the output device.

Miscellaneous Comments

If you run this program, you will see that `puts()` always appends a newline to the output, whereas `fputs()` does not. If you need to suppress the newline, `printf()` is a convenient alternative.

Function Names

`fread()` `fwrite()`

Standard Met

ANSI, SYSV

Purpose

For buffered reading and writing.

Prototypes

```
size_t fread(void *buff, size_t big, size_t number, FILE *fp)
size_t fwrite(const void *buff, size_t big, size_t number, FILE *fp)
```

Required Header

`#include <stdio.h>` ANSI/SYSV

Usage

```
size_t fread(void *buff, size_t big, size_t number, FILE *fp)
```

The `fread()` function reads `number` data items, each of which is of size `big`, into the buffer pointed to by `buff` from the stream associated with FILE pointer `fp`. The function continues to read from the stream until: (1) `number` items have been read, (2) EOF is sensed, or (3) a read error is detected. The function returns the number of data items read from the stream.

For ANSI, if an error occurs, the state of the file position indicator associated with the file is indeterminate. If a partial member is read, the member's value is indeterminate.

For ANSI, if the values for variables `big` or `number` are zero, `fread()` returns zero and the contents of `buff` and the file position indicator remain unchanged. For SYSV, on a nonpositive value for `big` or `number`, `fread()` also returns zero and guarantees the file position indicator is unchanged and implies that the contents of buff remain unchanged.

int fwrite(const void *buff, size_t big, size_t number, FILE *fp)

The fwrite() function writes number data items, each of which is of size big, from the buffer pointed to by buff to the stream associated with FILE pointer fp. The function continues to write to the stream until: (1) number items have been written, or (2) an error is sensed. The function returns the number of data items written to the stream, which may be less than number only if a write error occurred.

Caution

Because the fread() function is not designed to return EOF on reaching end-of-file, fread() should be used with the feof() function to be able to sense EOF, and the ferror() function to detect a read error. Likewise, because the fwrite() function is not designed to return an error code, fwrite() should be used with the ferror() function to sense any error condition.

Keep in mind that these functions return the number of items (for example, number) read from or written to the file, not the number of bytes read from or written to the file.

Note that SYSV uses a character pointer for buff (char * buff), while ANSI uses a void pointer (void *buff). Also, SYSV uses an integer for big and number when these variables are defined, but ANSI uses size_t. Both differences are an ANSI attempt to use data type specifiers that can be defined to a value that makes sense for the machine being used.

Illustration

```
/*
                                    fread(), fwrite()
*/

#include <stdio.h>
#include <stddef.h>
#include <string.h>
#include <stdlib.h>

#define MAXSTR 200
```

```
FILE *fpin, *fpout;                      /* I/O FILE pointers       */

void dofor(void), dofow(void), dofrw(void), doend(void);

int main()
{
     dofrw();                            /* Test putc()             */
     doend();
}

void dofrw(void)
{
     char string[MAXSTR], buff[MAXSTR];
     size_t big;

     strcpy(string, "This tests the fread() function.\n");

     dofow();                            /* Open a test file        */

     big = strlen(string) + 1;           /* Also keep the null      */

     if ((fwrite(string, big, 1, fpout)) != 1 || (ferror(fpout) != 0) ) {
          printf("Error writing string to file.\n");
          exit(1);
     }
     fclose(fpout);                      /* Close it                */

     dofor();                            /* Reopen it               */

     if ((fread(buff, big, 1, fpin)) != 1 || (feof(fpin) != 0) ) {
          printf("Error reading string to file.\n");
          exit(1);
     }
     fclose(fpin);                       /* Close it again          */

     printf("\nstring = %s\n", buff);
}
```

```
void dofow(void)
{
     if ((fpout = fopen("filename.xxx", "w")) == (FILE *) NULL) {
          printf("Cannot open test file for writing.\n");
          exit(1);
     }
}

void dofor(void)
{
     if ((fpin = fopen("filename.xxx", "r")) == (FILE *) NULL) {
          printf("Cannot open test file for reading.\n");
          exit(1);
     }
}

void doend(void)
{
     printf("RETURN to continue: ");
     while (getchar() != '\n')
          ;
}
```

Program Comment

The program first `#include`s several header files needed by the program and then `#define`s several FILE pointers. The call to `dofrw()` begins by copying a test string into `string` and then calls `dofow()` to open the file for writing. Variable `big` is used to find the string length of `string`. We add one to the return value from `strlen()` so that the null is also included in the length calculation. The program then writes the string to the file associated with the `fpout` stream. Notice how we check the return value from `fwrite()` to verify that one string was written. We also use a call to `ferror()` to see that no other errors occurred (for example, disk full).

We then close the file and reopen it by the call to `dofor()`. The call to `fread()` then attempts to read one item of size `big` into `buff`. (We use `buff` so that we know that we are not simply reading what `string` contains.) We also do a call to `feof()` to check for end-of-file. The error message would be printed if we did not read one item of size `big` or if end-of-file is sensed.

The program then closes the file and prints the string contained in the file and read into `buff`.

Miscellaneous Comments

The calls to `ferror()` with `fwrite()`, and `feof()` with `fread()`, are necessary to ensure that we can capture error conditions or EOF if they occur.

Function Names

`fscanf()` `scanf()` `sscanf()`

Standard Met

ANSI, SYSV

Purpose

General-purpose input functions.

Prototypes

```
int fscanf(FILE *fp, const char *contl, ...)
int scanf(const char *contl, ...)
int sscanf(const char *str, const char *contl, ...)
```

Required Header

`#include <stdio.h>` ANSI/SYSV

Usage

```
int fscanf(FILE *fp, const char *contl, ...)
```

The `fscanf()` function reads its input from the stream pointed to by the FILE pointer `fp` using the format control pointed to by `contl`. The control string `contl` contains one or more conversion specifications, each of which is introduced by the % character, and determines what constitutes valid input. The argument associated with each conversion character resolves to a pointer to the data item being converted. See the `scanf()` discussion for the list of options.

The return value is the number of successful conversions, or EOF if an input failure occurs, before any successful conversions have been performed, excluding conversions read but not assigned (for example, %* and %n). The result of a conversion is undefined if the converted value is out of range.

```
int sscanf(const char *str, const char *contl, ...)
```

The `sscanf()` function reads its input from the string pointed to by `str` using the format control pointed to by `contl`. See the `scanf()` function for the list of options.

The return value is EOF if an input failure occurs prior to any successful conversions. Otherwise, `sscanf()` returns the number of successful conversions that were completed, excluding conversions read but not assigned (for example, %* and %n). The result of a conversion is undefined if the converted value is out of range.

```
int scanf(const char *contl, ...)
```

The `scanf()` function reads input from `stdin` using the control string pointed to by `contl`.

The return value is EOF if an input failure occurs prior to any successful conversions. Otherwise, `scanf()` returns the number of successful conversions completed, excluding conversions read but not assigned (for example, %* and %n). The result of a conversion is undefined if the converted value is out of range.

Control String Options

The control string may contain zero or more conversion specifications, one or more white-space characters, any nonconversion (that is, not %) character(s), or a conversion character (that is, %). The control string's general format looks like:

```
% [modifier] [data type]
```

The following are valid modifiers to the data types:

* Suppresses, or skips over, the assignment. Therefore, if the control string is:

```
char name[30];
scanf("%*s%s", name);
```

and the input is:

```
Hello world Jack.
```

the variable `name` will hold "world" (not `Hello` or `Jack`). Unless told otherwise, white space separates input fields, so the * causes "Hello" to be suppressed, "world" is written into `name[]`, and "Jack" is still sitting in the input buffer. If you wanted "Jack" to be written into `name[]` with the input given, the control string

```
scanf("%*s%*s%s", name);
```

would cause "Jack" to be assigned into `name[]`.

nnn A sequence of one or more decimal digits is used to specify the maximum field width for the conversion. For example,

```
scanf("%2d", &i);
```

says that a maximum of two digits shall be used for the input into variable `i`. Therefore, if the input is "123", `i` would be assigned the value 12.

h The `h` is used to indicate that the conversion shall be for a `short` integer type. Therefore,

```
scanf("%hd", &i);
```

causes a `short int` value to be assigned into `i`. We assume that `i` is defined to be a short integer. ANSI states that the `h` modifier may be used with the `d`, `i`, `o`, `u`, `x`, and `n` types discussed later. SYSV acts identically except for the `i` or `n` conversion characters, which SYSV does not recognize.

l An `l` is used to indicate that the conversion shall be into a `long` or `double` data type. Therefore, assuming that `i` has been defined as a `long` integer,

```
scanf("%ld", &i);
```

will assign the input as a `long` integer into `i`. ANSI states that the `l` modifier may be used with the integral conversion characters `d`, `i`, `o`, `u`, `x`, and `n` types discussed later. SYSV acts identically except for the `i` or `n` conversion characters, which SYSV does not recognize.

For floating types, an `l` may be used also with `e`, `f`, and `g` to denote a pointer to `double`, rather than a pointer to `float`.

Neither standard allows an uppercase L to be used for a `long` integer data type. (See next paragraph.)

L An uppercase L may be used when the data item being pointed to is a `long double`. The `long double` is a new data type provided by the ANSI standard and is at least as large as a `double` but may be larger. (See your `limits.h` header file.) If `lx` is a `long double`, then

```
scanf("%Lf", &lx);
```

assigns the input into the `long double` at `lx`. However,

```
scanf("%lf", x);
```

assigns a `double` into `x`, not a `long double`. Because `long double` does not exist in SYSV, the "%Lf" conversion is not part of SYSV.

Conversion Characters

In the list that follows, the matching data item resolves to a pointer to the data item. For nonaggregate data items, the name of the variable should have the address of operator (&) preceding the variable's name; so an lvalue is used for the argument. If the data item is an aggregate data type (for example, an array), the variable's name is an lvalue, and no address of operator is required. Therefore,

```
int i, alot[10];
scanf("%d%d%d", &i, alot, &alot[5]);
```

assigns integer values into: `i`, `alot[0]`, and `alot[5]`.

All of the following data type specifications preread white space, except `%c` and `[`. The control string may use the data types:

`d` A signed decimal integer value. For example, if `i` is an integer,

```
scanf("%d", &i);
```

assigns an integer into `i`.

`i` A signed integer, but the input may be used to determine the base used for the conversion. Therefore,

```
scanf("%i", &i);
```

can digest input strings of "012", "0xa", or "10" and have `i` yield identical values (that is, 10 decimal) for `i`.

This conversion character is not part of SYSV.

o A signed octal integer. For example, an input of "012" to

```
scanf("%o", &i);
```

writes a decimal 10 into variable i.

u An unsigned integer. Two modifiers may also be used with this type:

```
unsigned short int i;
unsigned long int big;
scanf("%hu%lu", &i, &big);
```

which places an unsigned short int and an unsigned long int into i and big.

x A signed hexadecimal integer. If the input is "0a",

```
scanf("%x", &i);
```

writes a decimal 10 into variable i. ANSI permits the x to be upper- or lowercase.

e, f, g A floating-point number. The valid sequence for a floating-point number is (1) a string of digit characters that may contain an optional sign, (2) an optional decimal point, (3) an optional exponent field with an e or E, followed by (4) an optionally signed integer. ANSI states that the e and g types are not case sensitive. SYSV does not state how uppercase g and f are treated.

If no modifier is used, the pointer must be to a float. Writing data into a double data type requires the l modifier:

```
double x;
scanf("%lf", &x);
```

However, ANSI also states that the ell is case sensitive when used with floating-point numbers. Therefore,

```
long double verybig;
scanf("%Lf", &verybig);
```

writes a long double into verybig. (The size of a long double is stated in limits.h and is at least as large as a double.)

s A character string of nonwhite space characters. You have the responsibility to ensure that the character array being assigned is sufficiently large to hold the input and the null-termination character, which is automatically appended to the input.

This type often produces surprises for first-time users. For example, if an address is wanted and the input looks something like "6413 N. College Ave.", the code fragment

```
char address[40];
scanf("%s", address);
```

with the input given will find address to hold "6413" when scanf() completes its call. The reason is that a white-space character terminates the input scan. The rest of the input entered by the user is still sitting in the input buffer. Therefore, a subsequent call to scanf() will find "N." entered as the input regardless of what the user types in as a response. Clearly, maintaining things in sync becomes important. How to get around this problem is shown in the discussion of the next data type.

[A character string is expected with the input limited to the characters defined by the scanset. The scanset is defined by the characters that follow the opening bracket. For example,

```
char answer[20];
scanf("%[012345]", answer);
```

states that only the character digits 0 through 5 are considered valid input. If any other character outside the scanset is entered, the scan is stopped.

To make things more simple, an implementation may use a hyphen to define a range of characters. Therefore,

```
scanf("%[0-5]", answer);
```

performs the same task as the previous example. The use of the hyphen to denote a range is implementation-defined for ANSI and a standard feature of SYSV.

If the hyphen is either the first or last character in the scanset, the hyphen itself is in the scanset. Therefore,

```
scanf("%[0-9-], answer);
```

says that we will accept any character digit 0 through 9, to include a minus sign.

Now let's use this to get a complete address. Using the same input string "6413 N. College Ave.",

```
char address[40];
scanf("%[a-zA-Z .0-9]", address);
```

says that we will accept upper- and lowercase letters, a blank space, a period, and the character digits 0 through 9. Any other character will end the scan. Therefore, this scanset allows the complete address to be entered, including the blank spaces and periods.

There is another option that may be used with a scanset. The circumflex (^) says to allow all characters *except* what is in the scanset. For example:

```
scanf("[^A-Z]", answer);
```

says we will keep accepting input until we sense an uppercase letter. Some care is needed in the example shown here because a carriage return is in the valid input scanset. This means that pressing the RETURN key doesn't end the input. The user would have to enter an uppercase letter to end the input. (Keep in mind that an uppercase letter used to end the input is still sitting in the input buffer. `scanf()` consumes only what it is told to consume.)

Now consider the following two special cases:

```
scanf("%[]]", answer);
scanf("%[^]]", answer);
```

The first example says that the right bracket is included in the scanset, and the second example says that everything *but* the right bracket is in the scanset. If the right bracket is to be included, it must be the first character in the scanset.

Finally, if we want a general-purpose input to a string, we might have something like the following:

```
printf("Enter the data now (# = end of input): ");
scanf("%[^#]", data);
```

which allows the user to enter any character, including carriage returns, and ends only when a pound sign (#) is read.

c A single character is entered unless a field width modifier is present. Therefore,

```
scanf("%c", &letter);
scanf("%10c", firstname);
```

In the first call, a single character (that is, an implied field width of one) is written into `letter`. In the second call, up to a maximum of 10 characters can be written to `firstname`, implying that the variable is a character array. Note that the second call is not the same as a "%s" because the null-termination character is not appended to the input.

p A pointer to a `void` pointer. This is an implementation-defined set of characters that may be used to define a pointer for the host operating system. For example,

```
scanf("%p", ptr);
```

may require on an MS-DOS machine an input of `xxxx:XXXX` in which `xxxx` is a hexadecimal segment address, a colon, followed by offset address in hexadecimal (that is, XXXX). The exact form should be stated in your library documentation.

This type is not included in SYSV.

n A pointer to integer. This is a special type in that no input is expected. Rather, when this conversion is used, the `scanf()` function writes into the integer the number of characters that have been entered thus far in the scan. Therefore, in the code fragment

```
char name[20];
int convdone, num;

convdone = scanf("%s%n", name, &num);
```

If the input is "Fred", `num` contains the value 4; and the variable `convdone`, which measures the conversions that have been done, equals 1. Note that the %n does not count as a conversion in the conversion count, nor is the null that is appended to the name included in the character count.

This conversion character is not part of SYSV.

% Read a percent sign. Therefore,

```
int ratio;
scantf("%d%", &ratio);
```

with an input of "20%" assigns that value of 20 into `ratio`.

If you try to perform an invalid conversion (that is, a conversion that involves an invalid data type, modifier, or combination thereof), the behavior is undefined.

Termination

A `scanf()` call is terminated when (1) end-of-file is read, (2) the control string has been exhausted, or (3) the input conflicts with the domain defined by the control string. If the input conflicts with the control string, the conflicting characters are left unread in the input stream, including all white-space characters.

Caution

Some differences exist between ANSI and SYSV in the scan function discussed in this section (for example, %p, %n). In addition, implementors have some freedom to assign meanings that are not specified in either the ANSI or SYSV specification. For example, some compilers state that an uppercase letter in the control string indicates that the data type is to be a `long` data type. Therefore, "%X%O%D%U" might expect `long` integers for the four variables. You should study your documentation to discover whether there are any potential surprises.

Illustration

```
/*
                                        scanf()
*/

#include <stdio.h>
#include <stdlib.h>
#include <stddef.h>

int main()
{
     char control[200], buff[200];
     int done, i;
     long int big;
     double x;

     printf("Enter a control string: ");
     gets(control);

     printf("\nEnter a string: ");
     done = scanf(control, buff);
     printf("\nbuff = %s\n", buff);

     printf("\ndone = %d\n", done);

     if (done == 0 || done == EOF)
          exit(0);

     printf("\nEnter an integer, a long, and a double with \n");
     printf("one or more spaces between each value.\n");
     done = scanf("%d %ld %lf", &i, &big, &x);

     printf("\ndone = %d\n", done);

     if (done == 0)
          exit(0);

     printf("%d %ld %lf", i, big, x);

}
```

Program Comment

The program begins with several #includes for the header files followed by the definition of several working variables in main(). The program then prompts the user to enter a control string to be used for testing a string conversion. Note that the primary purpose of this is to allow you to test variations of the %s and %[] options.

We call scanf(), using the user's input for the control string. The return value from scanf() is assigned into done to keep track of how many conversions were made. The program then displays the contents of buff to show the conversion. If no conversion was done, done may return EOF or 0, depending on how the failure occurred. If the conversion failed, the program ends by the call to exit().

If the conversion was successful, the user is asked to enter an integer, long integer, and a double. These values are then displayed if the conversions were successful, and the program ends.

There are so many possibilities for the scanf() function (and its relatives) that a program to exercise all of those options would be prohibitively lengthy. However, the example program could be used to allow various control strings with each of the possible data types.

Miscellaneous Comments

As you might expect, scanf() has considerable flexibility and power. The function also uses considerable code space. Many introductory C texts also use scanf() where a much simpler function would serve the same purpose. Using scanf() is often overkill for a given situation. We frequently see scanf() used to input a simple string. Clearly, code size would be significantly smaller if gets() were used. In other cases, scanf() is used to input a single integer value. This code fragment is much more efficient in terms of code size:

```
char buff[20];
int i;
printf("Enter an integer: ");
i = atoi( gets(buff) );
```

We encourage you to ask yourself whether a given input problem can be solved with a less code-intensive function before you automatically jump to `scanf()` or its relatives.

Also note that the `scanf()` family can be affected by the call to `setlocale()`. If the decimal-point character (LC_NUMERIC) is changed through the call to `setlocale()`, the `scanf()` family functions use the appropriate character for the decimal point.

Function Names

`fseek()` `ftell()` `rewind()`

Standard Met

ANSI, SYSV

Purpose

To allow manipulation of the FILE pointer in the stream.

Prototypes

```
int fseek(FILE *fp, long index, int relative_to)
long ftell(FILE *fp)
void rewind(FILE *fp)
```

Required Header

```
#include <stdio.h>
```

Usage

```
int fseek(FILE *fp, long int index, int relative_to)
```

The `fseek()` function causes the next character in the stream associated with FILE pointer `fp` to be read or written at the position determined by `index` bytes from the base position `relative_to`. The base position may assume these values (ANSI provides symbolic constants):

ANSI	SYSV	Description
SEEK_SET	0	Beginning of the file
SEEK_CUR	1	Current position in the file
SEEK_END	2	End of the file

The variable `index` is a `long` data type that may assume negative values under certain circumstances.

Because of the differences between a binary and text stream, ANSI places restrictions on the use of `fseek()`. For binary streams, an implementation need not support a seek using the end of the file (that is, a `relative_to` with a value of SEEK_END). For text streams where newline (and perhaps other record-oriented) translations may take place, an implementation need support only an `index` value of zero or a value returned from a previous call to `ftell()` with `relative_to` set to SEEK_SET.

For ANSI and SYSV, `fseek()` clears the end-of-file indicator. This means that an `fseek()` on a file: (1) causes `feof()` to return false for the file, (2) undoes the effect of an `ungetc()`, and (3) allows the next operation on a file opened for updating to be either a read or a write.

Both ANSI and SYSV return zero if successful or nonzero on an improper `fseek()`.

As examples of incorrect use of `fseek()`:

```
fseek(fp, -1L, SEEK_SET); /* Seek in front of beginning  */
                          /* of the file                 */

fseek(fp, 1L, SEEK_END);  /* Seek past end of file.      */
                          /* error if opened for reading */

fseek(stdout, ØL, SEEK_SET);  /* Can't seek on display   */
```

For the second example, an assumption is that the file is opened for reading only. The last example is improper, but the host environment may not generate a recognizable error condition. You can seek past current end-of-file for writing.

```
long int ftell(FILE *fp)
```

The `ftell()` function returns a long integer that is the number of bytes from the beginning of the file for the current position in the stream.

Because of the differences between binary and text streams, ANSI places different meanings on the result of `ftell()`. For binary files, `ftell()` returns the number of characters from the beginning of the file, which is identical to SYSV.

For text files, the return values of `ftell()` are unspecified. The return value is guaranteed to be usable only to a call to `fseek()`. Because of newline or record-oriented translations, the difference between two ftell() calls may not provide a meaningful measure of the number of characters between the two positions.

For ANSI, a value of -1L is returned on error, and errno is set to a nonzero, implementation-defined value. SYSV does not specify ftell()'s behavior on error.

```
void rewind(FILE *fp)
```

The rewind() function sets the next input or output operation at the beginning of the file associated with the FILE pointer fp. ANSI specifies that rewind() clears the error indicator for that file. The function does not return a value.

Caution

ANSI and SYSV conflict on the return values for fseek(). ANSI uses zero for success and SYSV uses nonzero for success.

A common programming error is to forget that the second argument to fseek() is a long data type—the programmer forgets to use the L (ell) modifier with a numeric constant for the index argument. That is, the programmer uses fseek(fp, 0, 0) instead of the proper fseek(fp, 0L, 0). A second mistake is to neglect that ftell() returns a long. Compilers that support prototyping will have less chance of making these kinds of errors.

Also note that a count of characters written to a file [for example, by putc()] may not agree with a position count from ftell() because of the way the newline character is written to a text file.

Illustration

```
/*
                        fseek(), ftell(), rewind()
*/

#include <stdio.h>
#include <string.h>
#include <stdlib.h>

#define MAXSTR 200

FILE *fpin, *fpout;             /* I/O FILE pointers        */
```

```
void dofor(void), dofow(void), dofsek(void), doend(void);

int main()
{
     dofsek();                    /* Test them all          */
     doend();
}

void dofsek(void)
{
     char string[MAXSTR];
     int   i;
     long where;

     strcpy(string, "There are two halves: this is the second half");

     dofow();                              /* Open a test file        */

     for (i = Ø; string[i]; i++)           /* Write to it             */
          putc(string[i], fpout);
     fclose(fpout);                        /* Close it                */

     dofor();                              /* Reopen it               */

     if (fseek(fpin, ØL, SEEK_END) != Ø) {
          printf("Error in fseek().");
          exit(1);
     }

     where = ftell(fpin);
     where /= 2;
     fseek(fpin, where, SEEK_SET);

     while ((i = getc(fpin)) != EOF)       /* Read middle of the file */
          putchar(i);

     putchar('\n');
     rewind(fpin);
     while((i = getc(fpin)) != EOF)        /* Read and show the file  */
          putchar(i);

     fclose(fpin);                         /* Close it again          */
}
```

```
void dofow(void)
{
     if ((fpout = fopen("filename.xxx", "w")) == (FILE *) NULL) {
          printf("Cannot open test file for writing.\n");
          exit(1);
     }
}

void dofor(void)
{
     if ((fpin = fopen("filename.xxx", "r")) == (FILE *) NULL) {
          printf("Cannot open test file for reading.\n");
          exit(1);
     }
}

void doend(void)
{
     printf("\nPress RETURN to continue: ");
     while (getchar() != '\n')
          ;
}
```

Program Comment

The program begins with several `#includes` for the files required by the program and defines the needed FILE pointers. The call to `dofsek()` does most of the work.

The `dofsek()` function starts by creating a working string that is written to a disk file and then closed. The `dofor()` function reopens the file containing the string and uses `fseek()` to go to the end of the file. The call to `ftell()` returns the number of bytes in the file and assigns that value into variable `where`. [Variable `where` does have the length of the file because the previous call to `fseek()` placed us at the end-of-file.]

The program divides `where` by two, which gives us the approximate position for the middle of the file. (Integer division may not result in the exact middle of the file because of truncation.) The program then calls `fseek()`, using the new value of `where` to position the file pointer in the middle of the file, and prints out the text found there by calls to `getc()` and `putchar()`. Finally, `rewind()` is called, and `getc()` and `putchar()` show the entire contents of the file.

Miscellaneous Comments

Notice that `where` is a `long` data type. The program may still work on some compilers and may draw no error messages if `where` is defined as an integer. However, using `fseek()` and `ftell()` on large files with `where` defined as an `int` could cause integer overflow and yield faulty results that might not show up on the small data file shown in the example.

Function Names

`getc()` `getchar()` `fgetc()` `getw()`

Standard Met

`getc(), getchar(), fgetc()`	ANSI, SYSV
`getw()`	SYSV only

Purpose

To get either single or word bytes from an input stream.

Prototypes

The `getc()` and `getchar()` routines are normally implemented as macros and, hence, prototypes do not apply. If these functions were implemented as functions, the following are the prototypes:

```
int getc(FILE *fp)
int getchar(void)
```

The following prototypes are for `fgetc()` and `getw()`:

```
int fgetc(FILE *fp)
int getw(FILE *fp)                /* SYSV only */
```

Required Header

```
#include <stdio.h>                 ANSI/SYSV
```

Usage

```
int getc(FILE *fp)
```

This macro gets the next character from the input stream associated with FILE pointer `fp`. The return value is the character read from the input stream. If end-of-file (EOF) or an error occurs on a call to `getc()`, EOF is returned. If EOF or an error does not occur, the pointer is incremented to the next character in the stream.

Also see the Caution section.

```
int getchar(void)
```

This macro gets the next character from the standard input device (for example, `stdin`), which is normally the keyboard. The `getchar()` macro is defined as `getc(stdin)`, so `getchar()`'s behavior is like the `getc()` macro.

```
int fgetc(FILE *fp)
```

The `fgetc()` function is identical to `getc()` with the exception that `fgetc()` is implemented as a function rather than as a macro. Because `fgetc()` is a function, you may use `fgetc()` in ways that are not permissible with macros (for example, you cannot have a pointer to a macro, but you can have a pointer to a function). The `fgetc()` function can be used in an expression where a macro would cause side effects.

```
int getw(FILE *fp)
```

The `getw()` function returns "word" bytes of data from the input stream associated with the FILE pointer `fp`. The number of bytes in a "word" is machine-dependent and can be determined by using the `sizeof()` operator [for example, `sizeof(int)`]. Special surprises are possible with this function. See the Caution section.

Note that the `getw()` function is not provided as part of the ANSI standard library.

Caution

Because `getc()` and `getchar()` are macros, they generate in-line code. As a result, you cannot take the address of a macro (for example, to initialize a pointer), nor is it a safe practice to do any operations on the argument to a macro.

The `getw()` function is machine-dependent and not part of the ANSI standard library. The function is defined in terms of a "word," the size of which varies among machines. A word may be 16 bits on one machine and 32 bits on another. Further, comparing against EOF poses a problem because EOF is a valid integer value. Because of this EOF identity problem, sensing EOF is often accompanied by use of the `ferror()` function (shown in the example program).

Illustration

```
/*
                    getc(), getchar(), getw(), fgetc()
*/

#include <stdio.h>
#include <string.h>
#include <stdlib.h>

FILE *fpin, *fpout;             /* I/O FILE pointers            */

void dofor(void), dofow(void), dogetc(void),
     doend(void), dogetw(void), dofgetc(void);

int main()
{

     dogetc();                  /* Test getc()                  */
     doend();
     dogetw();                  /* Test getw()                  */
     doend();
     dofgetc();                 /* Test fgetc()                 */

}

void dogetc(void)
{
     char string[50];
     int   i;

     strcpy(string, "\nThis is a test of the getc() function.\n");

     dofow();                   /* Open a test file             */

     for (i = 0; string[i]; i++)
          putc(string[i], fpout);
     fclose(fpout);             /* Close it                     */

     dofor();                   /* Reopen it                    */
```

```
     while((i = getc(fpin)) != EOF)        /* Read and show the file */
          printf("%c", i);
     fclose(fpin);                         /* Close it again         */
}

void dogetw(void)
{
     int   i;

     dofow();                              /* Open a test file          */

     for (i = 0; i < 100; i++)             /* Write some integers to it */
          putw(i, fpout);
     fclose(fpout);                        /* Close it                  */

     dofor();                              /* Reopen it                 */

                                           /* Read and show the file    */
     while ((i = getw(fpin)) != EOF && ferror(fpin) == 0) {
          printf("%d ", i);
          if (i % 20 == 0 && i != 0)       /* Do 20 per line            */
               printf("\n");
     }
     fclose(fpin);
}

void dofgetc(void)
{
     char string[50];
     int   i;

     strcpy(string, "\nTest the fgetc() function.\n");

     dofow();                              /* Open a test file          */

     for (i = 0; string[i]; i++)
          putc(string[i], fpout);
     fclose(fpout);                        /* Close it                  */

     dofor();                              /* Reopen it                 */
```

```
    while ((i = fgetc(fpin)) != EOF)      /* Read and show the file      */
        printf("%c", i);
    fclose(fpin);                         /* Close it again              */
}

void dofow(void)
{
    if ((fpout = fopen("filename.xxx", "w")) == (FILE *) NULL) {
        printf("Cannot open test file for writing.\n");
        exit(1);
    }
}

void dofor(void)
{
    if ((fpin = fopen("filename.xxx", "r")) == (FILE *) NULL) {
        printf("Cannot open test file for reading.\n");
        exit(1);
    }
}

void doend(void)
{
    printf("\nPress RETURN to continue: ");
    while (getchar() != '\n')
        ;
}
```

Program Comment

The program begins with the usual #includes for the functions used in the program, followed by the definition of two FILE pointers. The main() function calls the various functions that test the individual functions.

The dogetc() function writes a string out to a file named filename.xxx. (Use a different file name if you already have a file by that name, because the file's contents are destroyed by this program.) The dofow() [that is, do fopen() for write] is a function that attempts to fopen() the file for writing. The putc() function is used to write the characters contained in the string to the file. The dofor() [that is, do fopen() for reading] opens the file, and calls to getc() get the characters stored in the file.

The call to `getw()` does virtually the same thing as `getc()`, except that integers are written to the file. The only worthwhile difference is the use of `ferror()` to detect that we have sensed end-of-file. This function must be used because the integer returned from `getw()` can have the same value as EOF. By using `ferror()` with the test for EOF, we can sense end-of-file properly.

Finally, `dofgetc()` does the same thing that the `dogetc()` does, except that we call `fgetc()` instead of `getc()`. If they do the same thing, why use one over the other? First, you can safely use

```
fgetc(*fp++);
```

but not so with `getc()` because of the way macros are expanded by the preprocessor. Therefore, if you want to use an operator as part of an argument (for example, an increment operator in the previous example), you should use the function version. A disadvantage is that the `fgetc()` function will be somewhat slower than `getc()` because in-line code is not produced when `fgetc()` is used. On the plus side, repeated calls to `fgetc()` will probably generate slightly smaller code than the same number of calls to `getc()`.

Because `getw()` is not part of the ANSI standard, you must define the macro SYSV to include the portion of the program using this function.

Miscellaneous Comments

Be sure to read the cautions about macros versus functions and sensing EOF when `getw()` is used.

Function Name

`getcwd()`

Standard Met

SYSV only

Purpose

To return the current working directory path name.

Prototypes

```
char *getcwd(const char *buff, int howbig)
```

Required Header

None provided. SYSV

(See caution below.)

Usage

```
char *getcwd(const char *buff, int howbig)
```

The `getcwd()` function returns a pointer that points to the path name of the current working directory (`cwd`). The current working directory is written into the space pointed to by `buff`. The amount of storage allocated to `buff` must be at least two larger than the directory name to be returned. The integer variable `howbig` is used by the function as a limit for the size of the path name. Variable `howbig` must be two characters larger than the path name of the `cwd`.

The return value from `getcwd()` is a pointer to the `cwd` if the call is successful. If the argument `howbig` is too small to hold the `cwd` path name, `getcwd()` returns a `NULL` pointer, and `errno` is set to one of the following possible error values:

`EINVAL`	If `howbig` is zero
`ERANGE`	If `howbig` cannot hold the path name of the `cwd`

Caution

Your program can test for the NULL pointer to see whether `getcwd()` failed. If you also want to know the nature of the error, you will need to declare `errno` and `sys_errlist[]` in the program. (See the example program.)

The `getcwd()` function is not an ANSI function.

Illustration

```
/*
                                getcwd()
*/

#include <stdio.h>
#include <stdlib.h>

#define MAXPATH 65

                              /* These are for errno processing */
extern char *sys_errlist[];
extern int errno;

int main()
{
     void dogetcwd(void), doend(void);

     dogetcwd();              /* Test getcwd()                   */
     doend();
}

/*
                               dogetcwd()
*/

void dogetcwd(void)
{
     char oldpath[MAXPATH], *ptr;

                              /* Find out where we are now       */
     ptr = getcwd(oldpath, sizeof(oldpath) );
```

```
     if (ptr == NULL) {
          printf("Error number %d -- %s", errno, sys_errlist[errno]);
          exit(1);
     } else
          printf("The current working directory is: %s\n", oldpath);
}

/*
                              doend()
*/

void doend(void)
{
     printf("\nPress RETURN to continue: ");
     while (getchar() != '\n')
          ;
}
```

Program Comment

The program begins with #includes for several header files.

The dogetcwd() function does all of the work. We call getcwd() with the arguments oldpath and sizeof(oldpath). We set the symbolic constant MAXPATH to 65 in the example because 65 should be large enough to hold the path name of the current working directory (cwd). We assign the return value from getcwd() to ptr and then use ptr to see whether a NULL pointer was returned.

If ptr is NULL, an error occurred, and we use errno and sys_errlist[] to tell us what went wrong. An error will be unlikely because of the size of MAXPATH. If you want to force an error to see how your compiler handles such errors, change the #define for MAXPATH from 65 to something like 1.

If ptr is not NULL, the program prints the path name for the cwd and the program ends.

Miscellaneous Comments

If you want to use the symbolic constants EINVAL and ERANGE, you must #include the errno.h header file. This might be done so that you can print out an error message instead of what is stored in sys_errlist[]. This might be something like:

```
void dogetcwderr()
{
     switch(errno) {
          case EINVAL:
               printf("\nERROR -- second argument to getcwd() is 0\n");
               break;
          case ERANGE:
               printf("\nERROR -- not enough storage for path name.\n");
               break;
         default:
               printf("\nUnknown error in getcwd() call.\n");
               break;
     }
}
```

The example assumes that the program #includes errno.h and declares errno. You may prefer this approach because the default message associated with ERANGE often says that the error is in a math function, which may not be true in this situation. In the example, you dictate the nature of the error message rather than what is fixed in sys_errlist[].

Function Names

`gets()` `fgets()`

Standard Met

ANSI, SYSV

Purpose

To read a string of data.

Prototypes

```
char *gets(char *str)
char *fgets(char *str, int maxbytes, FILE *fp)
```

Required Header

`#include <stdio.h>` ANSI/SYSV

Usage

```
char *gets(char *str)
```

The `gets()` function gets characters from `stdin`, which is the standard input device as defined in the `stdio.h` header file. The characters are read into the character array pointed to by `str`. The `gets()` function continues to read characters until a newline character ('\n') or end-of-file is sensed. The newline character is not written into the string but is replaced with a null termination character ('\Ø').

The normal return value from the `gets()` function is a pointer to `str`. If no characters have been read into `str` or if no characters are read prior to sensing end-of-file, the return value from `gets()` is a `NULL` pointer and the contents of `str` are unchanged. If a read error is detected, a `NULL` pointer is returned and the contents of `str` are indeterminate.

```
char *fgets(char *str, int maxbytes, FILE *fp)
```

The fgets() function gets characters from the input stream ciated with FILE pointer fp and places them in the character pointed to by str. The function will read characters into str (1) maxbyte - 1 characters have been read; (2) a newline cha is read into str; or (3) end-of-file is read. When one of these conditions is met, a null terminator is placed in str.

The normal return value from fgets() is a pointer to str. A pointer, however, is returned if either: (1) no characters have read into str prior to sensing end-of-file (the contents of st unchanged); or (2) an error occurred during a read operation (the contents of str are indeterminate).

Caution

Note that calling gets() with a given string does not produce the same string as a call to fgets() using stdin as the FILE pointer. The reason is that gets() replaces the newline character with a null character. The fgets() function uses the newline to sense the end input and adds the null to the string after the newline is read. The string ends up with a newline when fgets() is used, but the newline is "eaten" by gets().

The gets() function can fail if reading a string that is too long. If a possibility exists that the input string may overflow, use fgets(), which terminates input when maxbyte-1 characters are read.

Illustration

```
/*
                                gets(), fgets()
*/

#include <stdio.h>
#include <stdlib.h>

#define MAXSTR 200                  /* Max string length           */

FILE *fpin, *fpout;                 /* I/O FILE pointers           */

void dogets(char *s), dofw(char *s), dofr(char *s);
```

```
int main()
{

     char   buffin[MAXSTR], buffout[MAXSTR];

     dogets(buffin);               /* Get the string            */
     dofw(buffin);                 /* Write to a test file      */
     dofr(buffout);                /* Read from the test file   */

     printf("The keyboard string is:  %s\n", buffin);
     printf("    The file string is:  %s\n", buffout);
}

void dogets(char *s)
{
     printf("Enter a string of less than 200 characters.\n");
     gets(s);                      /* Talk about simple!        */
}

void dofw(char *s)                 /* Open a file for writing   */
{
     if ((fpout = fopen("filename.xxx", "w")) == (FILE *) NULL) {
          printf("Cannot open test file for writing.\n");
          exit(1);
     }

     fputs(s, fpout);              /* Write the string to file  */

     fclose(fpout);
}

void dofr(char *s)                 /* Open a file for reading   */
{
     if ((fpin = fopen("filename.xxx", "r")) == (FILE *) NULL) {
          printf("Cannot open test file for reading.\n");
          exit(1);
     }

     fgets(s, MAXSTR, fpin);

     fclose(fpin);
}
```

Program Comment

The program begins by using an `#include` with the standard input/output header file `stdio.h`, followed by the necessary FILE pointers. The `dogets()` function asks you to enter a string by a call to `gets()`, which reads the standard input device (`stdin`). The `dofw()` call then writes the string to a file using the `fputs()` function (which is discussed in this chapter).

The call to `dofr()` then reads into a different character array named `buffout` the string that was previously written to the file. (We did this so that we know that the two strings are formed by different means.) After we return from `dofr()`, we print out both versions of the string (that is, one from `stdin` and one from the file) to show they are the same.

Miscellaneous Comments

In the example program, both versions of the string are the same. As mentioned in the Caution section, they may not always be the same. Both functions produce the same output in the example because we use `gets()` to create the string in the first place. If you use other means than `gets()` to construct the string and the newline is part of the string, `gets()` and `fgets()` may produce different results because of the presence of the newline character.

Function Name

`lseek()`

Standard Met

SYSV only

Purpose

To change file pointer.

Prototypes

```
long int lseek(int fd, long int offset, int pos)
```

Required Header

None provided.

Usage

```
long int lseek(int fd, long int offset, int pos)
```

Programmers use the `lseek()` function to move the file pointer (associated with file `fd`) `offset` bytes relative to position `pos`. Variable `pos` may assume one of three possible values:

pos	Meaning
0	Relative to the beginning of the file
1	Relative to the current position in the file
2	Relative to the end-of-file

Note that you can `lseek()` past end-of-file. (If the file was opened for reading, SYSV does not say that an error occurs, although an error should occur.) If an `lseek()` is done past end-of-file and a write occurs, gaps are present in the file. If a `read()` is done in these "gaps," the value of the bytes read are all zero.

If the `lseek()` is successful, the function returns a `long int` data type that is the value of the file location pointer relative to the beginning of the file. Only the file pointer is changed, not the physical device.

If an error occurs, `lseek()` returns -1, and the file pointer is not changed. In addition, `errno` will be set to one of the following possible values:

EBADF	The `fd` is not associated with an open file.
ESPIPE	Cannot `lseek()` on a pipe
EINVAL	Illegal value for `pos`

Because ESPIPE makes sense, what happens if an `lseek()` is performed on a terminal is not defined.

Caution

The most common error with `lseek()` is to forget to declare that the function returns a long data type and that `offset` must be passed as a `long`. ANSI does not support this function [use `fseek()` instead].

Illustration

```
/*
                                        lseek()
*/

#include <stdio.h>
#include <stdlib.h>
#include <fcntl.h>
#include <string.h>

#define MAXSTR          200
#define READ_WRITE      0       /* NOTE: Op system specific value */

int fdin, fdout;

void doclose(void), doow(void), dor(void), dowrite(void), doend(void);

int main()
{
     dowrite();
     doend();
}
```

```
void doow(void)
{
     if ((fdout = creat("filename.xxx", READ_WRITE)) == -1) {
          printf("Cannot create test file for writing.\n");
          exit(1);
     }
}

void dowrite(void)
{
     char string[MAXSTR], buff[MAXSTR];
     int big, done;
     long where;
     void doc(int fd);

     strcpy(string, "This is to be the test#string for the lseek().\n");

     doow();                               /* Open a test file        */

     big = strlen(string) + 1;             /* Also keep the null      */

     if ((done = write(fdout, string, big)) == -1 || done != big) {
          printf("Error writing string to file.\n");
          exit(1);
     }

     doc(fdout);                           /* Close it                */

     dor();                                /* Reopen it               */

     where = lseek(fdin, 23L, 0);

     big -= 23;

     if ((done = read(fdin, buff, big)) == -1 || (done != big) ) {
          printf("Error reading string from file.\n");
          exit(1);
     }
     doc(fdin);                            /* Close it again          */

     printf("\nstring = %s\n", buff);
}
```

```
void doc(int fd)                          /* The real file close      */
{
     if (close(fd) == -1) {
          perror("Close failure");
          exit(1);
     }
}

void dor(void)
{
     if ((fdin = open("filename.xxx", O_RDONLY)) == -1) {
          printf("Cannot open test file for reading.\n");
          exit(1);
     }
}

void doend(void)
{
     printf("\nPress RETURN to continue: ");
     while (getchar() != '\n')
          ;
}
```

Program Comment

The program #includes several header files, defines several working variables, and then calls dowrite() from main(). In dowrite(), we copy a character string into string. Note the pound sign (#) in the string. Next, we call doow() to create the file, followed by a call to write(), and then close the file.

The call to dor() reopens the file, and we then call lseek(). Note that we use 23L for offset relative to the beginning of the file (that is, pos equals 0). We then use read() to read the data, using the file pointer that was set from the lseek() call. We adjust big to reflect the lseek() that was done. The program then reads and displays the string on the console.

Miscellaneous Comments

Note how we used an uppercase ell in the lseek() call. You can, if you want, print out the value of where and inspect the return value from lseek().

Function Name

`open()`

Standard Met

SYSV only

Purpose

To do a low-level open of a file for reading or writing.

Prototypes

```
int open(const char *fname, int flags, int mode)
```

Required Header

`#include <fcntl.h>` SYSV only

Usage

```
int open(const char *fname, int flags, int mode)
```

The `open()` function attempts to open the file pointed to by `fname` and return a file descriptor that will be used for that file name in subsequent file operations (for example, reading, writing, and closing). The variable `flags` is used to set the status of the file at the time it is opened. The `fcntl.h` file header defines the available flags.

O_RDONLY	Opens for reading only
O_WRONLY	Opens for writing only
O_RDWR	Opens for reading or writing
O_APPEND	Sets the file pointer to end-of-file for writing
O_TRUNC	If file exists, truncate the file to a 0 length

O_CREAT	Creates a file. Access is set to the effective user-ID and group-ID, and the access bits are whatever mode is used. The values for mode are implementation-specific.
O_EXCL	If this flag and O_CREAT are set, a call to open() will fail if the file exists.
O_NDELAY	The effect of this flag depends on other flag values:

O_RDONLY or O_WRONLY: If the O_NDELAY flag is set, and if the file is opened for reading, open() returns immediately without delay. If open for write-only, an error is returned if no process presently has the file opened for reading. If O_NDELAY is not set, an open() for reading is blocked until the file is opened for writing. If open()ed for writing, the process is blocked until the file is opened for reading.

If the open() is done on a communication line, and O_NDELAY is set, the function returns without waiting for a carrier. If O_NDELAY is not set, open() will wait until a carrier is detected.

If more than one flag is used, the flag bits are logically ORed together to determine the proper mask to use. (See the program example and comment. Some of the flags are not available on certain operating systems. Consult your documentation to see what is supported.)

The return value is an open file descriptor if the open() is successful, and -1 on error with errno set to one of the following values:

ENOTDIR	Part of path name is not a directory.
ENOENT	Part of path name does not exist.
EACESS	Access permission denied (a part of the patter search denies search permission, the file does not exist and the directory denies writing, or the flags permission is denied for the file)

EROFS — Read-only file system and flags is write or read/write.

ETXTBSY — Tried to execute a shared text file

EISDIR — The file is a directory name and flags is write or read/write.

EMFILE — Maximum number of files is already open by this process.

ENXIO — Set if the file is a character- or block-special file and the device associated with the file doesn't exist; or if O_NDELAY and O_WRONLY are set and no process has opened the file.

EEXIST — If O_CREAT and O_EXCL are both set and the file already exists

ENOSPC — Directory is full.

ENFILE — Full file table

EINTR — A signal was caught during the open() operation.

The perror() function may be used in the error processing, if desired.

Caution

Note that some operating systems may not be able to sense all of the error conditions listed or use all of the flag values listed. Consult your documentation for specifics.

Illustration

```
/*
                                        open()
*/

#include <stdio.h>
#include <stdlib.h>
#include <fcntl.h>
#include <string.h>
```

```
#define MAXSTR     200
#define PMODE  0666          /* NOTE: Op system specific value */
                             /* Use 0 for MS-DOS              */
int fdin, fdout;

void doclose(void), doow(void), dor(void), dowrite(void), doend(void);
void doc(int fd);

int main()
{
     dowrite();
     doend();
}

void doow(void)
{
     if ((fdout = open("filename.xxx", O_WRONLY | O_CREAT | O_TRUNC, PMODE)) == -1) {
          printf("Cannot open or create test file for writing.\n");
          perror("Error in open");
          exit(1);
     }
}

void dowrite(void)
{
     char string[MAXSTR], buff[MAXSTR];
     int done;
     unsigned int big;

     printf("Enter a string of up to 100 characters:\n");
     gets(string);

     doow();                              /* Open a test file       */

     big = strlen(string) + 1;            /* Also keep the null     */

     if ((done = write(fdout, string, big)) == -1 || (done != big)) {
          printf("Error writing string to file.\n");
          exit(1);
     }
```

```
    doc(fdout);                          /* Close it              */

    dor();                               /* Reopen it             */

    if ((done = read(fdin, buff, big)) == -1 || (done != big) ) {
         printf("Error reading string from file.\n");
         perror("Second read failed");
         exit(1);
    }
    doc(fdin);                           /* Close it again        */

    printf("\nstring = %s\n", buff);
}

void doc(int fd)                         /* The real file close   */
{
    if (close(fd) == -1) {
         perror("Close failure");
         exit(1);
    }
}

void dor(void)
{
    if ((fdin = open("filename.xxx", O_RDONLY, PMODE)) == -1) {
         printf("Cannot open test file for reading.\n");
         perror("Cannot read");
         exit(1);
    }
}

void doend(void)
{
    printf("\nPress RETURN to continue: ");
    while (getchar() != '\n')
         ;
}
```

Program Comment

The program begins with several `#includes` for the necessary header files. The call in `main()` to `dowrite()` asks you to enter a string of characters. The call to `doow()` attempts to `open()` the file using several flags that are logically ORed together. Using the `O_WRONLY`, `O_CREAT`, and `O_TRUNC` flags accomplishes the same task as if `creat()` were called. (If we wanted to open the file only if the file did not already exist, we could have added the `O_EXCL` flag to the list.)

If the file is opened, a call to `write()` is made to write the string to the file, and the file is then closed by the call to `doc()`. We then reopen the file by the call to `dor()`, which uses the `O_RDONLY` flag in the `open()` call. If the file is opened successfully, we read the contents of the file into `buff`, `close()` the file, display its contents, and end the program.

Miscellaneous Comments

You may want to substitute other values for the flags used in the example to get some experience with the flags' impact on the `open()` call.

Function Name

`perror()`

Standard Met

ANSI, SYSV

Purpose

To display a predefined system error message.

Prototypes

```
void perror(const char *mess)
```

Required Header

`#include <stdio.h>`	ANSI
None provided	SYSV

Usage

```
void perror(const char *mess)
```

The `perror()` function causes a predefined error message to be displayed on `stderr`. Selection of the message is based on the value held in `errno` at the time the error is set. The function first displays the message pointed to by `mess`, followed by a colon, the `errno`-dependent error message, and a newline character. No value is returned from `perror()`.

SYSV programmers have more direct access to the error-processing mechanism. Under SYSV,

```
extern int errno;
extern const char *sys_errlist[];
extern int sys_nerr;
```

are external variables that control the error-processing facilities of `perror()`. Variable `errno` is set to a value that is implementation-defined and used to index into `sys_errlist[]`, which contains the related messages. Variable `sys_nerr` tells how many error messages exist for the system. Therefore, the code fragment

```
extern int errno;
extern const char *sys_errlist[];
extern int sys_nerr;
int i;

for (i = 0; i < sys_nerr; i++)
     printf("%d %s", i, sys_errlist[i]);
```

will display the error messages defined for the system. SYSV states that `sys_nerr` may change with new releases.

Caution

None.

Illustration

```
/*
                                              perror()
*/

#include <stdio.h>
#include <stddef.h>
#include <errno.h>
#include <stdlib.h>

FILE *fpin;

int main()
{

     printf("Try to open a file that doesn't exit:\n");

     if ((fpin = fopen("xxxxxx.xxx", "r")) == (FILE *) NULL) {
          printf("errno = %d\n", errno);
          perror("Cannot open xxxxxx.xxx");
          exit(1);
     }

     fclose(fpin);
}
```

Program Comment

The program `#includes` the required files plus `errno.h` because we want to access `errno`. On the assumption that there is no file named `xxxxxx.xxx` on the system, the call to `fopen()` to open the file for reading should generate an error. The error causes the `printf()` for `errno` to be displayed, followed by a call to `perror()`. The call to `perror()` displays "`Cannot open xxxxxx.xxx`", followed by a colon and the error message defined by the implementation. For example,

```
Cannot open xxxxxx.xxx: No such file or directory.
```

or a related message is displayed on `stderr`.

Miscellaneous Comments

None.

Function Name

`read()`

Standard Met

SYSV only

Purpose

To read data from a file.

Prototypes

```
int read(int fd, char *buff, unsigned int howmany)
```

Required Header

None.

Usage

```
int read(int fd, char *buff, unsigned int howmany)
```

This function reads `howmany` bytes of data from the file associated with file descriptor `fd` into the buffer pointed to by `buff`. The file descriptor should have been returned by a successful call to either `creat()` or `open()`.

If the `read()` is successful, the function returns the number of bytes that were read from the file. The number of bytes read may be less than `howmany` if the file descriptor is associated with a communications line, a pipe, or other special type of file. Furthermore, the actual number of bytes may be less if the number of bytes left to be read in the file are less than `howmany`.

You can seek to a position past end-of-file [for example, by a call to `lseek()`] and still write data to the file. This can leave "gaps" in the file where no data has yet been written and from which no data can be read. In these situations, a `read()` call from a position where a gap exists will return `howmany` bytes from the read, but all of the bytes will have a value of 0.

If end-of-file is sensed, the function returns 0. If an error occurs, errno is set, and the return value is -1. The possible values for errno include:

EBADF	The file descriptor is not a valid fd for reading.
EINTR	A signal was trapped during the read.
EIO	Physical input/output error
ENXIO	Set if the file is a character- or block-special file and the device associated with the file doesn't exist; or if O_NDELAY and O_WRONLY are set and no process has opened the file.

If these constants are to be used, the fcntl.h header file should be #included in the program.

The read() is started from the current position in the file [which is normally the beginning of the file, but could be anywhere if previous read()s have been done]. On its return from the read() function, the file pointer is incremented by the number of bytes that were read.

Caution

This function is not included in the ANSI specification.

Illustration

```
/*
                                        read()
*/

#include <stdio.h>
#include <stdlib.h>
#include <fcntl.h>
#include <string.h>

#define MAXSTR      200
#define PMODE       0666        /* NOTE: Op system specific value */

int fdin, fdout;
```

```
void doclose(void), doow(void), dor(void), dowrite(void), doend(void);

int main()
{
     dowrite();
     doend();
}

void doow(void)
{
     if ((fdout = creat("filename.xxx", PMODE)) == -1) {
          printf("Cannot create test file for writing.\n");
          exit(1);
     }
}

void dowrite(void)
{
     char string[MAXSTR], buff[MAXSTR];
     int done;
     unsigned int big;
     void doc(int fd);

     printf("Enter a text string:\n");
     gets(string);

     doow();                              /* Open a test file        */

     big = strlen(string) + 1;            /* Also keep the null      */

     if ((done = write(fdout, string, big)) == -1 || done != big) {
          printf("Error writing string to file.\n");
          exit(1);
     }

     doc(fdout);                          /* Close it                */

     dor();                               /* Reopen it               */

     if ((done = read(fdin, buff, big)) == -1 || (done != big) ) {
          printf("Error reading string from file.\n");
          exit(1);
     }
```

```
    doc(fdin);                              /* Close it again           */

    printf("\nstring = %s\n", buff);
}

void doc(int fd)                            /* The real file close      */
{
    if (close(fd) == -1) {
        perror("Close failure");
        exit(1);
    }
}

void dor(void)
{
    if ((fdin = open("filename.xxx", O_RDONLY)) == -1) {
        printf("Cannot open test file for reading.\n");
        exit(1);
    }
}

void doend(void)
{
    printf("\nPress RETURN to continue: ");
    while (getchar() != '\n')
        ;
}
```

Program Comment

The program begins with several `#includes`. The `fcntl.h` header is needed for the symbolic constants (`O_RDONLY`) used in the program. Several working variables are then defined, and the program begins with a call to `dowrite()`. We enter a string by the call to `gets()`, with our response stored in `string`. The `doow()` attempts to create and open the file, assigning the file descriptor to `fdout`.

The program then determines the length of the input by `strlen()`. We added one to the string length so that the null-termination character is also written to disk. We then write `string` to the file, using `write()`. Note that we test to see whether an error occurred, (that is, -1) as well as the number of bytes written (comparing `done` with `big`). If all goes well, we close the file by the call to `doc()`.

We then reopen the file by the call to `dor()` and attempt to read the file by the call to `read()`. We try to read `big` bytes from the file associated with `fdin` and place it into `buff`. Again, we check for an error and the number of bytes actually read. If an error occurs, an error message is displayed.

If everything goes as expected, we display the string and end the program.

Miscellaneous Comments

Low-level input/output routines are not included in the ANSI library. You can use the high-level equivalents of these routines [for example, `fopen()`, `fread()`, `fwrite()`, etc.].

Function Names

`remove()` `rename()` `unlink()`

Standard Met

`remove()`, `rename()`	ANSI
`unlink()`	SYSV

Purpose

To remove and rename a file.

Prototypes

```
int remove(const char *fname)      ANSI
int rename(const char *oldname, const char *newname)      ANSI
int unlink(const char *fname)      SYSV
```

Required Header

`#include <stdio.h>`	ANSI
None provided	SYSV

Usage

```
int remove(const char *fname)
int unlink(const char *fname)
```

The `remove()` function causes the file name pointed to by `fname` to be removed from the disk. If the file is open at the time the `remove()` call is made, the function's behavior is implementation-defined.

If the file is removed successfully, `remove()` returns zero. If the call fails, nonzero is returned.

The SYSV `unlink()` function behaves like the `remove()` function. If successful, the function returns 0. If unsuccessful, the function returns -1 and sets `errno` to one of the following:

ENOTDIR	The name path is not a directory.
ENOENT	The file does not exist.
EACCES	Search permission is denied to a directory in the path or write permission is denied to the directory containing the link.
EPERM	The file is a directory and the user-id is not the super-user.
EBUSY	The file is a mount point for a mounted file system.
ETXTBSY	The file is the last link to a shared text file currently executing.
EROFS	The file is part of a read-only file system.

```
int rename(const char *oldname, const char *newname)
```

The `rename()` function causes the file, whose name is pointed to by `oldname`, to be renamed with the name pointed to by `newname`. If a file has the name pointed to by `newname` prior to the call, the function's behavior is implementation-defined.

If `rename()` is successful, the return value is zero. If the call fails, nonzero is returned, and the file name retains `oldname`.

Caution

None.

Illustration

```
/*
                                        remove(), rename()
*/

#include <stdio.h>
#include <stdlib.h>
#include <ctype.h>

#ifdef SYSV
     #define remove(a) unlink(a)            /* To work with SYSV */
#endif
```

```
FILE *fp;

int main()
{
     char buff[10];
     int delete, i;

     printf("Do you want the junk file removed (y, n): ");
     gets(buff);
     delete = (toupper(buff[0]) == 'Y') ? 1 : 0;

     if ((fp = fopen("junk.txt", "w")) == (FILE *) NULL ) {
          puts("Error in opening file.");
          exit(1);
     }
     for (i = 0; i < 20; i++)
          putc('a', fp);
     fclose(fp);

     rename("junk.txt", "dummy.txt");
     if (delete)
          remove("dummy.txt");
}
```

Program Comment

The program `#includes` the necessary header files and then uses an `#ifndef` to define a parametized macro if a SYSV library is being used. This construction allows those writing under SYSV to use a call `unlink()` whenever `remove()` is called.

In `main()`, you are asked whether you want to have the junk file removed as part of the program. The ternary sets `delete` according to your response to the question. (If you answer "yes," there is no evidence that the program does anything.)

The program then calls `fopen()` to open a junk file for writing, using the clever name "`junk.txt`". The call to `putc()` writes 20 'a' characters to the file and then closes it. The call to `rename()` simply changes the name from "`junk.txt`" to "`dummy.txt`".

If you opt to have the junk file removed, `delete` will have a value of 1, which causes the call to `remove()` to be executed. This removes from the disk directory the file that is now named "`dummy.txt`". If you opt to keep the junk file, the `remove()` call is skipped, and "`dummy.txt`" remains intact.

Miscellaneous Comments

None.

Function Name

`setbuf()`

Standard Met

ANSI, SYSV

Purpose

To provide stream buffering.

Prototypes

```
void setbuf(FILE *fp, char *buff)
```

Required Header

`#include <stdio.h>` ANSI/SYSV

Usage

```
void setbuf(FILE *fp, char *buff)
```

The `setbuf()` function causes the array pointed to by `buff` to be used with stream `fp` instead of any buffer that may be allocated automatically by the host environment. The `setbuf()` function must be called after the file associated with `fp` is opened, but before the file has been either read or written.

The size of `buff` is `BUFSIZ`, which is defined in `stdio.h`. Therefore, the definition of `buff` is `char buff[BUFSIZ]`. If `setbuf()` is called with a null pointer, all input/output is unbuffered if the request can be honored.

Notice that `setbuf()` is the same as

`setbuf(fp, buff)` or `setvbuf(fp, buff, _IOFBF, BUFSIZ)`

for buffered input/output, or, if no buffering is wanted

`setbuf(fp, (char *) NULL)` or `setvbuf(fp, (char *) NULL, _IONBF, BUFSIZ)`

Also see the `setvbuf()` function.

Caution

Make sure that the call to setbuf() is done after the file is opened and before performing any other operations on the file.

Because some environments cannot honor a request for line-buffered or unbuffered file input/output, setbuf() can fail. Because setbuf() does not return a success or failure indicator, use setvbuf() when a failure to set a file to a different unbuffering mode is possible. Consult your compiler's documentation for further information.

Illustration

```
/*
                                        setbuf()
*/

#include <stdio.h>
#include <stddef.h>
#include <string.h>
#include <stdlib.h>

#define MAXSTR 200

FILE *fpin, *fpout;                          /* I/O FILE pointers        */

void dofor(char *s, size_t t), dofrw(void), doend(void);
size_t dofow(char *s);

int main()
{
     dofrw();                                /* Test putc()              */
     doend();
}

void dofrw(void)
{
     char string[40], buff[BUFSIZ];
     size_t big;

     strcpy(string, "This tests the setbuf() function.\n");
```

```
    big = dofow(string);                /* Open the test file        */

    dofor(buff, big);                   /* Reopen it                 */
    printf("\nstring = %s\n", buff);
}

size_t dofow(char *string)
{
    size_t big;

    if ((fpout = fopen("filename.xxx", "w")) == (FILE *) NULL) {
        printf("Cannot open test file for writing.\n");
        exit(1);
    }

    big = strlen(string) + 1;           /* Need to keep the null      */

    if ((fwrite(string, big, 1, fpout)) != 1 || (ferror(fpout) != 0) ) {
        printf("Error writing string to file.\n");
        exit(1);
    }
    fclose(fpout);                      /* Close it                  */
    return (big);
}

void dofor(char *buff, size_t big)
{
    if ((fpin = fopen("filename.xxx", "r")) == (FILE *) NULL) {
        printf("Cannot open test file for reading.\n");
        exit(1);
    }

    setbuf(fpin, buff);

    if ((fread(buff, (unsigned) big, (unsigned) 1, fpin)) != 1 || (feof(fpin) != 0) ) {
        printf("Error reading string to file.\n");
        exit(1);
    }
    fclose(fpin);                       /* Close it again            */
}
```

```
void doend(void)
{
     printf("\nPress RETURN to continue: ");
     while (getchar() != '\n')
          ;
}
```

Program Comment

The program #includes a number of header files that are needed by the program. We then define two FILE pointers that are used in the program.

We then copy a string constant into string and pass the string to dofow(). The dofow() function then writes the string to a test file and closes the file.

The call to dofor() passes the address of the buffer that we want to use for buffering (that is, buff), along with the number of characters that were written to the file (that is, big). After we open the test file, we call setbuf(), passing buff as the function's argument. As a result, the output is read into buff rather than a buffer space allocated by the operating system. We then print out the contents of the buffer, and the program ends.

Miscellaneous Comments

The obvious question is "What do I gain by using setbuf()?" Not a whole lot, actually. If your program does large, dynamic memory allocations to grab all of available memory, a normal fread() or fwrite() may not have sufficient space to allocate a file buffer. Therefore, use setbuf() to set aside a buffer prior to the memory allocations and ensure that space is already reserved (for example, as defined for buff) to open and use a file.

Function Name

`setvbuf()`

Standard Met

ANSI, SYSV

Purpose

To set input/output buffering.

Prototypes

```
int setvbuf(FILE *fp, char *buff, int howbuf, size_t big)
```

Required Header

`#include <stdio.h>`	ANSI/SYSV

Usage

```
int setvbuf(FILE *fp, char *buff, int howbuf, size_t big)
```

The `setvbuf()` function allows the programmer to control both the buffer and the way in which buffering is performed on the input/output stream associated with the file pointed to by `fp`. The `setbuf()` function must be called after the file is opened and before any input or output operations on the file. The type of buffering is set by `howbuf`, where the permissible types of buffering (as defined in `stdio.h`) are

`_IOFBF`	Fully buffered
`_IOLBF`	Line buffered
`_IONBF`	Unbuffered

When line buffering is used, the buffer is flushed when a newline character is read, when the buffer fills, or on an input operation.

If the second argument (for example, `buff`) is not a null pointer, the character array pointed to by `buff` is used instead of the buffer that is automatically allocated when the file is opened. The last argument in the `setvbuf()` function (for example, `big`) tells the function how large `buff` is. (See the Caution section on using this buffer.) If unbuffered input/output is used, the arguments for `buff` and `big` are ignored.

If the call to `setvbuf()` is successful, the function returns zero. If the call fails, the return value is nonzero. The call will fail if the request cannot be fulfilled or if invalid arguments for `big` or `howbuf` are used.

Caution

Because some environments do not support all modes of buffering, using `setvbuf()` is preferred to using `setbuf()`. If your compiler's documentation indicates that some modes may not be available, your programs should check the return value from `setbuf()` to ensure successful operation.

Like `setbuf()`, `setvbuf()` must be called for a file after the file is opened but before the file is read or written. If you use your own character array for buffering, you should ensure that the array remains in scope for the life of the open file. Therefore, the `auto` storage class may be inappropriate if the file is to be used at different scope levels (for example, in different function blocks).

Illustration

```
/*
                                        setvbuf()
*/

#include <stdio.h>
#include <stdlib.h>
#include <stddef.h>

#define    BUFFER    4 * BUFSIZ
```

```
int main()
{

    int     i;
    char    buff[BUFFER];
    FILE    *fp;

    if ((fp = fopen("filename.xxx", "r")) == (FILE *) NULL) {
        puts("Error opening file");
        exit(1);
    }

    if (setvbuf(fp, buff, _IOFBF, (size_t) sizeof(buff)))
        puts("Using smaller buffer.\n");
    else
        puts("Using big buffer.\n");

    while ((i = getc(fp)) != EOF)
        putchar(i);
    fclose(fp);
}
```

Program Comment

The program `#include`s the requisite files and `#define`s several constants used in the program. In `main()`, the call to `fopen()` opens the file for reading, displaying an error message if the file cannot be opened.

In the call to `setvbuf()`, we attempt to activate a large buffer (for example, 4096 bytes) for the input/output operations associated with the `fp` file. If the request cannot be honored, `setvbuf()` returns nonzero, and the program displays "`Using smaller buffer.`" If the request is honored, the return value is zero and a message is displayed stating that we are using the larger buffer. (The default buffer size is set by `BUFSIZ` in `stdio.h`. A typical value is 512.) The program then proceeds to read the file, display its contents on `stdout`, close the file, and terminate the program.

Miscellaneous Comments

For a given file size, and if the file is larger than BUFSIZ and the buffer is also larger than BUFSIZ (probably an even multiple of BUFSIZ), the larger buffer should result in less disk input/output. On the other hand, we may be so close to running out of memory that there is not enough room for even a BUFSIZ buffer for the file. In that case, unbuffered input/output may be the only viable solution. In sum, setvbuf() provides a way for coping with a variety of input/output situations.

Function Names

`tmpfile()` `tmpnam()`

Standard Met

ANSI, SYSV

Purpose

To provide temporary file names.

Prototypes

```
FILE *tmpfile(void)
char *tmpnam(char *s)
```

Required Header

`#include <stdio.h>` ANSI/SYSV

Usage

```
FILE *tmpfile(void)
```

The `tmpfile()` function creates a temporary file that is automatically removed from the disk when the temporary file is closed or the program terminates. The file is opened for updating in binary mode (for example, "wb+").

The `tmpfile()` function returns a FILE pointer to the input/output stream that was created for that file. If the file cannot be created, a null pointer is returned.

```
char *tmpnam(char *s)
```

The `tmpnam()` function generates a string that may be used as a file name and that does not match an existing file name. Each time `tmpnam()` is called, a unique file name is created and written into the character string pointed to by `s`. The maximum number of unique file names that can be generated is defined by the symbolic constant TMP_MAX, which is defined in `stdio.h`. (ANSI says TMP_MAX shall be at least 25. The result of attempting to get more than TMP_MAX names is implementation-defined.)

If tmpnam() is called with a null pointer,

```
char *sptr;

sptr = tmpnam(NULL);
```

the function returns a pointer to an internal static data item that will hold the temporary file name. If the argument is not a null pointer, the argument is a character array that is large enough to hold a valid file name. The number of characters required for the valid file name is defined in stdio.h as L_tmpnam. Therefore, you might use

```
char tname[L_tmpnam];

tmpnam[tname];
```

which writes a temporary file name into tname. The return value from such a call is a pointer to the argument tname.

Caution

Note that the tmpnam() function discussed here is not the same as the SYSV function tempnam(), which allows some control over directory placement. SYSV provides both tmpnam() and tempnam().

Illustration

```
/*
                              tmpfile(), tmpnam()
*/

#include <stdio.h>
#include <stdlib.h>


int   main()
{
     char name[L_tmpnam], *sptr;
     FILE *fp, *fp2;
     int c, i;
```

```
        sptr = tmpnam(name);        /* Show example of temporary filename  */
        printf("Sample temporary file name: %s or %s\n", name, sptr);

        fp = tmpfile();             /* Get a temp FILE pointer...          */
        for (i = 0; i < 20; i++)
             putc('a', fp);         /* ...and write some a's to it         */

        rewind(fp);

        fp2 = tmpfile();            /* Get another temp FILE pointer...    */
        for (i = 0; i < 20; i++) {
             printf("%c", c = getc(fp));
             putc(c, fp2);          /* ...and copy the a's                 */
        }
}
```

Program Comment

The program #includes the requisite header files. In main(), several working variables are defined (note the use of L_tmpnam in the definition of name[]).

The call to tmpnam() results in a temporary file name being written into name[], and we assign sptr to the value returned by tmpnam(). We then print out what sptr points to and name[]—they both should display the same file name. This gives you some idea of the nature of the temporary name that is generated.

The call to tmpfile() returns a FILE pointer and, assuming we did get a valid FILE pointer, we use fp to write 20 letter a's to the file. When that is done, we rewind() the file to the beginning of the file and then call tmpfile() a second time. Assuming that we receive a valid FILE pointer back, we use fp2 to copy the contents of the first temporary file (that is, associated with fp) to the second temporary file (that is, associated with fp2). The program shows each letter as the letter is being copied. The program ends after the copy is complete.

The program does not show that the two files actually exist. The reason is that any file created by tmpfile() is automatically removed when the file is closed or when the program terminates. If you would like to see the files, you might insert just before the closing brace of `main()` a call to the `system()` function, using whatever command syntax is necessary to show the file directory. (If hidden files are used for temporary files, the `system()` call isn't going to show much.)

Miscellaneous Comments

Temporary files can be useful when there isn't enough memory to hold intermediate results for some subsequent process.

Function Name

`ungetc()`

Standard Met

ANSI, SYSV

Purpose

To push a character back to the input stream.

Prototypes

```
int ungetc(int c, FILE *fp)
```

Required Header

```
#include <stdio.h>        ANSI/SYSV
```

Usage

```
int ungetc(int c, FILE *fp)
```

The `ungetc()` function writes a single character `c` back to the input stream pointed to by the FILE pointer `fp`. That character is returned on the next read of the stream pointed to by `fp`, but a call to an `fseek()`, `fsetpos()`, `rewind()`, or `fflush()` ignores the character that has been pushed back.

The position of the file indicator maintained in the FILE structure remains unchanged by a successful call to `ungetc()`. ANSI states that, for a text file, a successful pushback by `ungetc()` is unspecified until all pushed-back characters are read. On a binary stream, however, the position indicator maintained in the FILE structure is decremented with a successful call to `ungetc()`. If the position indicator was zero prior to the call to `ungetc()`, behavior is indeterminate after the call to `ungetc()` is completed.

Only one call to `ungetc()` between a read or positioning call is guaranteed to operate successfully. If a call to `ungetc()` is made with `c` equal to `EOF`, the call fails.

The return value is the character pushed back if the call is successful, or EOF if the call fails.

Caution

None.

Illustration

```
/*
                                        ungetc()
*/

#include <stdio.h>
#include <ctype.h>

int main()
{
     int i = 0;
     char *readtok(char *), result[100], *s;

     result[0] = '\0';

     s = result;

     printf("Enter a string of characters:\n");

     while (s = readtok(s)) {
          *s++ = ':';
          *s = '\0';
     }
     puts(result);
}

/*
                                        readtok()
*/
```

```
char  *readtok(char *s)
{
     int i;

     while (isspace(i = getc(stdin)) )
          if (i == '\n' )
               return NULL;

     do {
          *s++ = i;
     } while ( isspace(i = getc(stdin) ) == Ø);

     ungetc(i, stdin);

     *s = '\Ø' ;
     return s;
}
```

Program Comment

The program #includes stdio.h and ctype.h [because of the call to isspace()]. The program defines several working variables and then asks you to enter a string of characters [which is implemented by a series of calls to readtok()].

The purpose of readtok() is to read a token that is delimited by white space. The first while in readtok() has the effect of stripping out any leading white-space characters entered by calls to getc() from stdin. Once a nonwhite-space character is read, we break out of the while loop. (If the white-space character read was a newline character, we return a null character pointer.)

Assuming a nonwhite-space character was read, the do-while is executed. This loop reads nonwhite-space characters into the character array s, which was passed into readtok(). We stay in the do-while loop until a white-space character is read, which causes program control to break out of the do-while.

The call to ungetc() then pushes the white-space character back into the input stream (that is, stdin in this example). A null terminator is then written into the string, a pointer to the string is returned from the readtok() call, and control returns to main().

In main(), a colon is written into the stream, followed by a null-terminating character, and another call to readtok() is made. This sequence continues until you enter a carriage return and a NULL is returned from readtok(). A NULL will terminate the while loop in main(), the string will be printed out, and the program will end.

If you input: "This is a test.", the contents of result[] are "This:is:a:test.:".

Miscellaneous Comments

This example of using ungetc() is fairly common. In many instances, the programmer wants to detect a delimiter (for example, a blank space) and then do some processing. Because the program may need to use the delimiter again farther down in the program, the ungetc() function is used to "restore" the delimiter back into the input stream. In many situations, this approach is the simplest and most direct way to accomplish the task.

Function Names

`vfprintf()` `vprintf()` `vsprintf()`

Standard Met

ANSI, SYSV

Purpose

To format output with variable arguments.

Prototypes

```
int vfprintf(FILE *fp, const char *contl, va_list args)
int vprintf(const char *contl, va_list args)
int vsprintf(char *str, const char *contl, va_list args)
```

Required Header

```
#include <stdarg.h>      ANSI
#include <stdio.h>       ANSI

#include <stdio.h>       SYSV
#include <varargs.h>     SYSV
```

Usage

```
int vfprintf(FILE *fp, const char *contl, va_list args)
```

The `vfprintf()` function sends its output to the file associated with the FILE pointer `fp`. The behavior of `vfprintf()` is similar to that of `fprintf()`, except that, instead of being called with a specified argument list, `vfprintf()` is called with an argument list which is initialized by the `va_start()` macro contained in `stdarg.h` (or `varargs.h` in SYSV). The first argument to `va_start()` is a parameter of type `va_list`, and the second argument is the list of data that will be used. If a control string (or some other data item) is being processed, a call using the `va_arg()` macro is used. The first argument to `va_arg()` is the `va_list` variable followed by the type of argument that is about to be processed. After all processing is done, the `va_end()` macro is called with the `va_list` variable as its argument.

The `vfprintf()` function returns the number of characters that were written if the call is successful, or a negative number if an error occurred.

See the program comment for a discussion of how each macro is used.

```
int vprintf(const char *contl, va_list args)
```

The `vprintf()` function performs the same as `vfprintf()`, except the output is sent to `stdout`. The `vprintf()` function returns the number of characters that were written if the call is successful, or a negative number if an error occurred. See the program comment for a complete description.

```
int vsprintf(char *str, const char *contl, va_list args)
```

The `vsprintf()` function performs the same as `vfprintf()`, except the output is sent to the character array pointed to by `str`. The `vsprintf()` function returns the number of characters that were written if the call is successful, or a negative number if an error occurred. See the program comment for a complete description.

Caution

The sequencing of the macro used in `vprintf()` and its relatives is important. See the program comment.

Illustration

```
/*
                    vprintf(), vsprintf(), vfprintf()
*/

#include   <stdio.h>
#include   <stdlib.h>
#include   <string.h>
#if SYSV                                /* For SYSV */
#include <varargs.h>
#else                                   /* For ANSI */
#include <stdarg.h>
#endif
```

```
void   error(int, ...);                /* prototype for error function  */

int   main()
{
     char buff[20];
     int   i, j;                       /* working counters              */

     printf("Enter a number: ");
     i = atoi( gets(buff) );

     j = i % 4;

     switch (j) {
          case 0:
              error(j, "This is error 0\n");
              break;
          case 1:
              error(j, "This is error %d\n", j);
              break;
          case 2:
              error(j, "This is error %d and i = %d", i, j);
              break;
          case 3:
              error(j, "This %s with j = %d i = %d", "is case 3", j, i);
              break;
          default:
              break;
     }
}

/*
                                  error()
*/

void   error(int value, int data)
{

     int   i;
     char   buff[200];
     char   *control;
     va_list   parms;                  /* Must be of type va_list    */

     /* use vfprintf or vprintf to put out error based on exit code */
```

```
    va_start(parms, data);            /* Initialize parms           */

    control = va_arg(parms, char *);

    switch (value) {
        case 0:                       /* use vprintf for error zero */
           vprintf(control, parms);
           va_end(parms);
           return;

        case   1:                     /* use vsprintf for error one */
           vsprintf(buff, control, parms);
           for(i =0; buff[i]; i++)
                putchar( (int) buff[i]);
           va_end(parms);
           return;

        default:            /* vfprintf to stderr on all other errors */
                            /* exit with value                        */
           vfprintf(stderr, control, parms);
           va_end(parms);
           exit(value);
    }
}
```

Program Comment

The program starts with the #includes necessary for vprintf() to work properly and must at least #include stdio.h and stdarg.h. The user is then asked to enter a number, which is then assigned into j after a mod 4 operation. The switch on j determines which variation of arguments are passed to the error() function. Note in main() that if j is 0, there are no arguments after the string, then one, two, and three arguments.

The interesting stuff takes place in error(). First, notice that the definition of error() has only two integer arguments. Because a function definition cannot use an ellipsis, we must state the minimum number of arguments that might be sent to the function.

Now notice the sequence of events. First, we must define a variable of type va_list. This definition sets up certain overhead information necessary for vprintf() to function properly. Indeed, we can draw a parallel between the va_list typedef and the FILE typedef—both are required before their related function can be used.

Second, we must call `va_start()` using the `va_list` variable `parms` as the first argument, and the `data` variable as the second argument. [The astute reader will notice that `data` is actually receiving a pointer to `char` from `main()` even though it is defined as an integer in the `error()` function.] Because we want to do further processing on the second argument that was passed to `va_start()`, which contains our control string, we call `va_arg()`, using `parms` as the first argument and what we expect to get as the second argument. Because we expect a pointer to `char`, we use `char *` as the second argument. [If we were just passing a string into `error()`, we wouldn't even need to call `va_arg()`. We could simply call `vprintf()` directly.] Because the second argument is a `char` pointer, that is what is returned from `va_arg()`, and it becomes the pointer to the control string.

Now that everything is properly set up, we use the first argument to `error()`, or `value`, to decide which version of `vprintf()` is used.

Inside the `switch`, one of the versions of `vprintf()` is called, using the control string pointer returned from the call to `va_arg()`. The second argument is `parms`, which has aligned the data properly by the previous call to `va_start()`. We then display the variable data that was passed into `error()` from `main()`.

Also note that, in each case, we call `va_end()`, using `parms` as the argument. This is the third step in the sequence that must be followed for things to work properly.

The use of the macros in `vprintf()` is similar to that for files. First, there must be a definition of a `va_list` data type, similar to defining a FILE type. Second, the list must be initialized by `va_start()`, much like `fopen()` establishes a file. Third, `va_arg()` is used to retrieve the specific data type we want to use from the `va_list` variable, similar to an `fread()`. Fourth, we stop using the data list by `va_end()`, like `fclose()` when using files.

The programmer need not worry about how `va_start()`, `va_arg()`, and `va_end()` work, only that they are to be called in that order.

Miscellaneous Comments

Also note that the `vprintf()` family can be affected by the call to `setlocale()`. If the decimal-point character (`LC_NUMERIC`) is changed through the call to `setlocale()`, the `vprintf()` family functions use the appropriate character for the decimal point.

Function Name

`write()`

Standard Met

SYSV only

Purpose

To write to a file.

Prototypes

```
int write(int fd, char *buff, unsigned howmany)
```

Required Header

None.

Usage

```
int write(int fd, char *buff, unsigned howmany)
```

The `write()` function writes `howmany` bytes from the buffer pointed to by `buff` to the file associated with file descriptor `fd`. The file is assumed to have been opened for writing by a call to `open()`. The write takes place from the current file position. An exception occurs when the `O_APPEND` flag is used to open the file. In that case, writing always occurs at the end of the file. When the write is completed, the file pointer is incremented by the number of bytes written.

If the `write()` is to a pipe for more bytes than the pipe can process (but less than `PIPE_BUF`), several results are possible:

If the `O_NDELAY` flag is not set, the process will block until `howmany` of free space is available and then process the `write()`.

If `O_NDELAY` is set, the process will not block, and the return value from `write()` is 0.

If the `write()` to the pipe was for greater than PIPE_BUF bytes, the alternatives include:

> If the O_NDELAY flag is not set, the process will block if the pipe is full. The request is then fulfilled as space becomes available in the pipe. The `write()`s, therefore, may be interleaved.
>
> If O_NDELAY is set and the pipe is full, the process will not block, and the return value from `write()` is 0.
>
> If O_NDELAY is set and the pipe isn't full, no blocking occurs, and the function writes as much data as the pipe can hold. The return value is the number of bytes written. No interleaving takes place. This means that some of the data is not written to the pipe.

Not all operating systems support pipes.

If the `write()` is successful, the function returns the number of bytes that were written to the file. If the number of bytes requested to be written (that is, `howmany`) is more than the file can hold, `write()` will write as many bytes as the file device can hold. (This can be checked because the return value from the call will not equal `howmany`.) Any subsequent call to `write()` with a nonzero value for `howmany` will produce a `write()` failure as indicated by a return value of -1. If an error does occur, the file pointer is left unchanged, and `errno` is set. The possible values for `errno` include:

EBADF	The file descriptor is not a valid `fd` for writing.
EPIPE	Attempt made to write to a pipe that is not open. Consistent with SIGPIPE signal
EFBIG	Attempt to write to a pipe that exceeds the size limit or file size for the process or file
EINTR	A signal was trapped during the write.
ENOSPC	Device is out of free space.
EIO	Physical input/output error
ENXIO	Set if the file is a character- or block-special file and file pointer is out of range.

If these constants are to be used, the `errno.h` header file should be `#included` in the program.

The `write()` is started from the current position in the file [which is normally the beginning of file, but could be anywhere if previous `write()`s, `read()`s, or `lseek()`s have been done]. On its return from the `write()` function, the file pointer is incremented by the number of bytes that were written.

Caution

This function is not supported by ANSI. The preferred ANSI function is `fwrite()`.

Illustration

```
/*
                                        write()
*/

#include <stdio.h>
#include <stdlib.h>
#include <fcntl.h>
#include <string.h>

#define MAXSTR       200
#define PMODE  0666                 /* NOTE: Op system specific value */
                                    /* Use 0 for MS-DOS               */
int fdin, fdout;

void doclose(void), doow(void), dor(void), dowrite(void), doend(void);

int main()
{
     dowrite();
     doend();
}
```

```
void doow(void)
{
     if ((fdout = creat("filename.xxx", PMODE)) == -1) {
          printf("Cannot create test file for writing.\n");
          exit(1);
     }
}

void dowrite(void)
{
     char string[MAXSTR], buff[MAXSTR];
     int done;
     unsigned int big;
     void doc(int fd);

     printf("Enter a text string:\n");
     gets(string);

     doow();                              /* Open a test file          */

     big = strlen(string) + 1;            /* Also keep the null        */

     if ((done = write(fdout, string, big)) == -1 || (done != big)) {
          printf("Error writing string to file.\n");
          perror("Write error");
          exit(1);
     }

     doc(fdout);                          /* Close it                  */

     dor();                               /* Reopen it                 */

     if ((done = read(fdin, buff, big)) == -1 || (done != big) ) {
          printf("Error reading string from file.\n");
          perror("Read Error");
          exit(1);
     }
     doc(fdin);                           /* Close it again            */

     printf("\nstring = %s\n", buff);
}
```

```
void doc(int fd)                          /* The real file close      */
{
     if (close(fd) == -1) {
          perror("Close failure");
          exit(1);
     }
}

void dor(void)
{
     if ((fdin = open("filename.xxx", O_RDONLY)) == -1) {
          printf("Cannot open test file for reading.\n");
          exit(1);
     }
}

void doend(void)
{
     printf("\nPress RETURN to continue: ");
     getchar();
}
```

Program Comment

The program starts with the necessary header files to include the `fcntl.h` file. In `main()`, the `dowrite()` call asks you to enter a string. The call to `doow()` opens the file for writing. (Again, the symbolic constant `READ_WRITE` varies among environments.)

The call to `write()` in `dowrite()` first checks to see that an error did not occur during the `write()` operation, but also checks to ensure that the number of bytes we wanted to write (that is, `big`) equals the number of bytes actually written to the file (that is, `done`). If these tests are passed, we can be fairly certain the data was successfully written to the file.

The rest of the program verifies that the `write()` was successful by opening the file, reading it, and displaying the contents on the console.

Miscellaneous Comments

Because high-level input/output usually ends up going through the low-level input/output, smaller code size can sometimes be realized by using the low-level routines [for example, `open()`, `read()`, `write()`, `close()`]. For example, the following code fragment:

```
char buff[50];

strcpy(buff, "This is a test of code size.\n");
printf(buff);
```

usually will generate significantly more code than the equivalent code:

```
char buff[50];

strcpy(buff, "This is a test of code size.\n");
write( fileno(stdout), buff, strlen(buff));
```

Both write the string to the display device, but the second version will generate less code and will execute slightly faster. Such a change can be useful when code size and speed are important.

8

Miscellaneous Utility Functions

This chapter describes a number of unique but useful functions.

Function Name

`abort()`

Standard Met

ANSI, SYSV

Purpose

To cause abnormal program termination.

Prototypes

```
void abort(void)
```

Required Header

`#include <stdlib.h>`	ANSI
None provided	SYSV

Usage

```
void abort(void)
```

The `abort()` function causes abnormal program termination to occur. For ANSI, the function causes the call `raise(SIGABRT)`. SYSV issues a `SIGIOT` signal instead. For both, a value is returned to the host environment to indicate an (implementation-defined) unsuccessful program-termination status. If `SIGABRT` is being trapped, any further processing is implementation-defined.

The ANSI specification states that any attempt to close open files is implementation-defined, whereas SYSV states that there will be an attempt to close all open files. SYSV does not provide a `raise()` function, although `alarm()` may be used.

Caution

A call to `abort()` can cause a wide variety of things to happen, ranging from nothing to a full core dump. The result of `abort()` is implementation-defined. Also see the `exit()` function for an alternative to `abort()`.

Illustration

```
/*
                              abort()
*/

#include <stdio.h>
#include <stddef.h>
#include <stdlib.h>

int main()
{
     FILE *fp;

     if ((fp = fopen("filename.xxx", "r")) == NULL) {
          fprintf(stderr, "Could not open filename.xxx");
          abort();
     }
     printf("Opened filename.xxx successfully.");
     fclose(fp);
}
```

Program Comment

The program `#includes` the required header files and then tries to open a file named "`filename.xxx`". If the file does not exist on the system, the `fprintf()` call is executed, followed by the call to `abort()`. What happens because of the call to `abort()` is implementation-specific and may vary from nothing taking place to some form of diagnostics being displayed on `stderr`.

If `filename.xxx` exists on the system, the program displays a message, closes the file, and terminates the program.

Miscellaneous Comments

Also see the `exit()` function.

Function Name

`abs()`

Standard Met

ANSI, SYSV

Purpose

To get the absolute value of an integer.

Prototypes

```
int abs(int val)
```

Required Header

`#include <stdlib.h>`	ANSI
None provided	SYSV

Usage

```
int abs(int val)
```

The `abs()` function returns the absolute value of the argument `val`. If the argument is not within the domain of an integer (see the `limits.h` header file), the function's behavior is undefined.

Caution

None.

Illustration

```
/*
                                      abs()
*/

#include <stdio.h>
#include <stdlib.h>

#define MAXSTR 20

int main()
{
      char buff[MAXSTR];
      int i;

      printf("Enter a number: ");
      i = atoi( gets(buff) );

      printf("The absolute value of %d is %d\n", i, abs(i) );
}
```

Program Comment

The program `#includes` the necessary header files and `#defines` the symbolic constant `MAXSTR` for use in the definition of `buff[]`. The program asks you to enter a number by a call to `gets()` and `atoi()`. The number's value is assigned to `i`, and the absolute value is displayed by the call to `abs()` in the `printf()` call.

You might want to enter a value greater than that of a signed integer to see the results produced by your version of the `abs()` function.

Miscellaneous Comments

None.

Function Name

`assert()`

Standard Met

ANSI, SYSV

Purpose

To test program expression.

Prototypes

```
void assert(int expres)
```

Required Header

`#include <assert.h>` ANSI/SYSV

Usage

```
void assert(int expres)
```

The `assert()` macro evaluates the expression `expres`. When the `assert()` macro is evaluated, if `expres` is logical `True`, no diagnostics are displayed. When `expres` evaluates to logical `False`, the `assert()` macro causes the following diagnostics to be displayed on the standard error device, `stderr`:

```
assertion failed: text, file filename, line nnn
```

in which `text` is the text for the `assert()` argument `expres`, `filename` is held by the preprocessing macro __FILE__, and the line number in __LINE__. After the diagnostics are displayed by a failed assertion, the `assert()` macro calls the `abort()` function, and the program terminates. (The capitalization of the message, including the file name, will vary between implementations.)

You may remove the `assert()` macro calls from the program by using the `-dNDEBUG` or `-DNDEBUG` compile-time switch provided by many compilers, or placing a `#define NDEBUG` preprocessor directive before the #include <assert.h> directive. Either method removes the assertions from the compiled code without removing the assertions from the source code file.

Caution

If the assert() macro is the object of an #undef directive or assert() is redefined as a macro or function, the behavior is undefined.

Illustration

```
/*
                                   assert()
*/

#include <stdio.h>
#include <stdlib.h>
#include <assert.h>

int main()
{

     int a, b, i;

     a = 3;
     b = 2;

     printf("\nIn for loop:\n");
     for (i = 0; i < 10; i++) {
          printf("%d\n", i);
          assert( (a + b) != i);
     }
}
```

Program Comment

The program #includes several header files. The stdlib.h file is needed because assert() calls abort() on a failed assertion.

In `main()`, we define several working variables and enter a `for` loop that controls a `printf()` call and the `assert()` macro. On each pass through the loop, we print the value of `i`, followed by the `assert()` test. As long as `i` does not equal 5 (that is, `a` + `b`), the loop continues to execute. When `i` equals 5, the assertion that `a` plus `b` is not equal to `i` fails, the diagnostics are displayed, and the program ends.

Miscellaneous Comments

None.

Function Name

`atexit()`

Standard Met

ANSI

Purpose

Special program termination sequence.

Prototypes

```
int atexit(void (*function)(void) )
```

Required Header

`#include <stdllib.h>` ANSI

Usage

```
int atexit(void (*function)(void) )
```

You can use the `atexit()` function to register up to 32 functions that are to be executed before normal program termination. The argument to `atexit()` is a pointer to function. The registered functions may not have an argument nor return a meaningful value (both `void` data type and argument).

If the registration succeeds, the return value is zero; otherwise, nonzero is returned if the function is not registered.

Before the program terminates normally, the functions are executed in the reverse order of their registration. You can use this function to perform special program termination tasks in addition to any tasks that are done by default. [Also see the `exit()` function.]

Caution

Some pre-ANSI compilers provide this function under the name `onexit()`.

Illustration

```
/*
                                    atexit()
*/

#include <stdio.h>
#include <stdlib.h>

int main()
{
     void func1(), func2(), func3();

     atexit(func1);
     atexit(func2);
     atexit(func3);
     exit(0);

}

void func1(void)
{
     printf("This is func1()\n");
}

void func2(void)
{
     printf("This is func2()\n");
}

void func3(void)
{
     printf("This is func3()\n");
}
```

Program Comment

The program starts with the required #include header files. In main(), we call atexit() three times, each time using the name of a function that is to be called on program termination. Because we use the name of the function without parentheses as the argument to atexit(), the function's name is a pointer to the function (that is, the function's lvalue) that is being passed to atexit(). The atexit() function can store at least 32 such pointers.

When the program is run, the output is

```
This is func3().
This is func2().
This is func1().
```

This shows that the functions are called in the reverse order of their registration in the program.

Miscellaneous Comments

The limitation of atexit() is that the functions may not have either arguments or return values.

Function Name

`bsearch()`

Standard Met

ANSI, SYSV

Purpose

To perform a binary search on a list of data.

Prototypes

```
void *bsearch(const void *find, void *root, size_t howbig,
            size_t elesize, int(*compar)(void *, void *)
```

Required Header

```
#include <stdlib.h>        ANSI
#include <search.h>        SYSV
```

Usage

```
void *bsearch(void *lookfor, void *root, size_t howbig,
     size_t elementsize, int (*compare)(void *, void *))
```

The function performs a binary search on a list of data that has been previously sorted into ascending order. The following are arguments to the function:

1. A `void` pointer that points to the data item we want to find (`looknfor`)
2. A `void` pointer that points to the start of the list of data to be searched (`root`)
3. The number of items in the list we are searching of type `size_t` (`howbig`)
4. The size of one element in the list of type `size_t` (`elementsize`)

5. A pointer to a function that returns an `int`. The function is responsible for converting the `void *` to the appropriate data types and performing the comparison of the elements from the list. The actual function must be supplied by the programmer. The return value from the function must be an integer value of less than, equal to, or greater than 0 according to whether the first argument is less than, equal to, or greater than the second argument [This is the way `strcmp()` works.] (`compare`)

The return value is a pointer to `void` that points to the matched data item. If the return value is a NULL pointer, the data item sought was not found in the list. Because the search may be performed on any data items, the return value must be cast to match the attribute list of the data being searched. The program illustration and discussion shows how this might be done for a list of data items that have the attribute list: "array of pointers to `char`."

Caution

The return value must be cast to match the type of data being searched.

SYSV, which does not have the `void *` data type or `size_t` typedef, uses this prototype for `bsearch()`

```
char *bsearch( char *looknfor, char *root, unsigned howbig,
               unsigned elementsize, int (*compare)() )
```

Although the ANSI version uses new data types in the prototype for `bsearch()` and the SYSV version expects the inclusion of the `search.h` header file, there is no functional difference between the two versions.

Illustration

```
/*
        Program to demonstrate bsearch()
*/

#include <stdio.h>                 /* Standard I/O header file    */
#include <stdlib.h>                /* Prototype header file       */
#ifdef SYSV
     #include <search.h>           /* Needed by bsearch() for SYSV */
#endif
#include <string.h>                /* Needed by string functions */

char *function[] = {               /* Define some function names */
     "abs",                        /* Note: these must be in
     "acos",                          ascending sorted order     */
     "asin",
     "atol",
     "bsearch",
     "ceil",
     "close",
     "cos",
     "printf",
     "sin",
     "strcpy",
     "tolower",
     "toupper",
     "vprintf",
};

                         /* compute the number in the array */

#define  NUMBER  (sizeof(function) / sizeof(function[Ø]))

int main(int argc, char *argv[])
{
     char **p;
     int compare(char **a, char **b);

     if(argc < 2) {
          puts("Usage: bsearch function-name\n");
          exit(1);
     }
```

```
     if((p = (char **) bsearch(&argv[1], function, NUMBER,
             sizeof(function[0]), compare)) != (char **) NULL) {
          puts("Found the function");
          puts(*p);
          exit(0);
     } else {
          puts("Did not find the function");
          puts(argv[1]);
          exit(1);
     }
}

/*
                              compare()
*/

int compare(char **a, char **b)
{
     return ( strcmp(*a, *b) );
}
```

Program Comment

When the program is invoked from the command line, one command line argument is used as a function name for a search. Note that the `search.h` header file is included in the program if the `SYSV` macro is defined. We then initialize the `function[]` array to hold a sample list of function names to be searched.

Notice how the `compare()` function is declared. The function has two arguments, both of which are pointer to pointer to `char` (same as an array of pointers to `char`). When the `compare()` function is first called, the key used in the search is the command line argument `argv[1]`. In the `compare()` routine, `argv[1]` corresponds to variable `a`.

When the `bsearch()` function is called, the second argument (`function[]`) tells `bsearch()` where to find the root of the list that is to be searched. The `bsearch()` function determines what item in the list ends up being variable `b` in the `compare()` function. If you want to see what `bsearch()` passes to `compare()`, place the following statement in the `compare()` function:

```
printf("a = %s b = %s\n", *a, *b);
```

The `bsearch()` function returns a nonnull pointer if the item being searched is found in the list. Since `bsearch()` returns a pointer to `char` and we are searching an array of pointers to `char`, the program uses a cast so that the data types match [that is, `(char **)`]. After the pointer is cast to the proper data type, the pointer is assigned into `p`. If the item is found, `p` is a nonnull pointer, and the program tells you that the item was found. If the item is not found, a `NULL` pointer is returned, the `if` statement is `False`, and the "`not found`" message is displayed.

The reason for using a pointer to function in `bsearch()` is so that we do not have to tell `bsearch()` about the type of data being searched. The `compare()` function can be made to compare whatever type of data is used in the current task.

Miscellaneous Comments

Many programmers overlook `bsearch()` and write their own binary search function. If your library has a `bsearch()` function, use it. The function has been debugged, and there is no sense writing it again.

Function Names

`calloc()` `malloc()` `realloc()` `free()`

Standard Met

ANSI, SYSV

Purpose

The functions `calloc()`, `malloc()`, and `realloc()` provide several ways to request storage dynamically from the operating system. The storage allocated "on the fly" can be deallocated with `free()`.

Prototypes

```
void *calloc(size_t num, size_t how_big)
void *malloc(size_t num)
void *realloc(void *root, size_t new_size)
void free(void *root)
```

Required Header

```
#include <stdlib.h>      ANSI
#include <malloc.h>      SYSV
```

Usage

```
void *calloc(size_t num, size_t how_big)
```

This function requests sufficient storage for `num` data items, each of which is of size `how_big`. That is, the number of bytes of storage requested is the product of how many elements times the size of each element. For example, to request sufficient storage for 100 `doubles`, you might use:

```
ptr = (double *) calloc(100, sizeof(double) );
```

The function returns either (1) a pointer to the storage requested if sufficient storage was available, or (2) a NULL pointer if there was not enough storage to meet the request. If a valid pointer is returned from the call to `calloc()`, the data area just allocated will be initialized to zero. If the number of elements (`num`) or size of each element (`how_big`) is 0, the function returns one of these two implementation-defined values: a NULL pointer or a valid (nonnull) pointer that points to no storage.

Note how a cast must be used on the pointer returned from `calloc()` to match the type of storage we want `ptr` to point to.

```
void *malloc(size_t num)
```

The `malloc()` function is similar to `calloc()`, except that the argument is the number of bytes of storage requested.

This function returns either (1) a pointer to the requested bytes of storage if the request can be filled, or (2) a NULL pointer if the request cannot be satisfied. If the number of requested bytes (`num`) is zero, the implementation-defined return value is either a NULL pointer or a valid pointer to an area with no storage.

Again, because `malloc()` returns a pointer to `void`, a cast must be used if the requested storage was for some other data type.

```
void *realloc(void *root, size_t new_size)
```

The primary use of the `realloc()` function is to "resize" the block of storage pointed to by `root` to `new_size`. For example, if `root` points to 100 bytes of storage,

```
ptr = realloc(root, 150);
```

is asking the function to resize the (previously obtained) storage upward by 50 bytes. If the request cannot be satisfied, a NULL pointer is returned and assigned to `ptr`.

If the request is successful, a valid pointer to the new area is returned. If the request cannot be honored, a NULL pointer is returned. The contents of the storage area remain unchanged, even if the contents are moved to a different area of memory. The exception is if the new storage area is smaller than the previous area. The `realloc()` function preserves (or copies) the old storage data to the new one, up to the limits of either the old or new request, whichever is smaller. If a smaller area is used, the contents are preserved to the limit of the smaller area.

The arguments to `realloc()` can be NULL and zero, respectively. If `root` is a NULL pointer and `new_size` is positive, `realloc()` works like `malloc()` and allocates storage. If `root` is NULL and `new_size` is zero, realloc() works like free() and deallocates the storage pointed to by root. When using realloc() to free memory, if root does not point to area allocated by calloc(), malloc(), or realloc() or was previously freed the behavior is undefined.

If root is NULL and new_size is zero, the function returns one of the two possible implementation-defined values, a NULL pointer or a valid pointer to an area with no storage.

```
void free(char *root)
```

This function deallocates the storage pointed to by root.

Caution

Note that each allocation function is associated with a size argument that tells the operating system how many bytes of storage to set aside for the request. If you overflow the requested storage space given back by the operating system, strange things can happen. The same behavior can be expected if free() is handed something other than a previously allocated pointer.

Illustration

```
/*
 *   calloc(), malloc(), realloc(), free()
 */

#include    <stdio.h>
#ifdef SYSV
     #include   <malloc.h>
#else
     #include   <stdlib.h>
#endif
#include    <string.h>

#define MAXTABLE  1000          /* Up to a thousand entries         */
#define MAXLEN    100           /* Max string length                */

char    **root;                 /* Base memory location for array   */

int doinput(void);              /* A couple of prototypes           */
```

```
void look(int i),
     clrscr(void),
     release(int i);

int   main()
{          /* root defines a base memory location which will hold */
           /* an array of pointers. It will be increased in size  */
           /* as each new string is input                         */

     int i;

     root = (char **) NULL;  /* initialize root to point to nothing */

     i = doinput();              /* get input strings to be matched  */
     look(i);                    /* Now find one                     */
     release(i);                 /* Free up everything               */

}

int doinput(void)
{
     char  buff[MAXLEN],         /* General purpose input buffer     */
           *newvalue;            /* newvalue pointer                 */
     int i;

     clrscr();
     printf("Enter up to %d strings:\n\n", MAXTABLE);
     for (i = 0; i < MAXTABLE; i++) {     /* get up to 1000 inputs   */
          printf("\nentry #%d: ", i);
          gets(buff);
          if (strlen(buff) == 0)      /* if a blank line, we're done */
               break;
          if (root) {            /* if we have root then expand size */

               newvalue = (char *)realloc(root, (size_t)(i + 1) * sizeof(char *));

               if (newvalue) {  /* If not a null pointer             */
                    root = (char **) newvalue;
               } else {          /* if newvalue == 0,  out of memory */
                    printf("memory is full.\n");
                    break;
               }
```

```
            } else {  /* get memory for first one - use calloc to demonstrate use */

                 root = (char **) calloc( sizeof(char *), (size_t) 1);
            }
                                                      /* get string space */
            if ((newvalue = malloc(strlen(buff) + (size_t)1) ) == 0) {
                 printf("memory is full.\n");
                 break;
            }
            root[i] = newvalue;        /* add pointer to array            */
            strcpy(newvalue, buff);    /* copy in string                  */
       }
       return i;
}

void look(int i)
{
     char buff[MAXLEN];
     int j;
                                       /* now get input to match strings   */

     for (;;) {                        /* done so get matches              */
          printf("\nEnter string to be found: ");
          gets(buff);                  /* get the string                   */
          if (strlen(buff) == 0)       /* if no string then terminate      */
               return;

          for (j = 0; j < i; j++) {                        /* search list */
               if (strcmp(root[j], buff) == 0) { /* if match, print-out */
                    printf("Matched: %s\n", root[j]);
                    return;
               }
          }                            /* End of for (j = 0;...)           */
          printf("No match: %s\n", buff);  /* if j == i, didn't find       */

     }                                 /* End of for (;;)                  */
}

void release(int i)
{      /* demonstrate the use of free to get rid of memory obtained by */
       /* malloc(), calloc() and realloc()                              */
```

```
        int j;

        for (j = 0; j < i; j++) {          /* unnecessary frees of memory      */
            free(root[j]);
        }

        free(root);                        /* free the root                    */
}
```

Program Comment

Because functions that allocate memory are widely used, we will discuss the sample program in detail.

The first thing to notice is that the header file associated with the allocator function is `stdlib.h` for ANSI or `malloc.h` for SYSV. The correct header should always be `#include`d when storage requests are made in your program. If the macro SYSV is defined, `malloc.h` header file is included. If SYSV is not defined, `stdlib.h` is included instead. Because the program also uses some of the string functions, we have included the `string.h` header file as well.

After the `#include`s, several prototypes are given for functions in the program. There is one global variable named `root`, which is a pointer to pointer to `char`. The first thing we do in `main()` is initialize this pointer to NULL. This ensures that `root` is not pointing to valid data at the start of the program.

Next, we call the `doinput()` function, which asks you to enter up to MAXTABLE strings. The strings are entered by the `gets()` function and placement of the input into a temporary buffer named `buff`. A `strlen()` on `buff` is done to make sure that a string was entered. If the string length is zero, the input is taken to signal the end of input.

If a string was entered, we test `root` to see whether it is a nonzero (that is, not equal to NULL) pointer. If the first string has just been entered, `root` will fail this `if` test and fall into the `else` part of the statement. This failure causes the following line to be executed:

```
root = (char **) calloc( sizeof(char *), (size_t) 1);
```

This call to `calloc()` requests enough storage for one character pointer. Note that this approach is more portable than using an integer constant for the first argument to `calloc()`. Some compilers use two bytes for a pointer, whereas others may use four. Using the sizeof() operator ensures that the correct number of bytes for a character pointer is made in the call. The second argument uses the cast operator to the integer constant 1 for similar reasons.

If you look at the prototype for calloc(), you will see that it returns a pointer to void. Since we need a pointer to pointer to char, a cast (char **) is used so that the correct data is assigned to root. This becomes the base of the pointer for the data being entered.

The next line:

```
if ((newvalue = malloc(strlen(buff) + 1)) == (char *)0) {
   printf("memory is full.\n");
   break;
}
```

is a request to malloc() for enough storage to store the string that was just entered. Why the "+ 1" at the argument to malloc()? Because strlen() does not include the null character at the end of the string in the calculation of the string length, we add one more byte to hold the null terminator for the string.

If malloc() cannot find enough storage for the string, a null pointer (that is, a value equal to 0) is returned, and an error message stating that we have run out of memory is displayed.

If all goes well and a nonnull value is returned from malloc(), the operating system has given us enough storage for the string you just entered. (The string is still sitting in buff.) The pointer in newvalue is then copied into the appropriate index in root. Once that is done, we copy the string from buff into that area of memory pointed to by newvalue. You may want to convince yourself that an array of pointers to char (char *root[i]) is the same as pointer to pointer to char (char **root) in an expression evaluation. (Then again, maybe you don't want to convince yourself of that.)

Once strcpy() has copied the string into memory, we loop back for your next entry. The second time through the for loop, root will not be a null pointer. Therefore, the if (root) becomes logical True, and we execute:

```
newvalue = (char *)realloc(root, (size_t)(i + 1) * sizeof(char *));
if (newvalue) {
   root = (char **) newvalue;
} else {
   printf("memory is full.\n");
   break;
}
```

The program executes a call to realloc(), which attempts to increase the storage presently associated with root so that another character pointer can be held.

Because variable i is initialized to 0, there are actually i + 1 strings entered at any given point. Further, since we now need another pointer, we are asking realloc() to give us enough storage for one more character pointer. Note what this means. Instead of (perhaps) using:

```
char *root[MAXTABLE];
```

which has a fixed limit to the number of pointers root can handle, we use realloc() to change dynamically the amount of storage given to root.

If realloc() returns a null pointer, we must be out of memory, and we break out of the for loop. If realloc() gives us a valid pointer for newvalue, we cast that pointer to be a pointer to pointer to char as required. The rest of the function behaves the same as during the first pass through the loop.

Eventually, either you will end the loop by entering an empty string or MAXTABLE will be reached. In both cases, the number of strings entered (i) is passed back to main().

The look() function asks you to enter a string. That string is used as a key to search the string data that was entered during the call to doinput(). The call to strcmp() does most of the work and determines whether the search is successful or not. Program control then returns to main() once again.

The program then does a call to release(), passing the number of table entries (i) as the function's argument. The release() function goes through the root array and deallocates each of the pointers stored there by calls to free() with the appropriate pointer as its argument. When j equals i, the loop terminates, and all of the storage will have been released back to the operating system. The final call to free() outside the for loop frees the root pointer, and the program ends.

Miscellaneous Comments

The only danger you might face in using the allocation functions is doing a call to free() without a corresponding (successful) call to either calloc(), malloc(), or realloc(). In such a case, a variety of things can happen—usually none of them good.

Function Names

`div()` `ldiv()`

Standard Met

ANSI

Purpose

To find a quotient and the remainder.

Prototypes

```
div_t div(int num, int denom)
ldiv_t ldiv(long int num, long int denom)
```

Required Header

`#include <stdlib.h>` ANSI

Usage

```
div_t div(int num, int denom)
```

The `div()` function divides `num` by `demon` and stores the quotient and remainder in a structure of type `div_t`. The `div_t` structure has the members:

```
int quot;
int rem;
```

The `div()` function returns a structure of type `div_t`. The sign of the quotient is determined by the algebraic quotient. The value of the quotient is the largest integer that is less than the mathematical quotient. That is, if the number is 21 and the denominator is 4, the algebraic quotient is 5.25. The contents of the `div_t` structure, therefore, are an integer quotient (`quot`) of 5 and a remainder (`rem`) of 1.

```
ldiv_t ldiv(long int num, long int denom)
```

The `ldiv()` function behaves the same as `div()`, except the values are all `long` integer data types. The return value is a structure of type `ldiv_t`, which has the members:

```
long int quot;
long int rem;
```

Caution

None.

Illustration

```
/*
                              div(), ldiv()
*/

#include <stdio.h>
#include <stdlib.h>

int main()
{
    char buff[20];
    int num, denom;
    long int newnum;
    div_t answer, div();            /* For integers      */
    ldiv_t lanswer, ldiv();         /* For long integers */

    printf("Enter a number: ");
    num = atoi( gets(buff) );
    printf("Enter the denominator: ");
    denom = atoi( gets(buff) );

    answer = div(num, denom);
    printf("\nFor div():\n");
    printf("quotient = %d, remainder = %d\n", answer.quot, answer.rem);
```

```
        newnum = 100000L + (long int) num;          /* Make it a long     */
        printf("\nFor ldiv():\n");
        lanswer = ldiv(newnum, (long int) denom );
        printf("quotient = %ld, remainder = %ld", lanswer.quot, lanswer.rem);

}
```

Program Comment

In this example, we `#include` the required header files. Note that `stdlib.h` contains the declarations for the `div_t` and `ldiv_t` structure types.

Inside `main()`, we define several working variables, including one for each of the structure types `div_t` and `ldiv_t`. The program then asks you to enter a number and a denominator. These values are then passed to the `div()` and `ldiv()` functions. Since `div()` and `ldiv()` return a structure, we need to define `answer` and `lanswer` to hold the result.

Note that we added 100,000 to the number you entered, so that we would generate different answers for the integer and `long` integer data types.

Miscellaneous Comments

None.

Function Name

`exit()`

Standard Met

ANSI, SYSV

Purpose

Normal program termination.

Prototypes

```
void exit(int endval)
```

Required Header

`#include <stdlib.h>`	ANSI
None provided	SYSV

Usage

```
void exit(int endval)
```

The `exit()` function causes the program to terminate in a normal fashion. This means that the following sequence of steps occurs:

1. All functions that were successfully registered by call(s) to `atexit()` are executed in reverse order compared to the order in which they were registered. [See the `atexit()` function.]

2. All open output streams (for example, `FILE` pointers) are flushed and then closed. Any temporary files created by calls to `tmpfile()` are removed.

3. System control is returned to the host environment. (In most cases, this is the operating system.) The argument to exit() informs the host environment whether the program termination is successful (endval = 0 or the macro from stdlib.h, EXIT_SUCCESS) or unsuccessful (endval = EXIT_FAILURE). The value returned to the operating system for any other value for endval is implementation-defined.

If the end of the main() function is reached and no exit() function has been called, the closing brace of main() causes the equivalent of an exit(EXIT_SUCCESS) function call.

Caution

None.

Illustration

```
/*
                                        exit()
*/

#include <stdio.h>
#include <stdlib.h>

int main()
{
     printf("Do something.\n");
     exit(0);
     printf("Never to be seen.\n");
}
```

Program Comment

The program #includes the required header files, does a printf() call, and then calls exit() with zero as the argument (that is, successful program termination). The second `printf()` is never executed because of the prior call to `printf()`. If the `exit(0)` call were deleted from the program, the closing brace would eventually produce the same effect as that of the `exit(0)` call, except the second `printf()` would be displayed.

A more common use of the `exit()` function is shown in the functions that use input/output streams. In these examples, `exit()` is often called with an error condition when the input/output stream cannot be opened, read, or written to. [See, for example, the `fopen()`, `fread()`, `fwrite()`, and related functions.]

Miscellaneous Comments

None.

Function Name

`getenv()`

Standard Met

ANSI, SYSV

Purpose

To get an environment value.

Prototypes

```
char *getenv(const char *str)
```

Required Header

`#include <stdlib.h>`	ANSI
None provided	SYSV

Usage

```
char *getenv(const char *str)
```

This function searches an implementation-defined environment list for a match on the string pointed to by `str`. The function returns a pointer to the member in the list if a match is found; otherwise, a null pointer is returned.

Caution

None.

Illustration

```
/*
                                getenv()
*/

#include <stdio.h>
#include <stdlib.h>
#include <ctype.h>

#define MAXSTR 128

int main()
{
     char buff[MAXSTR], *ptr;
     void getus(char *s);

     printf("Enter the search string: ");
     getus(buff);

     ptr = getenv(buff);
     if (ptr == NULL)
          printf("\nString not found\n");
     else
          printf("\nThe match on %s is %s\n", buff, ptr);

}

/*
                          getus()
*/

void getus(char *s)
{
     gets(s);
     while (*s != NULL)
          *s++ = toupper( (int) *s);
}
```

Program Comment

The program begins with the required `#include` header files and `#defines` the `MAXSTR` symbolic constant that is used to set the buffer size to hold your input.

The program then calls the `getus()` function to get the string to be used in the search of the environment list. Because some operating systems are case-sensitive, we convert the input received by the `gets()` call to uppercase letters. If your operating system is not case-sensitive, the `getus()` call could be replaced in `main()` with a single call to `gets()`, and the `getus()` function code could be deleted.

After the search string is entered, we call `getenv()` with the input you just entered. We test `ptr` to see whether a match was found and print out the appropriate message, depending upon whether a match was found. If, for example, we typed in "`path`" on an MS-DOS machine, we might get something like "`C:\bin`" displayed on the screen.

Miscellaneous Comments

None.

Function Name

`getopt()`

Standard Met

SYSV only

Purpose

Parse command line arguments.

Prototypes

```
int getopt(int argc, char *argv[], char *optstring)

extern char *optarg;
extern int optind, opterr;
```

Required Header

None provided. SYSV

Usage

```
int getopt(int argc, char *argv[], char *optstring)
```

The purpose of `getopt()` is to parse arguments passed to the program from the command line. The valid option characters are held in `optstring`. The case of the characters is significant. (A `d` is not the same as a `D`; you must use `dD` or `Dd` for both to be valid in the option string.)

(Although the SYSV documentation does not say, the command line precedes each option or option pair with a dash (-). If a colon follows a character in the option string, that character is expected to have an argument. It may be separated from the character by white space. Therefore, the option string:

```
char *optstring = "df:l";
```

may look for the command line arguments:

```
program -d -f test.c -l
program -dl -ftest.c
```

Both versions of the command line result in the same processing.

If an option in the option string (optstring) is followed by a colon, getopt() sets a pointer name optarg to point to the argument following that option on the command line. In the example, after the -f option is read, optarg will point to "test.c".

The variable optind is initialized to 1 before the call to getopt(). Each time getopt() is called, optind gets the argv[] index of the next argument to be processed.

As a special case, a double-dash (--) is recognized as ending the list of option arguments to be parsed by getopt(). This can be useful when you want getopt() to parse a number of arguments and then stop at the double-dash, but allow other command line arguments to be processed by another function.

When all arguments have been parsed or an unrecognized option is read, getopt() returns EOF. If getopt() senses an option letter not contained in optstring, the function returns a question mark (?) and prints a predefined error message on stderr. If you want to disable the printing of the error message, set opterr to 0 before the call to getopt().

Caution

This is not an ANSI function.

Illustration

```
/*
                              getopt()
*/

#include <stdio.h>
#include <stdlib.h>
#include <ctype.h>

int main(argc, argv)
int argc;
char **argv;
```

```
{
     char answer[10];
     int i;

     extern char *optarg;
     extern int optind, opterr;

     static char *optstring = "cCeEzZm:M:";

     printf("Should you defeat built-in error checking (y, n): ");
     gets(answer);

     if (toupper( (int) answer[0]) == 'Y' )
          opterr = 0;

     while((i = getopt(argc, argv, optstring)) != EOF) {
          switch(i) {
               case  'c' :
               case  'C' :
                    printf("The letter C was pressed\n");
                    break;
               case  'e' :
               case  'E' :
                    printf("The letter E was pressed\n");
                    break;
               case  'z' :
               case  'Z' :
                    printf("The letter Z was pressed\n");
                    break;
               case  'm' :
               case  'M' :
                    printf("\noptarg = %s\n", optarg);
                    printf("The letter M was pressed.\n");
                    break;
               case '?' :
                    printf("Unrecognized command-line argument.\n");
                    break;
              default:
                    break;
          }
     }
}
```

Program Comment

The program starts with several `#includes`. Note that we have declared `argc` and `argv` as the command-line arguments for `main()`. Next, we have defined an option string that will recognize the upper- or lowercase letters `c`, `e`, `m`, and `z`. The colon after the `m` options says that we expect to find an argument associated with option `m`.

The program then asks whether we want to suppress the default of printing an error message to `stderr` if an illegal option is detected. If you enter a 'y', `opterr` is set to zero to disable the default error message.

After that, we parse out what you entered and display the appropriate message.

Given the options in `optstring`, some sample command-line arguments generate the following results (in the examples the assumptions are that we do not defeat the default value for `opterr` and that the first argument on the command line is the program name, which is not shown below):

Command Line	*Output*

`-e -mtest.c -z`	`The letter E was pressed.`
	`optarg = test.c`
	`The letter M was pressed.`
	`The letter Z was pressed.`

`-e -mz f`	`The letter E was pressed.`
	`optarg = z`
	`The letter M was pressed.`

`-e -d -m`	`The letter E was pressed.`
	`: illegal option -- d`
	`Unrecognized command-line argument.`
	`: option requires an argument --`

The exact nature of the error messages that you receive on non-valid options is implementation-defined.

Miscellaneous Comments

Although `getopt()` is not part of ANSI, it is a useful function that significantly simplifies parsing command-line arguments.

Function Names

`hcreate()` `hdestroy()` `hsearch()`

Standard Met

SYSV only

Purpose

Search using hash table.

Prototypes

```
int hcreate(unsigned num)
void hdestroy(void)
ENTRY *hsearch(ENTRY key, ACTION dowhat)
```

Required Header

`#include <search.h>` SYSV

Usage

```
int hcreate(unsigned num)
```

The call to `hcreate()` is used to establish a search table of `num` elements in size. The `hcreate()` function returns nonzero if it can allocate sufficient space for the table; otherwise, 0 is returned.

```
void hdestroy(void)
```

The `hdestroy()` function destroys the search table that was created by the call to `hcreate()`.

```
ENTRY *hsearch(ENTRY key, ACTION dowhat)
```

The `hsearch()` function is used to search the hash table that was created by the call to `hcreate()`. The `strcmp()` function is used for the comparisons that take place when `hsearch()` is called.

The SYSV `search.h` header file contains several `typedef`s that are used by the `hsearch()` function. First, the `ENTRY` `typedef` is for a structure that holds the data that is ultimately searched. The ACTION typedef is an enum data type with the two values FIND and ENTER. If dowhat has the value of FIND, the table is searched. If the item being searched for (for example, key) is found in the table, a pointer of type ENTRY to key is returned. If the item is not found, a NULL pointer is returned. If dowhat has the value of ENTER, the item in key is placed into the table. If key already exists in the table, it is not added a second time. When ENTER is used in the call to hsearch(), it returns a pointer of type ENTRY to the item just added.

Caution

You should not make a second call to hsearch() before making a call to hdestroy(). At the present time, only one hash table can be alive at one time.

Note that this function is not in the ANSI standard library.

Illustration

```
/*
                              hsearch()
*/

#include <stdio.h>
#include <stdlib.h>
#include <search.h>
#include <string.h>

                    /* Define some function names in any order */

char *function[] = {
     "bsearch",
     "abs",
     "cos",
     "acos",
     "asin",
     "ceil",
     "close",
     "tolower",
     "printf",
     "sin",
```

```
	"atol",
	"strcpy",
	"toupper",
	"vprintf",
};

#define MAXSIZE 30                          /* space for hash table */

ENTRY data[MAXSIZE];

                              /* compute the number in the array */
#define  NUMBER  (sizeof(function) / sizeof(function[0]))

int main(int argc, char *argv[])
{
	ENTRY *p, lookup;
	int  i;
	ACTION mode;

	if (argc < 2) {
		puts("Usage: hsearch function-name");
		exit(1);
	}
	if (hcreate( (unsigned) MAXSIZE) == 0) {
		puts("Insufficient memory for hash table");
		exit(1);
	}
	mode = ENTER;
	for (i = 0; i < NUMBER; i++) {
		data[i].key = function[i];
		if (hsearch(data[i], mode) == (ENTRY *) NULL) {
			puts("Error entering function");
			puts(data[i].key);
			exit(1);
		}
	}
	lookup.key = argv[1];
	mode = FIND;
	p = hsearch(lookup, mode);
	if (p) {
		puts("The function was found");
		puts(p->key);
		exit(0);
```

```
        } else {
            puts("The function was not found");
            puts(argv[1]);
            exit(0);
        }
        hdestroy();
}
```

Program Comment

The program starts with the usual #includes followed by the definition of an array of pointers to several function names. We also define data[] to be an array of type ENTRY data items.

The call to hcreate() attempts to create the hash table and prints an error message if the attempt is not successful. On the assumption that the table is created, we set mode to ENTER and use a for loop to stuff data[] with the function names. At the same time, we build a hash table by calls to hsearch(), using the data[] array and mode as the arguments.

Variable lookup.key is set to the command-line argument of the item to be searched and mode is set to FIND. We then call hsearch() to see whether lookup.key is in the table. If the item is found in the table, p will be nonnull, and "The function was found" message is displayed. If the item is not found, p will be NULL and "The function was not found" is displayed.

When we have finished, hdestroy() is called to remove the table.

Miscellaneous Comments

Because hcreate() does call malloc() for table space and hdestroy() releases that space, you should always call hdestroy() to free that space used for the table before exiting from the program.

Function Name

```
labs()
```

Standard Met

ANSI only

Purpose

To find long integer absolute value.

Prototypes

```
long int labs(long int bignum)
```

Required Header

```
#include <stdlib.h>        ANSI
```

Usage

```
long int labs(long int bignum)
```

The function returns a `long` integer that is the absolute value of the argument `bignum`. If the result cannot be expressed as a `long` integer, the behavior of the function is undefined.

Caution

None.

Illustration

```
/*
                                        labs()
*/

#include <stdio.h>
#include <stdlib.h>

int main()
{
     char buff[20];
     long bignum;

     printf("Enter a number: ");
     bignum = strtol( gets(buff), (char **)0, 10 );

     printf("The absolute value of %ld is %ld\n", bignum, labs(bignum));

}
```

Program Comment

The program begins with the necessary `#include` files. A few working variables are defined, and you are asked to enter a number. The call to `strtol()` converts the value you entered to a base-10 `long` integer. The value is then printed out, followed by the absolute value by the call to `labs()`, and the program ends.

Miscellaneous Comments

You might want to try this program with a value that is larger or smaller than permitted by the `long` data type, to see what your implementation does with the value. (The largest and smallest values may be found in the `limits.h` header file under the symbolic constants `LONG_MAX` and `LONG_MIN`. More than likely, these two values are plus or minus 2,147,483,647.)

Function Names

`lsearch()` `lfind()`

Standard Met

SYSV only

Purpose

To do a linear search of a list of data.

Prototypes

```
char *lsearch(char *goal, char *root, unsigned *num,
              unsigned elesize, int (*compare)() )

char *lfind(char *goal, char *root, unsigned *num,
              unsigned elesize, int (*compare)() )
```

Required Header

`#include <search.h>` SYSV

Usage

```
char *lsearch(char *goal, char *root, unsigned *num,
         unsigned elesize, int (*compare)() )
```

The `lsearch()` function performs a linear search for variable `goal` in a list of data items that are stored where `root` points when the function is called. Variable `num` tells the function how many items are in the list when the function is called, whereas `elesize` tells the function how many bytes are required for an item in the list. The fifth argument is a pointer to a `compare()` function that is required to return 0 if the arguments match, and nonzero if they do not match. If the item being searched for (`goal`) is not found, that item is added to the list.

The `lsearch()` function returns a pointer to the item being searched for if the item is found in the list or added to the list.

Note that num is a *pointer* to unsigned. The reason is that, if the item is not in the list and it is added to the list, lsearch() will increment num to reflect the current number of items in the list to include the new item just added.

```
char *lfind(char *goal, char *root, unsigned *num,
        unsigned elesize, int (*compare)() )
```

The lfind() function works in the same manner as lsearch() except that, if the item being searched for (goal) is not found in the list pointed to by root, the item is not added to the list. If lfind() cannot find the item, a NULL pointer is returned.

Caution

At the present time, there is no direct way for lsearch() to know whether it has sufficient space to add safely a new item to a list; it adds the item if the item is not already in the list. It is your responsibility to ensure that enough storage space is left to add a new item safely.

Note that these two functions are not in the ANSI standard library.

Illustration

```
/*
                        lfind(), lsearch()
*/

#include <stdio.h>
#include <search.h>             /* SYSV */
#include <string.h>
#include <stdlib.h>

                    /* First define some function names */
                    /* Note: unlike bsearch(), these    */
                    /* may be in any order              */
```

```
char *function[] = {
      "bsearch",
      "abs",
      "cos",
      "acos",
      "asin",
      "ceil",
      "close",
      "tolower",
      "printf",
      "sin",
      "atol",
      "strcpy",
      "toupper",
      "vprintf",
};

/* create an array to put values in */

#define MAXSIZE 30

char *newfunction[MAXSIZE];

                         /* compute the number of items in the array */
#define  NUMBER  (sizeof(function) / sizeof(function[0]))

int nel = 0;

int main(int argc, char *argv[])
{
      char **p;
      int  oldnel, i, compare(char **a, char **b);

      if (argc < 2) {
            puts("Usage: lsearch function-name");
            exit(1);
      }
      for (i = 0; i < NUMBER; i++) {                /* Make a copy */
            lsearch(&function[i], newfunction, &nel,
                      sizeof(newfunction[0]), compare);
      }
```

```
        oldnel = nel;
        p = (char **)lsearch(&argv[1], newfunction, &nel, sizeof(newfunction[0]),
             compare);

        if (nel > oldnel) {
             puts("The function was added");
             puts(*p);
             exit(0);
        } else {
             puts("Found the function");
             puts(*p);
             exit(0);
        }
}

/*
                              compare()
*/

int compare(char **a, char **b)
{
        return ( strcmp(*a, *b) );
}
```

Program Comment

The program uses a command-line argument for the item to be searched for. Notice the `#include` for the `search.h` header file.

Also notice what was done in the `for` loop. Because we call the `lsearch()` function using the address of `function[i]` and set the list root equal to `newfunction[]`, we end up comparing every element in the `function[]` array to the "empty" `newfunction[]` array. Further, because we set `nel` equal to 0, we end up copying the contents of the `function[]` array into the `newfunction[]` array.

Next, we set `oldnel` to `nel` because both arrays now have the same number of elements in them. Having done that, we again call `lsearch()`, but using `argv[1]` as the search item. The return value from `lsearch()` is then cast to the proper attribute (array of pointers to `char`) and assigned into `p`.

On return from the function, `p` is a pointer to the item. Since the return value points to the item regardless of whether the item was in the list, the only way to tell whether the item was added to the list is to compare `oldnel` and `nel`. If `oldnel` is larger, we know that the item was added to the list.

We could have used a call to `lfind()` to do one search to find whether the item was in the list. If `lfind()` returned a NULL pointer, we would then know that the item was not in the list. However, if the item was not in the list, `lfind()` would not add it to the list the way `lsearch()` does. The method presented here gives one way of telling whether the item was previously in the list.

Miscellaneous Comments

You might also want to read about the `bsearch()` routine. Remember that the `lsearch()` function (1) does not require the items to be in sorted order, and (2) will add an item to the list automatically if the item is not in the list already (provided that there is sufficient memory to hold the item).

Function Name

`offsetof()`

Standard Met

ANSI only

Purpose

To determine the offset of a structure member.

Prototypes

The `offsetof()` is a macro and, therefore, does not have a prototype.

Required Header

```
#include <stddef.h>        ANSI
```

Usage

```
size_t offsetof(structurename, membername)
```

The `offsetof()` macro returns an integral value of `size_t`, which represents the number of bytes `membername` is from the beginning of `structurename`. The `structurename` must be a type specifier (for example, a structure tag or `typedef` name). If the member is the name of a bitfield member, the behavior is undefined.

Caution

This macro is not provided in SYSV.

Illustration

```
/*
                                    offsetof()
*/

#include   <stdio.h>
#include   <stddef.h>

struct   test {
     int     i;
     char    c[20];
     int     j;
     long    l;
} p;

int main()
{
     printf("i:%d c:%d j:%d, l:%d\n",
             offsetof(struct test, i),
             offsetof(struct test, c[0]),
             offsetof(struct test, j),
             offsetof(struct test, l));
}
```

Program Comment

The program `#includes` the required header files and defines a structure variable named `p` with four members. In `main()`, we print out the values returned from `offsetof()` for the members of the type `struct test`.

Miscellaneous Comments

Keep in mind that, because the `offsetof()` macro must use a cast to find the first element of the structure, the first argument must be some form of a type specifier.

The current sentiment of the ANSI committee is to make `offsetof()` a keyword rather than a macro. The formal outcome is not expected until early 1988.

Function Name

`qsort()`

Standard Met

ANSI, SYSV

Purpose

To sort data.

Prototypes

```
void qsort(void *base, size_t num, size_t big,
           int (*comp)(const void *, const void *))
```

Required Header

`#include <stdlib.h>`	ANSI
None provided	SYSV

Usage

```
void qsort(void *base, size_t num, size_t big,
           int (*comp)(const void *, const void *))
```

The `qsort()` function performs a sort on a list of data items pointed to by `base`. There are `num` items in the list, each of which is `big` bytes in size. The sorting order is ascending.

The final argument is a comparison function that you must supply. The comparison function is written for the type of data to be sorted in the list, and the argument is a pointer to function. The comparison function receives two pointers to the items to be sorted. The return value from the function must be an integer value that is less than zero, equal to zero, or greater than zero if the first argument to the comparison function is less than, equal to, or greater than the second argument. (See the example.)

Caution

None.

Illustration

```
/*
                                qsort()
*/

#include <stdio.h>
#include <stddef.h>
#include <stdlib.h>

#define MAXELE 100

int dirflag;

int main()
{
     char buff[20];
     int array[MAXELE], i, icomp(int *, int *);
     void showarray(int *s);

     for (i = 0; i < MAXELE; i++)
          array[i] = rand();

     showarray(array);

     printf("\n\nWhat order (1 = ascending, 2 = descending): ");
     dirflag = atoi(gets(buff));

     if (dirflag != 2)               /* Default is ascending */
          dirflag = 1;

     qsort( (char *) array, (size_t) MAXELE, (unsigned) sizeof(int), icomp);
     showarray(array);
}
```

```
int icomp(const int *v1, const int *v2)
{
     if (dirflag == 1)
          return (*v1 - *v2);
     else
          return (*v2 - *v1);
}

void showarray(int *s)
{
     int i;

     for (i = 0; i < MAXELE; i++) {
          if ( (i % 10) == 0)
               printf("\n");
               printf("%7d", *s++);
     }
}
```

Program Comment

The program begins with several `#include` files that contain information needed in the program. The symbolic constant `MAXELE` is used to set the number of data items in the list. Inside `main()`, we use `MAXELE` to define an array of integers.

The first thing we do inside `main()` is to fill `array[]` with a series of random integer numbers by calls to `rand()`. The `showarray()` function displays the numbers.

The program then asks you to indicate whether you want the list in ascending or descending order. The direction flag variable `dirflag` is set depending on the sort order desired. We did this to show that altering the sort order is simple. [Look at the `icomp()` function to see how `dirflag` is used to alter the sort order.]

The call to `qsort()` passes the required arguments to `icomp()`. Note how a pointer to function is passed to the function: the function name is passed. The `qsort()` function keeps track of the necessary details.

A final call to `showarray[]` then shows the sorted array.

Miscellaneous Comments

This is one of the few functions that has a pointer to function as one of its arguments. It seems strange to some that a function that requires two arguments is passed only the function name. Keep in mind, however, that internal code in `qsort()` calls the `icomp()` function directly—`icomp()` is not being called by the programmer in the `qsort()` call.

Whenever a function name is used without parentheses after the function name, the `lvalue` of the function is passed. In the `qsort()` function call, because we use `icomp` without any parentheses, `qsort()` receives the address, or `lvalue`, of where the `icomp()` function is stored in memory. The `qsort()` function calls the `icomp()` function with the proper arguments.

If you look at the arguments passed to `qsort()`: (1) the first argument tells `qsort()` where the array to be sorted starts in memory, (2) the second argument tells the function how many elements are in the array, (3) the third argument tells `qsort()` how big each element is, and (4) the fourth argument is a pointer to the function that performs the comparison of the data. Therefore, `qsort()` has all the information needed to perform the sort correctly.

The rule is simple: A function name without any parentheses passes the `lvalue` of the function, and a function name with the parentheses invokes the function.

Function Name

`raise()`

Standard Met

ANSI

Purpose

To send a signal.

Prototypes

```
int raise(int sig)
```

Required Header

`#include <signal.h>` ANSI

Usage

```
int raise(int onfire)
```

The `raise()` function sends the signal `onfire` to the executing program for subsequent processing. The `onfire` signal is assumed to be a signal that can be processed by `signal()`. The `raise()` function returns 0 if the request is satisfied, or nonzero if not.

Caution

The function is not available in SYSV, although `kill()` is similar. [The `kill()` function has two arguments: the first represents the process identification, and the second is the signal.]

Illustration

```
/*
                              raise()
*/

#include <stdio.h>
#include <signal.h>

int main()
{
     double d, e, divide(double x, double y);

     d = 3.14;

     for (e = 5.0; e >= 0.0; e--)
          printf("%f", divide(d, e) );
}

double divide(double a, double b)
{
     if (b == 0.0)
          raise(SIGFPE);
     return (a / b);
}
```

Program Comment

The program `#includes` the requisite header files, including `signal.h`, which contains the definition of the symbolic constant `SIGFPE`. In `main()`, the program defines several working variables and declares `divide()` to return a `double`. The `for` loop sets `e` to a value of 5 and then calls `divide()` with `d` and `e` as arguments. When `e` reaches a value of 0, the test for that condition in `divide()` becomes logical True, and `raise()` sends the signal that a floating-point error (`SIGFPE`) has occurred—division by zero in this example. [What happens beyond this point depends on how the `signal()` function processes the signal that was sent from the call to `raise()`. You may want to try this program to find out what your implementation does.]

The program may terminate at this point or, perhaps, issue an error message stating that a floating-point error occurred.

Miscellaneous Comments

Also see the discussion of the `signal()` function.

Function Names

`setjmp()` `longjmp()`

Standard Met

ANSI, SYSV

Purpose

To provide for a nonlocal `goto` by a saved environment.

Prototypes

```
int setjmp(jmp_buf environment)
void longjmp(jmp_buf environment, int val)
```

Required Header

```
#include <setjmp.h>        ANSI
#include <setjmp.h>        SYSV
```

Usage

```
int setjmp(jmp_buf environment)
```

The `setjmp()` function saves the environment that exists at the time `setjmp()` is called. The information necessary to preserve the environment is (implementation) defined by the `jmp_buf` type used as the argument to `setjmp()`.

The return value from `setjmp()` is 0.

```
void longjmp(jmp_buf environment, int val)
```

The `longjmp()` function restores the environment defined by the most recent call to `setjmp()` that used the `jmp_buf` environment variable. (This is equivalent to a `goto` where the `setjmp()` was made.) If `longjmp()` is called without a `setjmp()` call using a matching `jmp_buf` environment variable, the behavior of the function is undefined. Also, if the function that called `setjmp()` is out of scope at the time that `longjmp()` is called, the behavior is undefined.

The return value from a `longjmp()` is `val`. The value of `val` cannot be 0.

Caution

Keep in mind that the function that called `setjmp()` cannot have terminated before the execution of the corresponding `longjmp()`. Also, you should not `longjmp()` to an environment that was never set by a call to `setjmp()`. In both cases, the results are undefined. For example:

```
void func1(void)
{
      setjmp(env4);
}

void func2(void)
{
      longjmp(env4, 2);
}
```

will not work because the environment of the `setjmp()` in `func1()` is no longer valid when the `longjmp()` in `func2()` is executed. [We are assuming that `func1()` is called before `func2()`.] In other words, the stack information is no longer valid when we execute the `longjmp()`.

Illustration

```
/*
                          setjmp(), longjmp()
*/

#include <stdio.h>
#include <setjmp.h>

jmp_buf env1;
jmp_buf env2;
```

```
int main()
{
     void func1(void), func2(void), func3(void);

     if (setjmp(env1))
          func1();
     else {
          if (setjmp(env2)) {
               func2();
          } else {
               func3();
          }
     }
}

void func1(void)
{
     printf("First call.\n");
}

void func2(void)
{
     printf("Second call.\n");
     longjmp(env1, 1);
}

void func3(void)
{
     printf("Third call.\n");
     longjmp(env2, 2);
}
```

Program Comment

The program begins by including the `stdio.h` and `setjmp.h` header files. We then define two environment variables of type `jmp_buf` and begin executing the `main()` code.

When we execute the `setjmp(env1)`, we preserve the status of the environment at that point in the program. Because the return value from the `setjmp()` is 0, the `if` test fails, and we execute the second `setjmp()`.

The `setjmp(env2)` call saves the environment that exists when the second `if` statement is executed. Again, the return value will be 0, so we do not execute the call to `func2()` but rather fall into the `else` that causes `func3()` to execute.

Inside `func3()`, we display "`Third call.`" and execute the `longjmp(env2, 2)`. This causes control to resume with the environment that existed when `setjmp()` was called using `env2` as its argument. This is the same as going back to the second `if` statement in `main()` and replacing the `setjmp(env2)` with the value of `val` as given by the `longjmp()` call in `func3()`. Because `val` is 2 in the `longjmp()` in `func3()`, the second `if` test in `main()` becomes logical True, and we execute the call to `func2()`.

In `func2()`, we print "`Second call.`" and then call `longjmp(env1, 1)` to restore the environment that existed when `setjmp(env1)` was called. This is the environment that existed at the `setjmp()` in the first `if` in `main()`. Again, because `val` in `func2()` is 1, the `if` statement that does the first call to `setjmp()` is replaced by a logical True, and the call to `func1()` is made. The call to `func1()` displays "`First call.`", and the program ends.

The important thing to notice is what happens to the `setjmp()`s as we progress through the program. The following diagram shows the sequence of events, to be read from left to right.

```
Enter func3() ------->        After func3() ------->   After func2()

if (setjmp(env1))             if (setjmp(env1))          if (1)
     func1();                      func1();                  func1();
else {                        else {
     if (setjmp(env2)) {           if (2) {
          func2();                      func2();
     } else {                      }
          func3();            }
     }
}
```

In essence, when we execute `func3()`, it is as if the `setjmp(env2)` is replaced by a 2, which is the return value from `longjmp()`. Therefore, the "After `func3()`" snapshot shows the code as "`if (2)`", which means that we execute the call to `func2()`. The `longjmp()` in `func2()` restores the environment of `env1`, which means that the first call to `setjmp(env2)` is replaced by the 1 for `val` in the `longjmp()` call in `func2()`. Therefore, the last snapshot shows "`if (1)`", which will cause `func1()` to be executed.

Miscellaneous Comments

The `setjmp()` and `longjmp()` functions have a wide variety of uses. You can use the functions to return to a known status quickly. For example, if you have a recursive function that might go a hundred levels deep before the proper return condition is sensed, it is probably quicker to do a `setjmp()` going into the recursion, and a `longjmp()` back, than to return through those hundred levels.

Function Name

`signal()`

Standard Met

ANSI, SYSV

Purpose

To process a signal (interrupt).

Prototypes

```
void (*signal(int sig, void (*func)(int))) (int)    ANSI
int (*signal(int sig, int (*func)(int))) (int)      SYSV
```

Required Header

```
#include <signal.h>        ANSI/SYSV
```

Usage

```
void (*signal(int sig, void (*func)(int))) (int)
```

The `signal()` function gives the calling process three ways of processing a signal. The first argument, `sig`, states what signal has been received. The second argument, `func`, tells what is to be done about the signal. Therefore, `func` may resolve to one of three possibilities:

SIG_DFL	Uses default processing of the signal. This may mean aborting the program.
SIG_IGN	Ignores the signal
SIG_ERR	If the request for a signal process can be honored, returns the value of the function that was previously in effect. Otherwise, SIG_ERR is returned, and `errno` is set.

If the function is other than SIG_DFL or SIG_IGN, func is to process the signal. The only argument passed to func is the value of sig. If the second argument resolves to a pointer to function, the equivalent of a

```
signal(sig, SIG_DFL);
```

is executed, provided that the signal is not SIGILL for ANSI or SIGILL and SIGTRAP for SYSV. Then,

```
(*func)(sig);
```

is executed, which invokes the function that is to process the signal using sig as the function's only argument. What the function does from that point is implementation-defined. The function may call abort() or exit() and end the program, may attempt to execute a longjmp() to process the error, or may prompt you for some form of action. The function may also process the error in some predefined way and continue execution at the point at which the signal was sensed.

If the signal occurred by means other than raise() or abort() and the function func uses a function in the standard library other than signal() itself, the behavior is undefined. Likewise, if the function accesses any data item with the static storage class (other than assigning to a sig_atomic_t volatile static storage class), behavior is undefined.

When a program begins execution, the equivalent of a call to

```
signal(sig, SIG_IGN);
```

may be executed for those signals that are to be ignored for the implementation, whereas:

```
signal(sig, SIG_DFL);
```

is executed for those signals that are processed by the implementation.

If the signal can be processed, signal() returns the value returned by func. If the signal cannot be processed, SIG_ERR is returned, and errno is set to a value associated with the error.

Caution

SYSV interprets signals in a similar, but not identical, manner. You should consult your library documentation to determine what signals are processed by the system and how they are processed.

Illustration

```
/*
                                  signal()
*/

#include <stdio.h>
#include <signal.h>
#include <string.h>

int func();

int main()
{
    double d, e;

    d = 3.4;
    e = 0.0;

    signal(SIGFPE, func);

    for (;;)
        d / e;
}

int func(int sig)
{
    printf("Divide by zero error. Abort (Y, N)? ");

    if (toupper(getchar()) == 'Y')
        exit(1);
    signal(SIGFPE, func);
}
```

Program Comment

The program begins with `#includes` for the header files needed in the program. In `main()`, several working variables are defined and initialized. The call to `signal()` uses `SIGFPE` (that is, a floating-point error) as the first argument and sets a pointer to `func()` as the second argument. [Note that we declared `func()` prior to `main()`.] The program then enters an infinite `for` loop and proceeds to perform a division by zero. Because this is a floating-point error, `func()` is called and asks you whether you want to abort the program. If you answer Y (yes), the program ends.

If something other than Y is given, `signal()` is called, and control returns to the infinite `for` loop, which calls `func()` and asks the question again. This loop is repeated until you answer Y.

Miscellaneous Comments

The implementations of `signal()`, `raise()`, and the types of signals that are processed vary substantially across environments. You should consult your library documentation to see how the functions and what signals are implemented.

As a signal handler can be interrupted by another signal, the normal course is to disable unwanted signals as the first part of the signal handling function and then reenable signals before exiting the handler. Also, you should consult your documentation to see what library functions are wholly reentrant and eligible to be used in a signal handler. (Using nonreentrant library functions with interrupts can lead to interesting and undesirable results.)

Function Name

`system()`

Standard Met

ANSI, SYSV

Purpose

To perform a command processor directive.

Prototypes

```
int system(const char *str)
```

Required Header

`#include <stdlib.h>`	ANSI
`#include <stdio.h>`	SYSV

Usage

```
int system(const char *str)
```

The `system()` function takes the string pointed to by `str` and passes the string to the host operating system. The command processor of the host operating system then processes the command pointed to by `str`. If argument `str` is a null pointer and a command processor does exist, the `system()` function returns nonzero. If argument `str` is not a null pointer, an implementation-defined value is returned.

Caution

Under SYSV, the `system()` command causes whatever commands are in `str` to be passed to a new shell. Your documentation should explain the commands that may be used with the shell.

Illustration

```
/*
                                        system()
*/

#include <stdio.h>
#include <stdlib.h>
#include <stddef.h>

#define MAXSTR 128

int main()
{
     int i;
     char buff[MAXSTR];

     printf("Enter system command to be executed: ");
     gets(buff);

     i = system((char *)NULL);
     if (i == 0)
          printf("There is no command processor.\n");
     else
          system(buff);

}
```

Program Comment

The program `#includes` the required header files and calls `gets()` to get a system command from you. The program then calls `system()` with a null pointer to see whether a command processor exists. If it does, the return value from `system()` will be nonzero, and the `system()` call using `buff` is made. If `i` is zero, a message is displayed, and `system()` is not called.

Miscellaneous Comments

None.

Function Names

`tdelete()` `tfind()` `tsearch()` `twalk()`

Standard Met

SYSV only

Purpose

Functions to use binary search trees.

Prototypes

```
char *tdelete(char *key, char **rptr, int (*compar)() )
char *tfind(char *key, char **rptr, int (*compar)() )
char *tsearch(char *key, char **rptr, int (*compar)() )
void twalk(char *root, void (*action)() )
```

Required Header

`#include <search.h>` SYSV

Usage

Note: In the function below, it is your responsibility to allocate storage for the data items in the tree because the functions are manipulating pointers only, not the actual data itself. Likewise, you must provide the comparison function(s) for `tfind()`, `tsearch()`, and `tdelete()`. You can, of course, use a comparison function from the standard library, such as `strcmp()`.

```
char *tdelete(char *key, char **rptr, int (*compar)() )
```

This function is used to delete a node from a binary search tree. The pointer `key` points to the node that is to be deleted, `rptr` points to the root of the binary tree (a null pointer if the tree is empty), and `compar` is a pointer to the function that does the comparison between `key` and the tree node. You must provide the comparison function.

If a match is found for the node to be deleted, `tdelete()` returns a pointer to the parent of the node that was deleted. If no match is found, a null pointer is returned.

```
char *tfind(char *key, char **rptr, int (*compar)() )
```

The `tfind()` function searches the binary tree for the entry pointed to by `key`. You must supply the comparison function (`compar`). If `rptr` is a null pointer, the tree is empty. If a match on the entry is found, `tfind()` returns a pointer to the item. If the entry is not found, a null pointer is returned.

```
char *tsearch(char *key, char **rptr, int (*compar)() )
```

The `tsearch()` function behaves the same as `tfind()`, except that, if the entry is not found, the entry pointed to by `key` is inserted into the tree, and `tsearch()` returns a pointer to the entry just added to the tree. If there is not enough room to add the new entry, `tsearch()` returns a null pointer.

```
void twalk(char *root, void (*action)() )
```

The `twalk()` function traverses a binary tree, starting at the root pointed to by `root`. Note that `root` can be any node, not just the root node of the tree.

The `action()` function is supplied by the programmer and is a pointer to that function. The first argument of the `action()` function is a pointer to the root pointer. The second argument is an `enum` data type name `VISIT` of the set `preorder`, `postorder`, or `endorder`, which are defined in the `search.h` header file. The values for the `enum` types tell whether this is the first, second, or third time the node has been visited, or whether a leaf has been reached. The third argument for `action()` tells the level of the node in the tree. The root node is assumed to be level 0.

There is no return value from `twalk()`.

Caution

These functions are not part of ANSI.

Illustration

```
/*
            tdelete(), tfind(), tsearch(), twalk()
*/

#include   <stdio.h>
#include   <string.h>
#include   <search.h>

char   *root;                          /* provide a root for the tree */

void process_node();            /* function to process walk of nodes */

VISIT   order;               /* variable so process order may change */

char   *data[] = {           /* data to use */
     "gets()",
     "printf()",
     "strtod()",
     "strtol()",
     "strcpy()",
     "strcmp()",
     "gamma()",
     "tsearch()",
     "tfind()",
     "twalk()",
     "bsearch()",
     "lsearch()",
};

int   main()
{
     int   i;
                              /* fill in the tree with tsearch() */
     for(i = 0; i < sizeof(data) / sizeof(data[0]); i++) {

                              /* add data[i] to the tree from    */
                              /* root with strcmp as the compare */
                              /* routine                         */
          if(tsearch(data[i], &root, strcmp) == NULL) {
               printf("Unable to add item\n");
               exit(1);
          }
     }
```

```
                                /* print them sorted                */
                                /* set order so that they appear in */
                                /* sorted order                     */
    order = postorder;
    puts("POSTORDER");
    twalk(root, process_node);
                                /* delete printf() using tdelete    */
    tdelete(data[1], &root, strcmp);
                                /* print them in order encountered  */
    order = preorder;
    puts("PREORDER");
    twalk(root, process_node);
                                /* print them after all traversed   */
    order = endorder;
    puts("ENDORDER");
    twalk(root, process_node);
}

void process_node(char **node, VISIT visit, int level)
{
                            /* if at leaf (that is, no children) or */
                                /* at the correct traversal process */
                                /* the node                         */
    if(visit == order || visit == leaf) {

                                /* note that we get a pointer to    */
                                /* the node and not the node itself */
        printf("level:%d - %s\n", level, *node);
    }
}
```

Program Comment

The program `#includes` necessary header files and then defines several working variables. The `data[]` array is the list that we want to place into the binary tree. The variable `order` is the `enum` data type needed to be able to perform a `twalk()`.

In `main()`, the `for` loop searches the tree by repeated calls to `tsearch()`. Because the tree is empty, this loop has the effect of filling in the binary tree with the items in `data[]`. (Note the check for a null pointer just in case we run out of memory.)

The next thing we do is set order for a postorder search and call twalk(), using root [which was initialized by tsearch()] and a pointer to the action function we want to take, or process_node() in this example. The process_node() function is required to have the three arguments shown: (1) a pointer to the pointer to the node, (2) an enum data type of type VISIT, and (3) an integer that is the level of the tree we are in. The printf() shows the level of the tree and the node to which we are currently pointing.

The call to tdelete() deletes the item stored at data[1], or "printf()" in the list. Note how we use strcmp() for the comparison routine.

The program then reassigns order to be either a preorder or endorder search and calls twalk() again in the manner described above. You will note that printf() no longer appears in the list.

Miscellaneous Comments

Although the binary tree functions are shown processing character data types, any data type, such as structures, may be used with the tree functions. If a different data type is used, the root pointer must be the same type as the data to be manipulated, the pointers given to the tree functions must be cast to char *, and the comparison function must perform the comparison on the appropriate data item.

9 Time and Internationalization Functions

One of the interesting new features of the proposed ANSI standard is the recognition that different areas of the world present the same information in different ways. To allow for this "locale"-specific information, the concept of a run-time locale is introduced.

Although the C program is still written according to the rules of C grammar, the program has the run-time option of altering the way in which different parts of the standard library behave, based on a locale. ANSI specifies that there is a default locale named the "C" locale, which is in effect at run-time. (Other locales supported are implementation-specific, and even the default locale of "C" can vary, based on the place the code is expected to execute.)

The supported locale is a character array that represents a name. One typical way of providing varying locale information is to store the locale in a disk file. The next question is "What is locale, and how does it affect the standard libraries?" Simply stated, *locale* refers to the way in which certain information is presented in a specific geopolitical locality.

One effect a locale can have is on the format used to present the date and the time. In the standard library, the `asctime()` function uses a predefined way to generate the string that represents the date and time. On the other hand, ANSI provides a function to print out date and time information, using a format that is consistent with a locale. This function is called `strftime()`. It works much like a `printf()` but is for printing the date and time only. As an example, one locale may represent the time based on 24-hour world time (military time, as in 13:41:23), while another locale might use 12-hour time (as in 1:41:23 PM). Locale can dictate how the default time is represented.

A second way that locale can change the way the default library functions is in the "`ctype`" functions. Locale can redefine what constitutes uppercase or lowercase letters and their related conversions. For example, "What is the German B (which translates as ss), and what is its sort order? Is it upper- or lowercase, or both?" You can use locale to cope with these problems.

A third way in which locale is useful is in the collation order of the character set. In the example of the German B, the character's collation order is as if it were "ss". The function `strxfrm()` will generate the collation order of a character string based on locale. This function can generate up to four characters out for each character in, so that the collation sequence is mapped correctly.

Finally, the numeric radix character, the character that separates the integer and fractional digits of a numbering system, can be altered to suit the locale. In the United States, the character is normally a period (.), but in other parts of the world a comma is more common. Locale allows this character to be changed in input and output of numeric data. The functions affected are the `printf()`, `vprintf()`, and `scanf()` families, `atof()`, and `strtod()`. Remember, however, that locale does not change the way a compiler parses a floating-point number. Locale alters the way a floating-point number is parsed at run-time, when the program is processing data.

All or part of these locale-specific factors may be controlled by a function called `setlocale()`. The header file named `locale.h` defines the following constants:

`LC_ALL`	Get or set all locale types
`LC_CTYPE`	Get or set `ctype` locale data
`LC_COLL`	Get or set collation locale data
`LC_TIME`	Get or set date time locale information
`LC_NUMERIC`	Get or set the numeric radix character

Note that a get of `LC_ALL` will return only a locale identifier if all the locales are set to the same locale identifier.

This section discusses the time functions, many of which are affected by locale—hence, the reason for the previous discussion.

Time versus Time

The functions in this chapter deal with time on different levels. We need to distinguish between these levels at the outset. ANSI is quite clear in its terms.

1. *Calendar time.* This is the day of the week, the month, and the year for a given time. Calendar time also includes the hours, minutes, and seconds for the day of calendar time.

2. *Broken-down time.* This term refers to the components of the time structure that holds the calendar time. (The time structure was discussed in Chapter 2.) Broken-down time has variables to hold the various components of calendar time, plus several elapsed time variables and a flag for Daylight Savings Time. The structure that holds this information is usually referred to as a `tm` structure.

In many functions, the information that is held in broken-down time is used either to build a printable string from that information or to construct a single number, the value of which represents some element of time. Although all of this may seem a bit obtuse now, the function discussions that follow in this chapter should help to make things more clear.

For the ANSI time printing functions, unless otherwise stated for the return value of the function, if an implementation cannot determine the appropriate date or time, the function returns an implementation-defined date or time string. This means the returned date-time string has the proper form (for example, a time of 01:01:01), but the contents of the date or time will be defined and documented by the implementor.

Function Name

`asctime()`

Standard Met

ANSI, SYSV

Purpose

To get a time string.

Prototypes

```
char *asctime(const struct tm *tptr)
```

Required Header

`#include <time.h>` ANSI/SYSV

Usage

```
char *asctime(const struct tm *tptr)
```

The `asctime()` function creates a string that contains the time as held in the `tm` structure pointed to by `tptr`. In other words, the function takes broken-down time and converts it to a printable string. The format for the time string is of the specific form:

```
Day_name Month_name Day_of_month Hours:Minutes:Seconds Year\n\0
```

Note the newline and null-termination characters at the end of the string—for example,

```
Sun Jul  4 02:03:03 2001
```

ANSI states that the function shall use the following algorithm:

```
char *asctime(const struct tm *timeptr)
{
     static const char wday_name[7][3] = {
        "Sun", "Mon", "Tue", "Wed", "Thu", "Fri", "Sat"
     };
```

```
    static const char mon_name[12][3] = {
        "Jan", "Feb", "Mar", "Apr", "May", "Jun",
        "Jul", "Aug", "Sep", "Oct", "Nov", "Dec"
    };

    static char result[26];

    (void) sprintf(result, "%.3s %.3s%3d %.2d:%.2d:%.2d %d\n",
          wday_name[timeptr->tm_wday],
          mon_name[timeptr->tm_mon],
          timeptr->tm_mday,
          timeptr->tm_hour,
          timeptr->tm_min,
          timeptr->tm_sec,
          1900 + timeptr->tm_year);
    return (result);
}
```

(The definition of the `tm` structure is given in the `time.h` header file and also appears in Chapter 2.)

The `asctime()` function returns a pointer to the string (for example, `result`) holding the time information.

Caution

Because `asctime()` is to use the algorithm above, locale has no effect on the way the information is displayed when `asctime()` is called. Also note that the size of `wday_name[7][3]` is defined in such a way that no room is allocated for the null. This definition is legal under the ANSI specification, but non-ANSI compilers may choke on it.

The `asctime()` function can return a properly formed, implementation-defined date and time if the correct date and time cannot be determined from `tprt`.

Illustration

```
/*
                              asctime()
*/

#include   <stdio.h>
#include   <time.h>

struct   tm   timestr;

int main()
{
     timestr.tm_year = 2001 - 1900;      /* Years since 1900       */
     timestr.tm_mon = 7 - 1;             /* Months since Jan.      */
     timestr.tm_mday = 4;                /* Just make up the rest  */
     timestr.tm_hour = 2;
     timestr.tm_min = 3;
     timestr.tm_sec = 3;
     timestr.tm_isdst = 1;
     puts(asctime(&timestr));            /* Show what we have      */
}
```

Program Comment

The program `#includes` the necessary headers and defines a structure variable of type `tm` named `timestr`. We then assign values to the members of `timestr`, followed by a call to `asctime()` to create a printable time string from the data. The program generates the output:

```
Sun Jul  4 02:03:03 2001
```

Miscellaneous Comments

None.

Function Name

`clock()`

Standard Met

ANSI, SYSV

Purpose

To determine the processor time used.

Prototype

`clock_t clock(void)`	ANSI
`long int clock(void)`	SYSV

Required Header

`#include <time.h>`	ANSI
None provided	SYSV

Usage

```
clock_t clock(void)
```

The `clock()` function returns the amount of processor time used since the beginning of an implementation-defined period. The resolution of `clock()` is implementation-defined. When the value returned by `clock()` is divided by CLK_TCK, the result is the processor time expressed in seconds.

The function returns -1 (cast to type `clock_t`) if the processor time used is not available.

Caution

Note that SYSV returns a `long int` data type rather than ANSI's `clock_t`. Further, SYSV states that the return value is expressed in microseconds.

Illustration

```
/*
                                        clock()
*/

#include <stdio.h>
#include <time.h>

int main()
{
     clock_t start, past = 0;

     start = clock();
     printf("Press the ENTER or RETURN key when ready: ");
     getchar();
     past = clock() - start;              /* Get the count back  */

     past /= CLK_TCK;                     /* Make it into seconds */

     printf("\nThe response time was %ld ", (long) past);
     (past == 1) ? printf("second.\n") : printf("seconds.\n");

}
```

Program Comment

The program `#includes` the standard input/output and time header files and defines variable `past` as a `clock_t` data type. The first call to `clock()` assigns the starting value into `start`, which is followed by a message telling you to press the Enter or Return key. After the call to `getchar()`, a second call to `clock()` subtracts `start` from the return value of `clock()` and assigns the processor-time count to be assigned into `past`. [You could print this out with a `printf()` at this point in the program.]

To determine the number of seconds between the first and second calls to `clock()`, `past` is divided by CLK_TCK, and the result is assigned back into `past`. Note that if you don't wait long enough, the result will likely be zero. Because we do not necessarily know how to print a `clock_t` data item, but we do know that it is an integral data type, we cast `past` to a `long int` and display the result. The ternary causes the singular or plural of "`second`" to be displayed.

Miscellaneous Comments

If we make a third call to `clock()`, the return time is still relative to the first call to `clock()`, not the last call to `clock()`.

Function Name

`ctime()`

Standard Met

ANSI, SYSV

Purpose

To convert date and time to a string.

Prototypes

`char *ctime(const time_t *clk)`	ANSI
`char *ctime(long int *clk)`	SYSV

Required Header

`#include <time.h>` ANSI/SYSV

Usage

```
char *ctime(const time_t *clk)
```

The `ctime()` function converts the calendar time pointed to by `clk` to the local time in string form. The string has a format of

```
Day_name Month_name Day_of_month Hours:Minutes:Seconds Year\n\0
```

Note the newline and null-termination characters at the end of the string—for example,

```
Sun Jul  4 02:03:03 2001
```

This format is the same as that produced by `asctime()`.

The `ctime()` function returns a pointer to the time string.

The SYSV function is similar except that its argument is a pointer to a `long int` that holds the number of elapsed seconds since 00:00:00 GMT, January 1, 1970. The return value is a pointer to the time string, which has the same format as the ANSI `ctime()` time-string format.

Caution

Note the difference in the arguments for the ANSI and SYSV versions of this function (`clock_t` versus `long int`).

Illustration

```
/*
                                        ctime()
*/

#include    <stdio.h>
#include    <time.h>

int main()
{
     char *s;
     time_t value1;

     value1 = time( (time_t *) 0);          /* Get it from the system */

     s = ctime(&value1);
     puts(s);
}
```

Program Comment

The program `#include`s the two headers needed and `#define`s two working variables. The call to `time()` is made to get the system's current calendar time. [See the discussion of the `time()` function later in this chapter.] The call to `ctime()` then passes the information returned from `time()`, converts the information into a printable string of the required format, and assigns a pointer to the string to `s`. The call to `puts()` displays the result.

Miscellaneous Comments

A SYSV version of the program would use the same format; only the argument values would change.

Function Name

`difftime()`

Standard Met

ANSI only

Purpose

To find the difference between two dates.

Prototype

```
double difftime(time_t endtime, time_t starttime)
```

Required Header

`#include <time.h>` ANSI

Usage

```
double difftime(time_t endtime, time_t starttime)
```

The `difftime()` function determines the elapsed time between `starttime` and `endtime`. The `difftime()` function returns the difference between the two times as a `double` data type expressed in seconds.

Caution

SYSV does not provide this function.

Illustration

```
/*
                              difftime()
*/

#include <stdio.h>
#include <time.h>
#include <stdlib.h>

int main()
{
     char   buff[100];
     static const char *d[] = {"Sun", "Mon", "Tue", "Wed",
                              "Thu", "Fri", "Sat"};
     struct   tm   time_val;
     time_t   value, value1;

     printf("Let's find out how many seconds since you were born.\n");
     printf("    Enter year (for example, 1949): ");
     time_val.tm_year = atoi(gets(buff)) - 1900;
     printf("Enter month (for example, 5 = May): ");
     time_val.tm_mon = atoi(gets(buff)) - 1;
     printf("       Enter day (for example, 23): ");
     time_val.tm_mday = atoi(gets(buff));
     time_val.tm_hour = 0;
     time_val.tm_min = 0;
     time_val.tm_sec = 1;
     value = mktime(&time_val);                        /* Start time */
     printf("Born on %s, or the %d day of the year\n",
             d[time_val.tm_wday], time_val.tm_yday);

     value1 = time((time_t *) 0);                      /* End time   */

     printf("difference in seconds is: %g\n", difftime(value1, value));

}
```

Program Comment

The program #includes the necessary header files and defines several working variables in main(). The program then prompts you to enter your birth date and fills in the members of the type tm structure with appropriate values. The mktime() function uses the information in the structure to generate a time value. The mktime() function fills in the proper value for time_val.tm_wday and time_val.tm_yday, which are used to show the day of the week on which you were born. The value of time_val.tm.ytd is the number of days between the beginning of the year and your birthday.

The call to time() uses the clock maintained by the host environment to produce a time value similar to that returned from mktime(). These two time values are then passed to difftime() to compute the number of seconds that have elapsed between the birth date and the current date. (It is discouraging to see one's age expressed in billions of seconds, although it beats the alternative!)

Miscellaneous Comments

None.

Function Name

`gmtime()`

Standard Met

ANSI, SYSV

Purpose

To convert time to Greenwich Mean Time.

Prototype

`struct tm *gmtime(const time_t *clk)`	ANSI
`struct tm *gmtime(long int *clk)`	SYSV

Required Header

`#include <time.h>` ANSI/SYSV

Usage

```
struct tm *gmtime(const time_t *clk)
```

The `gmtime()` function converts the time pointed to by `clk` into the components of calendar time held in the `tm` time structure. That is, the function takes calendar time from the host system's clock and converts the calendar time to broken-down time for storage in a `tm` structure. The results are expressed in Greenwich Mean Time (GMT). The `gmtime()` function returns a pointer to a `tm` time structure, or to a null pointer if GMT cannot be determined.

Caution

None.

Illustration

```
/*
                                        gmtime()
*/

#include <stdio.h>
#include <time.h>

int main()
{
     time_t value;

     value = time((time_t *) 0);               /* Time from host         */
     puts(ctime(&value));                       /* Time display for host  */
     puts(asctime(gmtime(&value)));             /* Time display for GMT   */
}
```

Program Comment

The program `#include`s the usual header files and defines a single variable `value` of type `time_t`. The call to the `time()` function returns the current time kept by the host environment and assigns the current time to `value`. The `ctime()` function receives `value` as a pointer and forms a printable version of the time. The call to `puts()` displays the time.

The program then calls the `gmtime()` function, using `value` as the function's argument. Since the value returned from `gmtime()` is not directly printable, the value is used as the argument to `asctime()`, which does return a printable value. The `puts()` then prints the time.

Miscellaneous Comments

GMT is sometimes used outside the time zone that comprises GMT. Some branches of the government use GMT rather than local time for time-keeping purposes. There is a trend in some areas to refer to GMT as "coordinated universal" time.

Function Name

`localtime()`

Standard Met

ANSI, SYSV

Purpose

To convert calendar time to local time.

Prototype

```
struct tm *localtime(const time_t *clk)        ANSI
struct tm *localtime(long int *clk)            SYSV
```

Required Header

```
#include <time.h>        ANSI/SYSV
```

Usage

```
struct tm *localtime(const time_t *clk)
```

The `localtime()` function takes the calendar time being pointed to by `clk`, converts the calendar time to local time, and stores the resulting broken-down time in a `tm` structure. The function returns a pointer to the `tm` structure.

Caution

The SYSV version of this function uses a pointer to `long int` as the argument.

Illustration

```
/*
                                localtime()
*/

#include <stdio.h>
#include <time.h>
#include <stdlib.h>

int main()
{
     time_t value1;

     value1 = time((time_t *) 0);
     puts( asctime(localtime(&value1)) );
}
```

Program Comment

The usual header files are `#included`, followed by the definition of a single `time_t` data type variable named `value1`. When `time()` is called with a null pointer, the host system provides a time count that is assigned into `value1`. The `localtime()` function uses a pointer to `value1` to convert the calendar time into broken-down time. The `asctime()` call converts the broken-down time into printable form, which then serves as the argument to `puts()` to display the local time.

Miscellaneous Comments

None.

Function Name

`mktime()`

Standard Met

ANSI only

Purpose

To convert broken-down time to calendar time.

Prototypes

```
time_t mktime(struct tm *tptr)
```

Required Header

`#include <time.h>` ANSI

Usage

```
time_t mktime(struct tm *tptr)
```

The `mktime()` function converts into calendar time the broken-down time stored in the `tm` structure pointed to by `tptr`. The values for the structure members `tm_wday` and `tm_yday` are assigned the proper values after the call to `mktime()`.

The return value is the calendar time for the contents of the `tm` structure when `mktime()` was called. If calendar time cannot be represented, `mktime()` returns -1 cast to type `time_t`.

Caution

The starting values for the `tm` structure members `tm_wday` and `tm_yday` are ignored by `mktime()`; the function fills in these values. Also, `tm_mon` and `tm_year` must be determined before `tm_mday` can be set. Therefore, if a valid weekday and yearday are to be used, mktime() should be called before these values are used. (See the Miscellaneous Comments section.)

This function is not supported in SYSV.

Illustration

```
/*
                                        mktime()
*/

#include    <time.h>
#include    <stdio.h>

int main()
{
     struct tm time_val;
     time_t value;

     time_val.tm_year = 1949 - 1900;      /* Stuff with some values     */
     time_val.tm_mon = 5 - 1;
     time_val.tm_mday = 23;
     time_val.tm_hour = 0;
     time_val.tm_min = 0;
     time_val.tm_sec = 0;
     time_val.tm_isdst = 0;
                                          /* See Misc Comm for insert   */
     value = mktime(&time_val);
     puts(ctime(&value));                 /* Show it's still the same   */
}
```

Program Comment

The program starts with #includes for the needed header files, followed by definitions for several working variables in main(). Simple assignment is used to assign a date into the members of the time_val structure. The call to mktime() passes the address of the time_val structure and, based on the broken-down time in time_val, returns the calendar time and assigns it into value. We then call ctime(), using value as the argument, and display the result with a call to puts().

Miscellaneous Comments

The call to mktime() fills in members of the structure that were not explicitly assigned. That is, the day of the week (tm_wday) and the number of days elapsed since January 1st (tm_yday) are filled in by the call to mktime(). Because these are available, you could print these out as well.

If you tried to use the tm_wday or tm_yday structure members before a call to mktime(), there is no guarantee that the results will be correct. For example, try placing the following line after the member assignments, but before the mktime() call (see the Program Comment),

```
puts(asctime(&time_val));
```

and examine the results. At this point in the program, the values for tm_wday and tm_yday have not been initialized, but asctime() needs tm_wday to print out the day of the week.

Function Name

`setlocale()`

Standard Met

ANSI

Purpose

To select a program's locale.

Prototypes

```
char *setlocale(int loctype, const char *loc)
```

Required Header

`#include <locale.h>` ANSI

Usage

```
char *setlocale(int loctype, const char *loc)
```

The `setlocale()` function selects the locale component requested by the argument `loctype` as stored in the locale pointed to by the variable `loc`. (The interpretation of locale and its components is discussed in Chapter 3.) There are five valid locale types available, as defined by the following symbolic constants in the `locale.h` header file:

LC_ALL	Set all the locale constants at one time
LC_COLLATE	Set the locale constant used for collation sequencing. [For example, produce consistent sort results with German character representations rather than English. See the `strxfrm()` function.]
LC_CTYPE	Set the locale constant for character representation. [For example, some functions in `ctype.h` are affected.]

LC_NUMERIC	Set the locale constant for numeric representation. [For example, a comma or a decimal point is used for radix operation. Setting this component will affect the `printf()`, `vprintf()`, and `scanf()` function families, and the `atof()` and `strtod()` functions.]
LC_TIME	Set the locale constant for time and date representation. [For example, much of Europe prefers 1.1.87, while the United States uses 1/1/87. See the `strftime()` function.]

The purpose of locale is to allow programmers to use functions in a generalized fashion, and allow the executing program to adjust to the changes in local conventions (date-time representation, character set, etc.). The `setlocale()` function provides an easy means of switching between those locales that have been defined for the host environment.

A call to `setlocale()` using LC_ALL as the first argument changes all of the locale constants with a single `setlocale()` call. (For example, LC_COLLATE, LC_TYPE, etc., are all changed.) You may also call `setlocale()` with any of the other symbolic constants and change only that element of the locale. If you were writing for a Canadian environment, perhaps only the LC_TIME constant in the locale should be changed.

The call

```
setlocale(LC_ALL, "C");
```

establishes the minimal environment necessary for C programs and is the effective `setlocale()` call at program start-up. If `loc` is an empty string [that is, `setlocale(LC_ALL, "")`], the locale will be the implementation-defined native environment.

The `setlocale()` function returns a pointer to the specified `loctype` for the new locale. If the selection cannot be fulfilled, a null pointer is returned, and the locale is unchanged.

If a null pointer is passed for `loc`, `setlocale()` returns a pointer to the current `loctype` locale; the present locale is not changed. A null pointer may be returned only if `loctype` is set to LC_ALL, and the last successful call to set the locale was something other than LC_ALL.

(This is consistent with the idea that some locale must be in effect at all times.)

The pointer to the string returned from `setlocale()` cannot be altered by the program but only by another call to `setlocale()`.

Note that the contents of `loc`, except for an empty string or "C", is implementation-defined.

See the program example.

Caution

This function is not provided in SYSV.

Illustration

```
/*
                                    setlocale()
*/

#include <stdio.h>
#include <locale.h>
#include <time.h>
#include <stdlib.h>
#include <stddef.h>

int main()
{

     struct   tm time_val;
     time_t   value1;
     char   buff[100];

     printf("LC_ALL:%s\n", setlocale(LC_ALL, (char *) NULL));
     printf("LC_COLLATE:%s\n", setlocale(LC_COLLATE, (char *) NULL));
     printf("LC_CTYPE:%s\n", setlocale(LC_CTYPE, (char *) NULL));
     printf("LC_NUMERIC:%s\n", setlocale(LC_NUMERIC, (char *) NULL));
     printf("LC_TIME:%s ", setlocale(LC_TIME, (char *) NULL));
```

```
        value1 = time((time_t *) Ø);
        time_val = *localtime(&value1);
        strftime(buff, sizeof(buff), "%c\n", &time_val);
        printf("%s\n", buff);

        printf("LC_TIME:%s ", setlocale(LC_TIME, "euro"));
        strftime(buff, sizeof(buff), "%c\n", &time_val);
        printf("%s", buff);
        printf("LC_ALL:%x\n", setlocale(LC_ALL, (char *) NULL));
}
```

Program Comment

The program starts with the `#includes` for those header files used in the program. The program then does a series of `setlocale()` calls to see what the "minimal" locale is at program start-up. The output will vary according to the implementation being used. [If a minimal environment is in effect, you will see a "C" displayed as the return string from the `setlocale()` calls.]

The program then calls several time functions, followed by a call to `strftime()` to show how time is displayed in the minimal environment. The call

```
printf("LC_TIME:%s", setlocale(LC_TIME, "euro"));
```

changes the way the locale processes the time functions. In this example, we are assuming that a European locale has been defined and is available using "`euro`" as the `loc` argument to `setlocale()`. The subsequent call to `strftime()` then displays the (implementation-defined) time using a European format for the time locale. The final call to `setlocale()` returns a null pointer because the last call to `setlocale()` did not use LC_ALL as the function's `loctype` argument (that is, we used LC_TIME). This tells us that we changed some component of the locale, but not all of it.

Miscellaneous Comments

The concept of a locale is explicit recognition that C is an international language. The introduction of a locale was done by ANSI X3J11 to simplify porting code between diverse programming environments.

Function Name

`strftime()`

Standard Met

ANSI

Purpose

To format date and time.

Prototypes

```
size_t strftime(char *str, size_t max, const char *ctrl,
                const char *tptr)
```

Required Header

`#include <time.h>` ANSI

Usage

```
size_t strftime(char *str, size_t max, const char *ctrl,
                 const char *tptr)
```

The `strftime()` function writes characters, as dictated by the control string `ctrl`, to the character array pointed to by `str`. The data used for the conversions specified in the control string are pointed to by `tptr`. The maximum number of characters that may be written to `str` is set by `max`.

The `strftime()` conversion process is similar to `printf()` in that a conversion character precedes any conversions that are to be made. The control string uses the percent character (%), followed by a control-directive character. Normal text characters are copied to the array unchanged. A list of valid conversion directives appears in table 9.1.

Table 9.1
Conversion Directives

%a	Locale's abbreviated weekday name
%A	Locale's full weekday name
%b	Locale's abbreviated month name
%B	Locale's full month name
%c	Locale's date and time representation
%d	Day of month as decimal number (01 - 31)
%H	Hour (24-hour clock) as decimal number (00 - 23)
%I	Hour (12-hour clock) as decimal number (01 - 12)
%j	Day of the year as a decimal number (001 - 366)
%m	Month as a decimal number (01 - 12)
%M	Minute as a decimal number (00 - 59)
%p	Locale's equivalent of AM or PM
%S	Second as a decimal number (00 - 59)
%U	Week number of the year (Sunday is first day of the week) as a decimal number (00 - 52)
%w	Weekday as a decimal number (0 - 6, Sunday = 0)
%W	Week number of the year (Monday as the first day of the week) as a decimal number (00 - 52)
%x	Locale's appropriate date
%X	Locale's appropriate time
%y	Year without century as a decimal number (00 - 99)
%Y	Year with century as a decimal number
%Z	Time zone name (no characters if no time zone exists)
%%	Display percent sign

If a conversion character other than one listed in the table is presented, behavior is undefined.

The `strftime()` function returns the number of characters that were written into array `str` (excluding the null-termination character), provided that the count, including the null, does not exceed `max` characters. If these conditions are not met, zero is returned, and the contents of the `str` array are undefined.

Caution

The `strftime()` function is not available in SYSV. Also note in the table that the locale in force when `strftime()` is used affects the output produced for several of the conversion options.

Illustration

```
/*
                                    strftime()
*/

#include <time.h>
#include <stdio.h>
#include <stdlib.h>

#define MAXSTR 500

int main()
{
     struct   tm   time_val;
     time_t   value, value1;
     size_t   i;

     char   buff[200], bigbuff[MAXSTR];

     for (;;) {
          printf("Enter a test string (# = end): ");
          gets(buff);
          if (buff[0] == '#')
               break;

          time(&value);
          time_val = *localtime(&value);
```

```
        printf("Local data:\n");
        i = strftime(bigbuff, sizeof(bigbuff), buff, &time_val);
        printf("%s\nCharacter count = %u\n\n", bigbuff, (unsigned)i);

        printf("\nNow do the same time for GMT.\n\n");

        value1 = value;
        time_val = *gmtime(&value1);

        i = strftime(bigbuff, sizeof(bigbuff), buff, &time_val);
        printf("%s\nCharacter count = %u\n\n", bigbuff, (unsigned)i);
    }
}
```

Program Comment

The program begins with #includes for the needed header files and a #define for the array size. In main(), the program enters an infinite for loop and prompts you for a sample control string to test. The call to time() fills in a calendar time for the variable value as provided by the host environment. The call to localtime() takes value, converts it to broken-down time, and assigns the results into time_val.

Because we have properly initialized the necessary variables, we can call strftime(), using the control string you entered, to display the time values. The call to strftime() writes whatever you entered into bigbuff. Variable i then receives a count of the number of characters written to bigbuff during the call to strftime(). The call to printf() then displays bigbuff and the total character count.

The program then shows the same time, using GMT, by a call to gmtime(). The displayed values will vary according to the control string you enter. If %c was used, for example, all times are corrected to reflect GMT.

For example, if you enter the control string

```
"%B  %x  %c%p"
```

a sample run would look like the following:

```
Enter a test string (# = end): %B %x %c%p
Local data:
November  Fri 11-28-1986  Fri 11-28-1986 08:13:11AM
Character count = 53
```

Now do the same time for GMT.

```
November  Fri 11-28-1986  Fri 11-28-1986 14:13:11PM
Character count = 53

Enter a test string (# = end): #
```

Use this program to enter sample test control strings. The program will end when you enter a '#' character as the first character. The output will vary with the locale in force when the program is run.

Miscellaneous Comments

The `strftime()` function will generate quite a bit of code. You should consider using some of the other time functions if code space is a problem.

Function Name

`time()`

Standard Met

ANSI, SYSV

Purpose

To get the calendar time.

Prototypes

`time_t time(time_t *clk)`	ANSI
`long int time(long int *clk)`	SYSV

Required Header

`#include <time.h>`	ANSI
None provided	SYSV

Usage

```
time_t time(time_t *clk)
```

The `time()` function gets the current calendar time. The return value is the calendar time. Therefore, the call

```
cctm = time( (time_t *) 0);
```

assigns the current calendar time into variable `cctm`. On the other hand,

```
time(&cctm);
```

returns and assigns the current calendar time into `cctm`. The SYSV version works the same, but the function arguments are `long int` data types.

Caution

Note that the argument types of the SYSV version are different from those of the ANSI version.

Illustration

```
/*
                                        time()
*/

#include <stdio.h>
#include <time.h>
#include <string.h>

int main()
{
     char buff[5];
     time_t value;

     printf("Enter Ø for null pointer version: ");
     gets(buff);
     if (buff[Ø] == 'Ø')
          value = time( (time_t *) Ø);
     else
          time(&value);

     printf(ctime(&value));             /* Show it's still the same   */
}
```

Program Comment

The program `#includes` the headers needed by the program and defines several working variables in `main()`. The program then asks you which variation of the `time()` function call to use—with or without the null pointer as the function argument. Either way, `value` ends up with the calendar time, which is then displayed by the `ctime()` and `printf()` calls.

Miscellaneous Comments

Note that we could also have a third version of the `time()` call

```
time_t val1, val2;

val2 = time(&val1);
```

and both variables, `val1` and `val2`, would hold the same values.

A
Function Index

Under SYSV an entry of stdlib.h indicates that the function exists and does not require a specific header.

Function	ANSI	SYSV	Page	Task
abort	stdlib.h	stdlib.h	311	Termination
abs	stdlib.h	stdlib.h	314	Math Function
acos	math.h	math.h	108	Math Function
asctime	time.h	time.h	388	Date/Time
asin	math.h	math.h	111	Math Function
assert	assert.h	assert.h	316	Debug
atan	math.h	math.h	114	Math Function
atan2	math.h	math.h	116	Math Function
atexit	stdlib.h		319	Termination
atof	stdlib.h	stdlib.h	52	Converter
atoi	stdlib.h	stdlib.h	52	Converter
atol	stdlib.h	stdlib.h	52	Converter
bsearch	stdlib.h	search.h	322	Searching - Binary
calloc	stdlib.h	malloc.h	327	Memory Management
ceil	math.h	math.h	119	Math Function
chdir		stdlib.h	172	Environment
clearerr	stdio.h	stdio.h	176	I/O
clock	time.h	stdlib.h	391	Timing
close		stdlib.h	180	I/O
cos	math.h	math.h	121	Math Function
cosh	math.h	math.h	124	Math Function
creat		stdlib.h	184	I/O
ctime	time.h	time.h	394	Date/Time
difftime	time.h		396	Date/Time

Function	ANSI	SYSV	Page	Task
div	stdlib.h		335	Math Function
exit	stdlib.h	stdlib.h	338	Termination
exp	math.h	math.h	127	Math Function
fabs	math.h	math.h	130	Math Function
fclose	stdio.h	stdio.h	189	I/O
fdopen		stdio.h	196	I/O
feof	stdio.h	stdio.h	176	I/O
ferror	stdio.h	stdio.h	176	I/O
fflush	stdio.h	stdio.h	189	I/O
fgetc	stdio.h	stdio.h	248	I/O
fgetpos	stdio.h		193	I/O
fgets	stdio.h	stdio.h	257	I/O
fileno	stdio.h	stdio.h	176	I/O
floor	math.h	math.h	132	Math Function
fmod	math.h	math.h	134	Math Function
fopen	stdio.h	stdio.h	196	I/O
fprintf	stdio.h	stdio.h	202	I/O
fputc	stdio.h	stdio.h	214	I/O
fputs	stdio.h	stdio.h	220	I/O
fread	stdio.h	stdio.h	224	I/O
free	stdlib.h	malloc.h	327	Memory Management
freopen	stdio.h	stdio.h	196	I/O
frexp	math.h	math.h	136	Math Function
fscanf	stdio.h	stdio.h	229	I/O - Converter
fseek	stdio.h	stdio.h	241	I/O - Positioning
fsetpos	stdio.h		193	I/O
ftell	stdio.h	stdio.h	241	I/O - Positioning
fwrite	stdio.h	stdio.h	224	I/O
getc	stdio.h	stdio.h	247	I/O
getchar	stdio.h	stdio.h	247	I/O
getcwd		stdio.h	253	Environment
getenv	stdlib.h	stdlib.h	341	Environment
getopt		stdlib.h	344	Environment - Parse Flags
gets	stdio.h	stdio.h	257	I/O
getw		stdio.h	247	I/O
gmtime	time.h	time.h	399	Date/Time
hcreate		search.h	349	Searching - Hashed
hdestroy		search.h	349	Searching - Hashed
hsearch		search.h	349	Searching - Hashed
isalnum	ctype.h	ctype.h	64	Character Handling
isalpha	ctype.h	ctype.h	64	Character Handling

Function	ANSI	SYSV	Page	Task
isascii		ctype.h	64	Character Handling
iscntrl	ctype.h	ctype.h	64	Character Handling
isdigit	ctype.h	ctype.h	64	Character Handling
isgraph	ctype.h	ctype.h	64	Character Handling
islower	ctype.h	ctype.h	64	Character Handling
isprint	ctype.h	ctype.h	64	Character Handling
ispunct	ctype.h	ctype.h	64	Character Handling
isspace	ctype.h	ctype.h	64	Character Handling
isupper	ctype.h	ctype.h	64	Character Handling
isxdigit	ctype.h	ctype.h	64	Character Handling
labs	stdlib.h		353	Math Function
ldexp	math.h	math.h	139	Math Function
ldiv	stdlib.h		335	Math Function
lfind		search.h	355	Searching - Linear
localtime	time.h	time.h	401	Date/Time
log	math.h	math.h	141	Math Function
log10	math.h	math.h	144	Math Function
longjmp	setjmp.h	setjmp.h	369	Program Control
lsearch		search.h	355	Searching - Linear
lseek		stdlib.h	261	I/O
malloc	stdlib.h	malloc.h	327	Memory Management
memchr	string.h	memory.h	90	Memory Manipulation
memcmp	string.h	memory.h	83	Memory Manipulation
memcpy	string.h	memory.h	73	Memory Manipulation
memmove	string.h		73	Memory Manipulation
memset	string.h	memory.h	100	Memory Manipulation
mktime	time.h		403	Date/Time
modf	math.h		147	Math Function
offsetof	stddef.h		360	Struct Offsets (intrinsic)
open		stdlib.h	265	I/O
perror	stdio.h	stdlib.h	271	I/O
pow	math.h	math.h	149	Math Function
printf	stdio.h	stdio.h	202	I/O
putc	stdio.h	stdio.h	214	I/O
putchar	stdio.h	stdio.h	214	I/O
puts	stdio.h	stdio.h	220	I/O
putw		stdio.h	214	I/O
qsort	stdlib.h	stdlib.h	362	Sorting
raise	signal.h		366	Control
rand	stdlib.h	stdlib.h	152	Math Function
read		stdlib.h	274	I/O

Function	ANSI	SYSV	Page	Task
realloc	stdlib.h	malloc.h	327	Memory Management
remove	stdio.h		279	I/O
rename	stdio.h		279	I/O
rewind	stdio.h	stdio.h	241	I/O - Positioning
scanf	stdio.h	stdio.h	229	I/O - Converter
setbuf	stdio.h	stdio.h	283	I/O
setlocale	locale.h		406	Locale Information
setjmp	setjmp.h	setjmp.h	369	Program Control
setvbuf	stdio.h	stdio.h	287	I/O
signal	signal.h	signal.h	374	Control
sin	math.h	math.h	155	Math Function
sinh	math.h	math.h	158	Math Function
sprintf	stdio.h	stdio.h	202	I/O
sqrt	math.h	math.h	161	Math Function
srand	stdlib.h	stdlib.h	152	Math Function
sscanf	stdio.h	stdio.h	229	I/O - Converter
strcat	string.h	string.h	79	String Manipulation
strchr	string.h	string.h	90	String Manipulation
strcmp	string.h	string.h	83	String Manipulation
strcoll	string.h		83	String Manipulation (locale)
strcpy	string.h	string.h	73	String Manipulation
strcspn	string.h	string.h	90	String Manipulation
strerror	string.h		100	String Manipulation
strftime	time.h		410	Date/Time
strlen	string.h	string.h	100	String Manipulation
strncat	string.h	string.h	79	String Manipulation
strncmp	string.h	string.h	83	String Manipulation
strncpy	string.h	string.h	73	String Manipulation
strpbrk	string.h	string.h	90	String Manipulation
strrchr	string.h	string.h	90	String Manipulation
strspn	string.h	string.h	90	String Manipulation
strstr	string.h		90	String Manipulation
strtod	stdlib.h	stdlib.h	56	Converter
strtok	string.h	string.h	90	String Manipulation
strtol	stdlib.h	stdlib.h	56	Converter
strtoul	stdlib.h		56	Converter
strxfrm	string.h		83	String Manipulation (locale)
system	stdlib.h	stdio.h	378	Opsys
tan	math.h	math.h	164	Math Function
tanh	math.h	math.h	167	Math Function
tdelete		search.h	380	Searching - Binary Tree

Function	ANSI	SYSV	Page	Task
tfind		search.h	380	Searching - Binary Tree
time	time.h	stdlib.h	415	Date/Time
tmpfile	stdio.h	stdio.h	291	I/O
tmpnam	stdio.h	stdio.h	291	I/O
tolower	ctype.h	ctype.h	70	Character Handling
toupper	ctype.h	ctype.h	70	Character Handling
tsearch		search.h	380	Searching - Binary Tree
twalk		search.h	380	Searching - Binary Tree
ungetc	stdio.h	stdio.h	295	I/O
vfprintf	stdarg.h	stdio.h	299	I/O
	stdio.h	varargs.h		
vprintf	stdarg.h	stdio.h	299	I/O
	stdio.h	varargs.h		
vsprintf	stdarg.h	stdio.h	299	I/O
	stdio.h	varargs.h		
write		stdlib.h	304	I/O

Index

Bold numbers indicate where the function's usage is discussed.

A

B

C

D

G

H

I

O

P

Q

R

S

T

FOLD HERE

Place
Stamp
Here

Que Corporation
P. O. Box 50507
Indianapolis, IN 46250

FOLD HERE

Place
Stamp
Here

Que Corporation
P. O. Box 50507
Indianapolis, IN 46250

FOLD HERE

Place
Stamp
Here

Que Corporation
P. O. Box 50507
Indianapolis, IN 46250